I0634555

Citadel
of LOVE

Pratibha Ray, formerly Professor in Education and former Member, Odisha Public Service Commission, is one of the leading fiction writers in India writing in her mother tongue Odia. Her literary focus is on psychosocial analysis of people, tribes and characters. She is powerfully drawn to history and legends and often builds intricate narratives around themes that are part of the racial consciousness. She has several novels, travelogues, short story, poetry and essay collections to her credit. She is the recipient of the Jnanpith Award for her contribution to Indian literature, the Moorti Devi Award, the Sahitya Akademi Award and the Padma Shri given by the Government of India.

Monalisa Jena was born in Odisha. She is the author of many books in various genres, including two collections of short stories, three books of poems and several volumes of translations. She has to her credit three collections of poems in Odia. Her short stories are collected in *Indramalatira Shoka* and *Nilamadhabi*. Ms Jena also wrote a biography of the noted Odia poet Ramakanta Rath besides translating and editing *Dasuram's Script*, a collection of contemporary Odia stories published in 2013.

By the same author

Yajnaseni

Citadel
Of
LOVE

Pratibha Ray

Translated by **MONALISA JENA**

RUPA

Published by
Rupa Publications India Pvt. Ltd 2015
7/16, Ansari Road, Daryaganj
New Delhi 110002

Sales Centres:

Allahabad Bengaluru Chennai
Hyderabad Jaipur Kathmandu
Kolkata Mumbai

Copyright © Pratibha Ray 2015
Translation Copyright © Monalisa Jena 2015

This is a work of fiction. Names, characters, places and incidents are
either the product of the author's imagination or are used fictitiously and any
resemblance to any actual person, living or dead,
events or locales is entirely coincidental.

All rights reserved.
No part of this publication may be reproduced, transmitted,
or stored in a retrieval system, in any form or by any means,
electronic, mechanical, photocopying, recording or otherwise,
without the prior permission of the publisher.

ISBN: 978-81-291-3724-1

First impression 2015

10 9 8 7 6 5 4 3 2 1

The moral right of the author has been asserted.

Printed and bound in India by Repro Knowledgecast Limited, Thane

This book is sold subject to the condition that it shall not,
by way of trade or otherwise, be lent, resold, hired out, or otherwise circulated,
without the publisher's prior consent, in any form of binding or cover other
than that in which it is published.

Dedicated to those immortal artists who made lotus bloom on stones.

The stream of time sweeps away errors, and leaves the truth for the inheritance of humanity.

GEORG BRANDES

One

~

'Om Jagannath Swamy nayana pathagami bhabatu me'[1]—his letters always began with this chant.

Is it you I have glimpsed through eternity—you who come a step or two closer each time, only to slip away forever into eternity? Is yours that face, Prachiprava? Is it you I have waited for through infinity?

I wandered the globe seeking my destiny, desperate to settle somewhere, desperate until I saw you. The first sight of you, standing on that beach at Konark—I couldn't believe my eyes, you—standing there—posed an impossible question for my soul. How could it be? Even though we didn't speak a word, I thought I'd found the answers I was looking for, though ever since all I seem to do is try to solve life's problems!

I left you behind in India, but I find you here, in the inner recesses of my soul. Space...time...everything fell apart before you. Since we've met, I've realized that even sadness is alluring and, now that I have seen Konark, that dilapidated monuments can be so majestic, magnificent and incredible.

I set my eyes on Konark and realized, perhaps for the first time, that the ruins of a structure which collapsed so long ago can still retain such magnificence, possess such grandeur.

---

[1]Translated as 'May that Jagannatha Svami be the object of my vision,' by Stephen Knapp at http://www.stephen-knapp.com/prayers_to_lord_jagannatha.htm

Isn't it strange that one is never absolutely cut off, nothing is absolutely finished; that in the wake of loss, one discovers an inner strength flowing like a never-ending stream? Who has given me such strength? Is it you, or Konark, or is it Lord Jagannath the Lord of Harmony? Perhaps you are one and the same. Every problem, discord, anxiety, fear, dissolves at His Diamond Throne. That is why whenever I think of you, thoughts of Lord Jagannath come to me, and when I think of Him, thoughts of you instinctively come to mind.

Prachiprava let me take leave of you for today.

Dehi pada pallava mudaram[2]
Yours truly,
Charles

Letters from Charles were always the same. They would begin with a hymn to Lord Jagannath and conclude quoting the beautiful line—Dehi pada pallava mudaram—from the *Gita Govinda*.

Ensconced in wealthy Washington DC, Charles was haunted by memories of the serene waters of the Chandrabhaga. All that he desired was all that was beyond his grasp, and DC was nothing like modest, underdeveloped Bhubaneswar.

Charles had reached the river front at Chandrabhaga after much wandering across the globe, his maxim in life being to live through fear and adventure. He moved from continent to continent, country to country, traversing numerous villages, rivers, forests, valleys and even mountains. He was not too sure

---

[2]A line from Jayadeva's *Gita Govinda* said to have been written by Lord Sri Krishna himself and is addressed to Radha. It may be translated as '[I] bow at your lotus feet'.

himself why he did this, nor what his goal was, or whether he ought to arrive at any conclusion, or simply lose himself in a maze of wonderment. Charles felt his soul lay in his infinite, purposeless journey—to wander from nothing to eternity.

Life held no meaning for him, yet was masked in enticing mystery. He could not imagine a life without travel and would probably continue to roam the globe till his last breath, yet was drawn to Konark, Chandrabhaga and Prachiprava by a tie he could not explain.

Apart or together, the dialogue continued.

Their conversations would span anything and everything that struck a chord with either, bridging viewpoints, opening vistas, defining their time together. A foreigner had travelled to her country in search of knowledge; had the heritage and tradition of her country not been so rich, would someone like Charles have bothered to come?

Though Prachiprava was often in awe of him, she was aware she held her own during wide-ranging conversations on art, culture, architecture, history, or the theology of Odisha.

She took issue with 'the unique trait of Indian women', as he dubbed it, 'of remaining in a state of bliss, even when they have lost everything in life. This trait gave them the strength to survive despite their pain,' said Charles, adding that such consolation was 'a sham'.

'Don't pity us Charles, sympathy doesn't build friendships,' she replied tartly. 'Only God can give, and yet remain a debtor—not man. Only God is the fount of love and mercy, yet longs for love.'

'Love, affection...' Charles smiled. 'We Americans don't see them the way you do. Our concepts of family and social life, or even sacrifice are very different, in many cases simply non-existent. We are rich, have more freedom, but everybody is lonely and unhappy, just like me. People break rules, have few or no permanent relationships, are always on the move; there's nothing like a final destination. Rules, restrictions, a life philosophy, or values simply don't exist for so many and that's just the way it goes. I haven't reached there yet, I guess. I'm a drifter, but I'm no hippie, I've come to India to explore myself, to go within and introspect.'

Charles was born into an affluent, elite family and had been blessed with a comfortable childhood. Edward Naïve, his father, lived in India for almost twenty years establishing a soybean protein plant, a technical institute, and a school to spread education in a remote village. Charles, then hardly eight or nine years old could speak a few Indian languages, though he was not very fluent, and could read a little too in those languages.

He had spent four years in Odisha with his family when his parents decided to separate. His mother wanted to go back to America his father did not, arguing there was nothing for him to do there. India could keep him busy for the rest of his life. He could easily manage his own shambles while being concerned about others. Back home people drowned themselves in wealth and seeking pleasure to cope with the burden of living, but too much comfort was an encumbrance too.

Charles's mother failed to see it that way. She filed for a divorce and quit India with her son. Charles was barely a year old when he came to India and was nine years old when she left. He carried some good memories; never forgot India, and missed his father.

After returning to the USA, Charles's mother remarried. Money was never the issue for Charles, but he was lonely and learnt to be self-reliant from an early age. He studied Architecture before completing a second Masters in History from the Open University. This was about the time that his father returned to America and set up an institution for developmental projects with the help of some non-resident Indians (NRIs). Charles met up with him and at his behest went to India to carry out research on ancient architecture.

And so it was that Charles found himself on the beach at Konark near the magnificent ruins of the seven-hundred year old Sun Temple. His fascination with the land of his early childhood had not just survived, but naturally brought him to Odisha again.

Charles had left many things behind on the American continent—his country, his parents, and his numerous girlfriends. Now rootless, he was completely on his own. He had been left to fend for himself ever since he was barely thirteen. He went on to have lots of girlfriends, but what was okay back home was not okay in India.

Any kind of intimacy between men and women was taboo before marriage, and had to be conducted clandestinely. This made the young women he met very nervous, and they behaved so prudishly that they doused ardour like a cold winter night. Girlfriends were not much of an option in India in the era in which Charles had chosen to return. A man could find certain women in metros like Mumbai, Delhi, Chennai, or Kolkata, but they could not be considered girlfriends; besides sleeping with a woman did not ensure a durable friendship. Companionship between men and women was almost non-existent then, even in Indian metros.

Charles came across plenty of nervous and stammering young women in India, no matter how educated and modern they might be. It must be distressing to be born a girl in India, he thought. Discrimination against the fairer sex was apparent everywhere—in what they wore and could not wear, what they ate, in the behaviour meted out to them by their families, and in social rituals.

Moreover Odisha was poor and backward and Charles initially thought he'd made a mistake choosing it for his project. His opinion, based on fond childhood memories, faltered; he wanted to abandon the project and flee. Heritage structures of high architectural and artistic merit didn't seem possible in such a place. But since he'd come all the way he decided to give the Sun Temple at Konark and the temple at Puri, a shot. He wanted to see Lord Jagannath the 'Juggernaut' for himself. The 'Lord of the Universe' whose chariot was pulled by thousands of ardent devotees, many being trampled underfoot, each year—such devotion! Charles was fascinated.

And so, fascinated Charles landed first at Puri and found his way to the temple. There he was called an untouchable on account of not being a Hindu and denied permission to enter. Astounded, he tried to comprehend a Deity who would advocate this. Eventually he concluded that a few opportunists had enthroned Him on an altar, and rendered Him dumb and immobile. Nevertheless, no one can stand between a fascinated devotee and God, and Charles carried on research from outside the temple, biding his time, growing ever more fascinated with what was inside.

Throngs of elated devotees would stream out of the temple, descending twenty-two flights of stairs, their faces ecstatic, possibly reflecting the glory of the divinity they'd interacted with. He'd been told the image was ugly, going by those radiant smiles he didn't think so. The carved face of God ought to be beautiful; realizing His actual presence ought to bring joy and bliss. Closing his eyes, Charles tried to visualize Him and feel His presence within his soul. A few days later, still staunchly being denied entry into the temple, Charles boarded a tourist bus and headed for Konark and its Sun Temple nearly 85 kilometres away.

The world-famous ruins stood majestically on the desolate sea-shore of the Bay of Bengal. Charles was awestruck by its beauty and ethereal grandeur. He tried to imagine what the Sun Temple must have looked like in its heyday—the wall carvings and the architecture of the sections still standing were striking and exquisite. Charles was very well-travelled and his passion had taken him to almost all important historical sites of note, nevertheless the craftsmanship at Konark stood out. The loveliness of this ruined temple was unsurpassed and it would have been the greatest among temples in the world had it survived, the architect in him felt.

He was very curious about the artisans and sculptors—how on earth had they accomplished such a Herculean task? How had they acquired such knowledge and mastery of architecture? Thirteenth century Odisha surely had no institutions teaching art or architecture yet had produced this magnificent architectural marvel. So well ahead of its time centuries ago thought Charles, but so backward in the modern age—when did poverty set in? At one point this obviously had been a very rich state. Charles fell in love with Odisha all over again, this time with its fabulous cultural heritage.

The exquisitely beautiful maidens dancing and playing mridang drums, erotic sculptures of men and women... they looked alive, so full of vitality, he almost felt they could breathe. One could almost feel their throbbing souls, and hear them reveal their tales about the temple. Charles, desperately wanting to perceive them in flesh and blood, stood as though mesmerized.

So completely immersed was he in his thoughts that the tourist bus left without him. He was now stranded at Konark, alone with the enchantingly sculpted damsels of the temple for company. He could almost hear the sound of their tinkling anklets. Charles was enraptured.

Before coming to Odisha, Charles had not thought much about the afterlife, let alone the concept of the soul and its eternal existence. But Konark drew him to its mysteries and raised questions that had never arisen before. Charles decided to heed the call and stay on.

It was raining. From his open window at the tourist lodge he saw the ruins of Konark silhouetted against the dark stretch of the sky. He was yet to see all the sculptures, or touch them with his hands. The sensual ambience of Konark was best experienced in the company of a woman, or so he'd been told. But the tourist influx had dwindled due to the monsoon and Charles missed Lillian, his girlfriend. The rains always made him romantic, on top of which he had the ruins of Konark to contend with. A heavy downpour like this was exhilarating, but depressing with no girlfriend in sight; though with Lillian for company Charles would not have really missed the rain. Right now the sky mirrored Charles's feelings, ark, clouded, heavy and despairingly lonely. Lillian would arrive only when the holidays began at University.

The ruins appeared solemn against the grey gloomy sky. Their allure beckoned Charles, and he walked out into the rain and towards the temple. Walking in the rain and getting drenched to the bone suddenly took him back to his childhood. Then, he would do anything to get his mother's attention—wander the streets for hours, bake in the sun, get drenched in the rain, do anything to get her to notice him—if only to scold him. He never got a reaction out of her, she never yelled at him, there were no restrictions on him. One side-effect of all this was that the rain and sun never bothered Charles thereafter, though the lack of his mother's attention still rankled.

He'd reached the ruins and was now walking atop the boundary wall of the temple. He was a stranger here, a fair-skinned foreigner whom no one knew and no one would want to ask why he walked alone, unprotected in the rain. His childhood reverie continued.

The monsoon had turned Konark into an enigma, it was as though the monument moaned desolately. Charles had just turned at the western corner of the temple when he was stopped by an old woman addressing him. He had picked up a smattering of the language but not enough to understand her completely. 'My son,' she said in Odia, 'Look at you, a grown-up man careless enough to get drenched in this lashing rain. Come here, let me wipe away the water. You are a foreigner here, who will look after you, if you fall sick?'

As though in a daze, Charles looked at her not quite understanding what she was saying but catching the gist and the fact that she was addressing him as she would a son. That was strange, to treat a stranger like a son. The old woman sat beneath a massive banyan tree, its foliage creating a huge canopy. He went to her. She seemed like a dried, wrinkled leaf from history—aged, emaciated and as ancient as the temple. She beckoned to him. Charles, out of deference to her age, obeyed and stood beneath the tree. She mimed as she spoke, telling him not to get wet in the rain.

He wondered why a stranger in Odisha would be so concerned about his well-being, cautioning him against catching a cold and fever; he doubted his own mother would have been so worried. Charles had no memory of his mother ever taking care of him when he was ill. In India, mothers nurtured and pampered their children even after they became adults, old enough to look after themselves. Charles liked the old woman.

The rain beat down on the banyan tree, but its dense foliage prevented even a single drop from falling on the ground. The tree had spread its boughs like the arms of a loving mother to shelter and protect, and the old woman looked like the tree—loving, caring and aged. She motioned him to sit down. He sat a little distance away. She held a basket of toys made of clay. Each toy was unique. Charles presumed she sold them and wondered how she could carry such a load at her age. Now the old woman stretched out the edge of her sari for Charles to wipe himself with. It was such an informal gesture as though it was an everyday affair. 'Dry yourself my son, or you will catch a cold.' Charles looked at her, amazed.

He wanted to take the edge of the sari and mop himself a bit, but it seemed a little soiled. She guessed the reason behind his hesitance and withdrawing, said, 'Wait, I will give you a clean cloth.' She unwrapped her shoulder bag and took out a clean piece of cloth, shook it open and gave it to him. She used clean cloth pieces to wipe her wares. Charles thanked her and wiped himself with it, albeit a little reluctantly.

Rainwater still rolled down his head. The old woman took the cloth from him and said rather irritably, 'Come here. You do not even know how to dry yourself.' Charles allowed her to wipe his wet hair. He could feel her gentle fingers and every drop of water was soon wiped off. She was as gentle as if she was wiping the clay idols in her bag. Initially, Charles felt awkward but soon began to thaw under her loving attention and care. To him, the old woman seemed the picture of Mother Mary. It was as if in India he had found the mother he had lost in America.

'I am Charles. You can call me Charlie. My people call me that.'

She could grasp his words. He faltered in Odia but was fluent in Hindi. In fact she had no difficulty in understanding some foreign languages because she had been interacting with tourists almost every day for years. She could understand a few words of Hindi and Bengali too. Gazing tenderly at Charles she said, 'How many names will I remember, my dear? Every day I meet so many people, who I never see again. I cannot even pronounce many of the names. For a mother, the name of her son is not necessary. If I call you my son, won't you respond?'

The woman smelled terrible. But her eyes, cataract-ripened and foggy, were filled with warm and affectionate tears. Charles muttered, 'I must have been your son in one of my previous births.'

'Arre paagla, are you not my son in this life? Otherwise why, despite being a foreigner, do you obey and sit near me?'

Charles did not understand what she meant by the word 'paagla'. But considering the kind expression on her face, she had addressed him with affection; and 'paagla' could be a word of love in this country. He later learnt it meant 'crazy'; had he known this and had anyone in his motherland addressed him as 'paagla', he would have immediately filed a suit. But from a mother, the word assumes much importance, it sounds sweet. India was great, thought Charles, just great.

The old mother's name was Kushabhadra and she lived in a village called Kheranga, about three miles from Konark. Her age was an enigma and she did not give any details about her family. She was popular as Kushi Mausi[3]. She herself had no clue about her age. When asked, she would guess, 'as old as the temple of Konark, may be the temple can tell you my age!'

The villagers said Kushi Mausi must have been born an old woman because there was nobody in the village who could remember her younger days. Everybody had seen her as an old woman, ancient and weather-beaten, like the ruins of the Sun Temple. She had not altered much over the years. Nobody could recall her as ever having been ill or tired. She would come with her wares and settle down under the shade of the old banyan tree expecting customers. When her wares were sold, she would go back to her village and return the next day with fresh stock.

If anyone asked her about her husband, she would simply smile her toothless smile and say, 'Lord Jagannath is my husband. He is the Lord of the Universe. Who does not know him? If you have not seen him as yet, then go and have a look. He resides at the Sri Mandira Temple at Puri. He smiles all the time. You will be blessed if you see him.'

If anyone asked about her parentage, she would say, 'My father is there, up in the sky. He is the Sun God. If he were not here, I would not have been here. The world would not have existed. And my mother is the good earth who holds me in her lap. She is the one who has kept me alive. She has given me clay to make the toys I sell. The Sun bakes them. My livelihood survives because of them, and I live because of them.'

If anyone asked about her sons, she would frown, 'You don't know my sons? You haven't recognized them even after seeing the temple? My sons may be deep in slumber now, but that is no excuse for not recognizing them! Their names are engraved on

---

[3]Aunt, a mother's sister.

the stone walls of the temple. Their footprints are imprinted on the sands of River Chandrabhaga. The temple may wither away with time, crumble and perish but my sons will be immortal. Those twelve hundred masons who built the Sun Temple are *my* sons. They do awaken! You can hear them carving in the dead of night. But mostly they roam the ruins in tears over the neglect of a temple they raised with such care, love, and above all with such sacrifice. They're waiting only to hand their legacy over, but the search for worthy inheritors in vain.'

Some said she was mad that was why she talked such nonsense. Some said that she was actually Goddess Ramachandi in disguise, keeping a vigil at the temple. She rescued people in trouble. She never rested, or slept during a storm, or when it was raining. She would sit under the banyan tree gazing endlessly at the temple, as if her hands and gaze would cast a protective shield around the temple.

No matter what the truth was, whether she was a goddess or mortal, the old woman was like an almanac, and one could read the history of Kalinga, as Odisha was once known, leaf by leaf on her palms. She could recall significant moments in history by exact dates, describing them as if they were still fresh in mind. Many believed she had a treasure of antique manuscripts and important documents with her, which she studied clandestinely. She neither denied nor confirmed such reports. And if anyone offered her money to part with those rare documents she would grin toothlessly and say, 'History is written in the dust, sand and hills all over Odisha. If you keep your eyes open, you can gather all of it. You should create history yourself and build another Konark temple for posterity. Why run after history? Why take pride only in the past? You should create your own future, search for the new and unexplored. It is not proper to turn historian overnight by collecting old manuscripts from others. That is no talent. True achievement lies in finding something new, creating something of lasting importance.'

Some treated her as a crazy woman, but those who understood knew she made sense. Charles wondered at her wisdom and then wondered at the younger Indian women he'd met—they would blush, get nervous and start stammering if you talked to them. Even highly-educated girls would falter when speaking in English. Could they ever be as brave as Kushi Mausi?

Kushabhadra, the old illiterate woman, changed his opinion about Indian women. With time, they became close friends. The old woman was living history and Charles her researcher. He praised the toys she sold and this endeared him to her further. He worked with her help. That was a fact.

Two

~

The River Chitrotpala was very much like a painting—beautiful and picturesque. Once upon a time, a prosperous city had thrived on its banks. It was a centre of wisdom and wealth. The river was mentioned in many old scriptures. According to a text called Prachi Mahatmya, in ancient times the river was also called Saraswati. It flowed past Arka Kshetra before merging into the Bay of Bengal. Prachi Valley had a flourishing civilization and Konark was a prosperous nearby village.

All this had passed. Konark was today a deserted township, forsaken and desolate. But Chitrotpala lived. No, not as a river; but as a young girl named Chitrotpala, fondly called Chitra.

Chitra sold flowers at the temple. She was always as cheerful as the flowers she sold, pure and innocent. Her flowers stayed fresh till the evening. She would sprinkle water on them from time to time. There was a great demand for her flowers by the tourists. She had a smiling face and never looked fatigued, just like the river she was named after. People felt invigorated in her presence. But she was also very shy and faint roses touched her cheeks when she blushed. Perhaps it was her beauty and youth that drew the tourists to her; they would keep asking if she had any flowers left! They loved to take pictures of her with the flowers, and promised her that her pictures would boost her trade in far-off lands. The innocent girl believed them and posed for them. The tourists would go back, and new tourists would come. They too bought flowers from thirteen-year-old Chitra. Sometimes, they would gaze at her admiringly as if she was a sculpture of the Konark temple!

Charles called her Chitra, which meant 'painting'. He thought she looked like a painting, meticulously created, uniquely beautiful. Charles wondered whether she would resemble the nayikas at the temple once she was grown up! Or was it Chitra herself who had inspired those immortal models in stone!

As if under some compulsion, he bought flowers from her every day. He loved to talk to her. He could understand a little of her language but most of it was beyond his comprehension. He gathered that Chitra was betrothed and set to marry in the near future. She had to earn enough from selling flowers to raise a dowry for her wedding

Charles would wonder how a simple young girl like Chitra could be a burden on her father. He could not understand why, if marriage was considered so central for a woman, she was not consulted when a groom was chosen for her. Charles would stare at her and say, 'Chitra, I wish that your life stays beautiful and fresh, happy and sweet, just like your flowers. Life should never be a burden on you.' Chitra did not understand a word of what he had said but she smiled, feeling that whatever the Saheb had said was good. She was a trusting soul. Chitra's innocence was endearing. Charles had rarely come across anyone with such innocence in his own country.

Charles felt that even the stones in India had souls, had life. The temple of Konark too had a soul, a heartbeat and it breathed. Although the main temple had collapsed and only the audience hall remained, this was not an ordinary temple.

Each stone reverberated with life. Each sculpture resonated. Horses, elephants, birds, plants, trees, creepers, flowers, gods and goddesses, men and women carved in stone came to life. They talked, sang and danced, the sound of bells filled the air during worship of the Sun God here; the chanting of hymns could still be heard echoing all over. Belled anklets on dainty feet jingled as seductive dancing girls captivated their audience. The fragrance of sweet-smelling flowers pervaded the air.

In the dead of night, the Konark temple came so vibrantly alive that the clip-clop of the royal horses could clearly be heard and their hoof prints seen on the sands of the Chandrabhaga. When the whole area slept, Konark awoke. And it was as though time went back eight hundred years. The centurion, Vishnu Maharana, would vouch for it.

Vishnu Maharana was the descendant of the masons who built the Konark temple. Some said that he was over a hundred years old. No one knew for sure what his actual age was, as no one had seen him growing up. He was the oldest man there. He claimed he was seven hundred years old, and that he too was a part of the team that had built the shrine. Each piece of stone was known to him. He could testify to its history. He could recall every detail about the large pieces of stone, how they were fetched, and from where.

He could remember everything and become sentimental while talking about them. His tears would flow past his long beard and a sad smile would flicker on his lips. Whether it was about the efforts of Sibei Samantrai to lay the foundation stone, or the rituals that took place in the temple, he would narrate episodes vividly. Memories of the days when the temple was vandalized and abandoned later would make him weep inconsolably. His tears flowed like a river.

Vishnu Maharana often talked about King Narasimha Deva; of his valour, magnanimity, compassion, wisdom and patriotism. The king was a great patron of the arts, of culture and literature. Sometimes, Vishnu Maharana would get so involved in his memories that he would stop midway. His audience, totally engrossed, would wait for him to resume.

'You have not seen him. Anyone who does not know King Narasimha Deva cannot understand this land. You have no idea about his bravery and heroism. You cannot even imagine the Kalinga that we had seen as a country. It is your misfortune.'

They said age had caught up with Vishnu Maharana. He had become senile. He claimed that he could see things in the dark and hear voices of bygone centuries. He said he could recognize the masons and could sympathize with their angst and comfort their troubled souls. He would inspire them, saying that the artisans of Kalinga could never die. 'I am eternal, what is there to fear,' he would add. If this was not madness, what was it? Some listeners however, would agree with Vishnu Maharana. They too had heard voices in the dark at Konark, they would say.

Death marks the end of life. Charles knew that. But after reaching Konark, he got the feeling that there was life even after death. The soul does not die. Vishnu Maharana's words filled his heart with a strange excitement. Charles hoped that someday he too would get a chance to see those beautiful damsels in the flesh. He dreamt of seeing them alive. King Narasimha Deva, Vishnu Maharana and those forgotten days of yore!

He would wake up in the middle of the night and step out of his hotel room in search of those images hovering in the dark, just as Vishnu Maharana had narrated them! He would walk as if in a trance and would search for them the whole night long in the casuarina groves, mango orchards and along the sandy beaches. It was as if some invisible spirit was carrying him along. In the morning, the villagers would find the foreigner in deep slumber on the high boundary walls of the temple or in the casuarina jungle or on the shore of the River Chandrabhaga. The tender morning sun would caress him and wake him. Then he would narrate his encounters of the night with the invisible souls to the people who thronged around him. He would ask them, 'Have you seen any ghosts? I have seen them. I followed them last night. They are all ghosts, but I have seen them,' and his blue eyes would turn heavy and he would become dreamy while describing the incidents. People thought that the Saheb was under some spell. Some said he was into ganja or other drugs.

Charles would smile in acknowledgement, saying, 'You are right. I am under the influence of drugs. But it is the drug of Konark, the influence of the artisans who built the temple.'

Vishnu Maharana resembled a rishi, an ancient sage, with his long, flowing beard and matted hair. He had a broad forehead and large, expressive eyes. His age had turned him into a sombre personality. He lived in a 400-year old monastery called Samba's Ashram, situated to the south, outside the boundary of the Konark temple. Charles would frequently go there to hear Vishnu Maharana speak. Before he began his research on the art and architecture of the temple, he had to gather historical evidence. He paid complete attention while listening to the history of the monastery and the temple. Each stone of the temple had a tale embedded in it, to listen to Vishnu Maharana!

Charles had become a sort of a disciple of Maharana. He would settle down near the fireplace inside the monastery and listen to him. Uninterrupted, Vishnu Maharana would go on narrating the story about his own life and that of the great temple.

About four thousand years ago, Maharana would say, Samba was born as the son of Sri Krishna from his eighth queen Jambabati, in the Dwapara era. He was very handsome and this made him haughty. He was so haughty that he once humiliated Brahmashri Narada. It was an unpardonable offence to show any kind of disrespect to a Brahman. Narada complained to Krishna that his son Samba indulged in immoral activities with the women of Gopa who were Krishna's gopis. This enraged Krishna. At the same time Narada played a trick and informed Samba that Krishna was waiting for him at Raibataka mountain. Samba reached the place but did not find his father. Instead he saw beautiful maidens engaged in water sports. They became enamoured of the handsome Samba and thronged to embrace him. Sri Krishna reached the spot accompanied by Narada and witnessed the sight himself and cursed Samba with a deadly disease, leprosy. This would make him ugly, cause him to lose his good looks. Samba was immediately afflicted with the disease.

Later, Narada advised Samba to worship the Sun God in the serene surroundings of the Maitreya jungles situated in the east of India. Only the Sun God could rid him of the curse. Samba left Dwarka and wandered for long before reaching the coast of Odisha and finally settled down in the Maitreya forests to meditate on the Sun God with single-minded devotion. He stood waist deep in the waters of the Chandrabhaga River without food and water. In course of time, the Sun God was pleased with his devotion and cured him of his leprosy. The sacred Maitreya Vana is actually the site which is now known as Konark, Padma Kshetra.

The Sun God blessed Samba saying, 'Whoever erects a temple for me on this earth will go to heaven.' The next day Samba, while bathing in the river, found an idol of the Sun God on the riverbed. He built a temple on the shores of the Chandrabhaga River and after installing the deity in it, worshipped it. From that day onwards, the Sun God has been worshipped on earth in the form of an idol.

The four-thousand-year-old Samba Sadhanapitha is now known as the Konark Kshetra Math. It is believed lepers who come here and worship the Sun God are cured of leprosy. At the monastery, the Sun is worshipped as Nirakari Brahma. There is an idol in black granite called Omkar Brahma. At the rear of the temple is a thatch-roofed hall where an eternal fire called Baishangni burns. In the courtyard of the monastery, are tombs of seven 'abadhuta sadhus' (saints who abandoned worldly life). When the priests worshipped these sadhus, Charles could really feel and believed that the soul never died, but was eternal and not subject to infirmities of old age or death. It is indestructible. He would slowly get up and walk to the pond located at the southern corner of the monastery and then roam through the mango orchard feeling very depressed.

Charles was waiting for Lillian to arrive. If it were not for her, he would have preferred to settle in one of the monasteries and sleep on the sands of Chandrabhaga River. He would wander amidst the casuarina forests or in the cashew orchard, with the blue sky above for a roof and the soft sand to serve as his bed. Konark would loom in silhouette, a phoenix.

Charles walked up to the sea on the narrow pucca road. The sky spread blue and boundless before him. The deserted path was bordered with rows of casuarinas. They shaded the path, offering a whiff of cool refreshing gentle breeze to travellers. Charles wondered if even the trees in India knew how to receive a guest!

There were two monasteries on either side of the

Chandrabhaga River. The one to the west was more ancient. The Kapila Samhita mentioned that the Sun God himself had assumed the form of an enormous banyan tree. The tree was formerly called the Arka Vata and was worshipped by devotees. It does not exist now. In its place, Bateshwara Mahadeva came to be worshipped in the form of a stone idol. A monastery called Chandrabhaga was located next to it. To the east was another monastery named Biranchi Narayana Math. Charles spent a lot of time in both these monasteries. He also visited the hamlets of the fishing community nearby. While strolling on the sandy beach of Chandrabhaga, he would look for the footprints of those masons and artists of Kalinga who had erected such a magnificent temple.

Vishnu Maharana would say, 'Saheb, listen to me, in the beginning cleanse your mind, be content and attain calmness and stability of mind. With single-minded devotion try to find the Kalinga that is now past its glory. You have to search deep and study earnestly to find the answers. Then you will find all you are looking for.' By the time Lillian arrived, Charles had acquired an impression about Konark and its surrounding areas.

He and Lillian had been in love for a long time. But they had never talked about marriage. Charles was against the concept of marriage and Lillian never broached the topic either. Whenever they got an opportunity, they lived together. Lillian travelled with him quite frequently.

She now came to India to be with Charles. She was eager to see Konark for she had heard a lot about the erotic images carved on the stone walls of the temple. The couples in amorous embrace would excite her. For Lillian, Konark symbolized images of erotic copulation. She had come to Konark to see the sculptures for herself. With Charles for company they would be delightful. Charles too had similar thoughts before he had actually arrived at Konark. But once he was there and had attained a deeper awareness, his preconceived ideas had altered. She was in Konark for a holiday but Charles had come on a research assignment.

For Lillian, Konark was like an album of pornographic pictures. She came across Dharmananda at the eastern gate of the temple. Twelve-year-old Dharmananda sold pictures of Konark in the temple grounds. He was clever for his age and could sense what could be sold for a profit. He would display erotic pictures to customers. His crafty information about the sculptures hooked the customers. He could converse with them in broken English and also a bit of Hindi. Although he was a talented student, he had to quit studies after Class VII because of poverty. He had to provide for seven siblings. He lived in Karamanga village, three kilometres away from Konark. He would leave home at dawn, after a breakfast of rice gruel. He would then sell pictures of sculptures at Konark. Mostly, foreigners bought his pictures. For lunch he would munch on a bada or pakoda at a nearby dhaba. On the days he earned well, he would treat himself to a proper meal with rice and fish curry in a hotel. Then, even the scorching heat would not trouble him. He would be preoccupied with finding ways of earning more so his family could get enough to eat every day.

Dharmananda would wait for tourists who came in cars or buses and stayed in the hotels and lodges. He would dream that one day he too would became rich like them, and be able spend lavishly and eat to his heart's content. He wondered why he was so poor. Why he had to run after the tourists and circle the temple at least twenty-five times a day repeating his sales speech and finally sell his pictures? Sometimes, he would accuse his mother; why on earth did she give birth to so many children? How could his father provide for so many mouths? His father was a simple man and was taking care of all of them.

But after abandoning school to help his family, Dharmananda soon realized that it was actually his father who was more to be blamed for the pitiable condition of his family. Dharmananda topped in school always but understanding of life came from his exposure to real life. He grew up swiftly and matured early.

Initially, he would feel depressed. While his classmates went to school every day, he had to bring his wares to sell at Konark. He felt ashamed and angry. He did not know whom he could vent his anger upon. But lately, those feelings did not affect him. He started liking his job which exposed him to many interesting events. Curiosity of the unknown brought excitement to his day-to-day life. He was exposed to things his contemporaries did not even have a clue about. He was indulging in activities forbidden to boys his age. But to be privy to the prohibited world made him feel at an advantage to his friends and colleagues. Slowly his feelings of dejection were replaced with this new-found enchantment. He began to pursue his job with alertness.

Catching sight of Lillian from a distance, Dharmananda could immediately sense that she was a potential customer. He took out more erotic photographs from his bag and exhibited them before Lillian. She checked them one after another. Dharma explained the meaning of the pictures to persuade her to buy. Lillian was impressed and bought the entire packet at a much higher cost and ordered twenty-five sets for her friends back home. They would surely be tempted to come to Konark after seeing those pictures, she thought.

For Dharama it was a rare occasion to earn so much in

a day. Foreigners did not haggle over money. He had even picked up some words and expressions to interact with them. He wished them 'Good morning' or 'Good evening'. He said 'sorry' when he made a mistake. He would introduce himself saying, 'Excuse me, Madam. I am Dharmananda Das…' After selling the goods, he would say 'Thank you, Sir, thank you, Madam.' Everyone liked him.

Lillian headed towards the Natamandira. Sridhar Behura, the guide, welcomed her and narrated the story behind the temple's architecture and sculptures. The guide paused before the erotic images and explained their meaning. Sometimes he even suggested, 'Ask Sir to accompany you, Madam. These sculptures are not to be seen alone.'

Lillian was quite at ease with the subject of erotica and would say, 'I will come to see them again with him. Let me have a peek first.' She tipped the guide handsomely.

Charles, on the other hand, would watch the sculptures with the eyes of a researcher. He would pause before some and stand motionless before others, like a philosopher. Next day, he would go again with Lillian in tow, just to make her happy.

While Lillian felt enthused with the sensuous sculptures, Charles became weary. How could these images be carved on the temple walls when Indians were so orthodox? Such statuettes must have been frowned upon in that bygone era too. These images corrupted people. The artists of Kalinga seemed to have been amoral. But strangely that did not affect the spiritual disposition of the people. But until he had deeper knowledge, Charles could not come up with any satisfactory explanation.

One needs a companion to view Konark's carvings with and Lillian fitted the bill perfectly. But she was good only at the physical level. Charles was a wonderful lover but he was not as passé about it as Lillian. Lillian had no scruples and treated the temple simply as an extension of her bedroom! This was where they differed. Charles was deeply committed in all his activities. While busy in research and serious work he would not contemplate love, sex and romance. And while making love, he would totally put away his study and research. But Lillian could never rise above being a slave to her lust. Scholarly activities held no meaning for her. She was happy seeking pleasures in life and loved every moment of it. In Konark she behaved in the same impulsive way.

She would wander around with Charles in the temple courtyard, in the casuarina jungles, along the seashore, and try and persuade him to give up his research work. 'Why waste your time in research? Konark symbolizes sex and one must enjoy one's life here. Konark has captivated me absolutely. But you have changed so radically. You have lost all your warmth and enthusiasm. Except the temple, there is nothing left here. Perhaps this desolate place has made you so lifeless! Let us go somewhere else. We can enjoy the pleasures of life. After spending two nights at Konark there is no charm left. Let us move away and explore something new.'

Charles would respond philosophically, 'You have not understood Konark properly, and I also do not. But what I have learnt so far is that Konark is everlastingly fresh. Every day it reveals a new face to me. Change your approach and you will find the temple absorbing, and find something new in it every day.' But Lillian was not about to amend her views, or her attitude. Konark no longer appealed to her and she felt her holiday was being wasted.

That afternoon, Konark had been vibrantly alive to Charles. They were sitting silently. Lillian, cigarette in hand, was studying the statuettes. Charles's eyes were on the intricate lace-like designs in a row just above the erotic figurines. They were each lost in their own worlds. The sky was overcast. The ambiance was profound. The sculptures seemed grave. Unexpectedly Charles noticed that one of the stone figures was stirring. The sight sent shock waves down his spine! And he got up and followed the damsel as if under a spell. It was getting desolate and dark. Finally, he came face to face with the figure. She was flawlessly built, exquisitely beautiful but she was not scantily dressed like the damsels of Konark. As if she had come to realize her bare body after coming to life and had covered her torso! Charles felt tempted to touch her but something stopped him. She was moving back. She was coy and gentle which enhanced her charm in Charles's eyes which were fixed in an unblinking stare; she turned away and began walking faster.

Charles came to his senses and shouted, 'Please excuse me. I was under the impression that it was a sculpture from the carved walls of the temple that was standing before me. If alive, all these stone images would look just like you.'

She stared at him for a while and replied, 'None of the sculptures are without souls here. They breathe every moment. You will hear their heartbeat if you try to sense their soul.' Her demeanour and voice was very cultured thought Charles, as he said, 'Please forgive me, I am Charles Naïve. May I take a photograph of you?' She agreed to pose without qualms and stood motionless as if she was a stone statue of stone. Charles quickly took a snap of hers against the temple, now shaded by the lingering shadows. But was it a human being or a sculpture that he was seeing through the camera lens? Before he could click she moved a few steps ahead. Charles felt let down. 'In my country it is considered ill mannered to behave in such a way once you agree for a pose.'

She smiled, 'You thought I am a damsel of Konark temple, and it is indeed a damsel of Konark temple who is captured in your camera. Why should I stand here? Won't that be inappropriate?'

Charles retorted, 'I wanted to take your photograph!'

'In that case you need permission from your girlfriend first. And I do not pose as a model. I am a student of history. I am doing research on the Sun Temple.'

The woman, now only seen in silhouette was walking away towards the Natamandir. Charles stared at her as though in a trance. It was raining and getting late but Charles was oblivious until Lillian's touch suddenly brought him back to his senses. 'Darling, the rain brings magic to Konark! It is so romantic! Let us go back to our lodge. Don't waste such a lovely evening, please.' But Charles's thoughts were elsewhere, 'Perhaps, I will find her; find the soul of that ghost, even if it takes the whole night. If she were not a ghost she would have told me her name. Any educated person would show that courtesy.' Charles had read that a ghost does not allow its image to be captured in a camera and it cannot be caught on film. The woman, although appearing to be in flesh and blood was certainly a ghost. He was absolutely sure about it.

Three

~

River Prachi—called Saraswati, Chitrotpala, Shola and Kadua, as she traversed through sacred places and habitats in the valley carved by her flowing waters—emerged from her source, the River Kushabhadra, at Balianta and flowed through Banamalipur, Niali, and Kakatpur, before attaining eternal union with the sea as Chandrabhaga at Konark—though today that union is more mystical than factual.

Many ancient scriptures such as the Brahma Purana, Samba Purana, Kapila Samhita and Chaitanya Charitamruta refer to Konark as 'Arka Kshetra' and 'Padma Kshetra'; the Prachi Mahatmya also refers to it as 'Ravi Kshetra'. There are references in these scriptures to places called Konaditya, Mitrabana, and Konark; according to a copper-plate inscription issued by King Narasimha Deva II, the region was called Konakona during his rule.

Flowing serenely down the centuries, the Prachi never questioned her fate. Even today, she is still captivating and seemingly beyond earthly decay. Her pristine majesty rejuvenates, as though filling a vow to do so. She flows after all, through the land of Jagannath who holds the power to change grief into joy, who guarantees all eternal bliss and a peaceful life.

Her incarnation as the Chandrabhaga though, reveals the ravages of time. Shrunken, emaciated, reduced to a pond, with her tributaries long since dried up, Chandrabhaga's union with the sea is today a long-forgotten dream.

Prachiprava was often to be found on the banks of the Chandrabhaga or amidst the ruins of Konark. A post-graduate in History, she was conducting research on the period when the Sun Temple was built, the process of its building, and the legends associated with it. She was also looking for information on the man who had it built—King Narasimha Deva II, a scion of the Ganga dynasty—without whom no study of Konark would be complete.

She spent her days among the carved and engraved stones at the temple ruins, or walked the Chandrabhaga riverfront looking for anything that would give her more information about the king. She also relied upon old and wise Kushabhadra, and universally called Kushi Mausi—an invaluable fount of knowledge on the legends and lore associated with the king, the temple and much else.

The fifth child and only daughter of her parents, Prachiprava had been born as a blessing of Goddess Mangala. Her youngest brother was ten years older than her, and the eldest twenty years older. When Prachi was born, her eldest brother already had a five-year-old son. She was doted upon by the whole family.

As a child Prachi had been under the impression that her family owned the entire province; that they were so wealthy that their riches would never end. They possessed acres of mango, coconut, jackfruit, jamun and guava orchards. They also had punanga trees, champak and oleander, hibiscus and tulip gardens. She used to feel like a princess wandering the orchards and flower gardens. In a family where even sons never completed schooling or stepped outside the boundary of their village, she, a daughter, had gone to study in a college far away.

Hitherto surrounded by love, beauty and comfort and never having experienced separation or deprivation, hostel life had come as a bit of a shock. Not that she'd been unhappy, but things changed when you moved away. She completed her postgraduation in History at Kalinga University and then decided to research the building of the Sun Temple at Konark, including the legends associated with it. It was decided that she should live with her aunt Charukala and uncle Dinabandhu Babu in the nearby township of Kakatpur famous for its patron goddess, Mangala.

The day Charles saw her for the first time on the beach at Konark, Prachi was utterly lost in contemplation of its grandeur and the enigma of its bygone glory. So totally absorbed was she that she remained motionless under the overcast sky. It was in that trance that her eyes met Charles's. He was mesmerized at the sight of her, as though she tanding so still and motionless was herself one of the stunning sculptures of that bygone era. He was to write to her much later, 'Even though we didn't speak a word, I thought I'd found the answers I was looking for.' Prachi was lost in the past at that moment, Charles Naïve was just another foreign tourist who did not really create any great impression on her.

She had come across many foreigners and tourists during research, was friendly with many of them, and that was that. As a serious historian she realized that most foreigners on holiday saw Konark's carvings only as sensuous entertainment. And saw nothing beyond the 'amorous couples' carved in stone. The spiritual essence behind the intricate artistry remained beyond their grasp. They would return home with photographs of the temple's erotic carvings, singing praises of the craftsmanship on view at Konark.

Night in the Konark ruins hypnotized Charles. That particular night the storm, the lashing rain, the thunder and lightning, as though put him under a spell. Lillian had done drugs and was out of it. Charles, unable to sleep and feeling lonely, informed the watchman that he was going out for a stroll. It was only ten at night, but the pouring rain and desolate surroundings made it seem like midnight. He could hear the faint tinkle of bells—not temple bells, but the tiny bells on anklets worn by the devadasi women dancers carved on the temple walls. He could definitely hear them from within the temple premises and he followed the sound down to the eastern gate of the temple. It was locked.

He saw a flickering diya burning feebly in the Navagraha Temple within the Konark complex, visible through the storm and rain. Faint footsteps could be heard and soon he recognized Kushi Mausi coming towards him from the Navagraha Temple. Behind her was another ghost-like silhouette. Was the old woman a ghost too?

As they came closer there was a sudden burst of lightning and the temple of Konark was illuminated brightly for a brief second. Before he realized it, Charles felt someone's hands pulling him away. The next moment there was a massive thud, as a huge branch of a banyan tree came crashing down where he had stood just a moment ago. It would have crushed him. The hands that saved him, withdrew just as quickly. 'Thanks,' stammered Charles.

'This is no time for thanks,' said the shadow moving briskly on, 'the storm will soon turn violent. Follow me.'

Kushi Mausi asked him to follow the shadowy figure, 'Go my son. I will take shelter in this temple. She had come to offer puja at the temple. It is already late and you can go back with her now.'

Prachi stopped at the hut which was Naru Uncle's 'Dharmapada Hotel'. This small, tattered edifice had withstood many a devastating storm. Inside, Dharmananda was drying some soggy photographs in a lantern's glow. There was another middle-aged man with a stick in hand. As he saw Prachi he said, 'How can we go out in such storm and rain? Had I known it would pour, I would have fetched another umbrella. Sir will be annoyed if you get drenched. It is getting late. Who knows when the rain will stop?'

'Charukala Mausi will definitely send someone with umbrellas to fetch us,' she said reassuringly sitting down on a wooden bench, motioning to Charles to sit as well. 'We have to wait till the storm stops,' she said turning to Charles. 'In coastal areas, it becomes unpredictable and wild. It is dangerous to venture out in such weather.'

Charles stared at the worn-out roof. 'It doesn't seem very safe here!'

Prachi sighed. 'In my country, many people do not have even a roof over their head. Have you ever visited the fishermen's colonies along the banks of the Chandrabhaga?'

Dharmananda piped up, 'Storms cannot harm this hut. I have seen this place since birth. It stands like a rock, just like the Konark Temple.'

Prachi laughed affectionately, 'And how old are you! How many stormy nights have you witnessed in your twelve years?' She turned to Charles introducing Dharmananda and briefly mentioning his daily, valiant struggle for survival.

Someone chuckled sarcastically in the gloom. It was Vishnu Maharana sitting in a corner. 'Grandpa, you here,' exclaimed Prachi, 'Why did you laugh?'

'What else do you expect me to do?' he replied. 'If another

temple to the Sun God were to be constructed here, would our Dharma be the one chosen to place the holy pitcher on the top[4]? How can boys like Dharma prosper in a country where even the men who built a Konark are no longer remembered?'

Charles, introducing himself as an architect from America said he would love to learn about the temple from him. But Vishnu Maharana shook his head, 'You do research, write heaps of books, but can you ever build another Konark? It is not a book. It's a symbol of dedicated sacrifice, of hundreds of masons and craftsmen who put their soul, sweat and blood into making it a sacred altar, an outstanding monument. Anyone who doesn't realize this is far from getting what Konark is all about.'

'Believe me,' replied Charles earnestly, 'Konark has cast such a spell that I was compelled to come out on this stormy night and have been wandering near the eastern gate. It was locked.'

Konark sprang to life at night said Vishnu Maharana, and dance performances took place in the Natamandir dance hall after dark.

So who had Charles heard dancing? A long dead devadasi, or a celestial maiden inviting Charles to watch her dance? Shaking off an imagination running wild, Charles turned to Prachi and said, 'And then this lady rescued me from certain death barely a few minutes ago.'

Prachi said softly, 'It was Lord Jagannath who saved you. Man only drives man to death. The Almighty alone can save

---

[4]Worship at the Sun Temple built in 1250 is said to have continued at least until 1508, before being abandoned in 1536. When the ruins were excavated, the tower over the sanctum sanctorum was found to be missing, as was the idol. Why worship stopped, why the tower over the sanctum sanctorum was missing, and why the temple was abandoned by 1536 are questions that have given birth to many legends.

him from death.'

'You're my saviour then, a representative of God! I am Charles Naïve, an American, and an architect by profession.'

Prachi politely replied, 'I am Prachi Mahapatra, an Odia, a History research student and my area of research is the Konark temple.'

'I am staying in the tourist bungalow with my friend, Lillian,' said Charles. 'I plan to stay on as a paying guest once Lillian leaves, until I complete my research. But I don't know if people keep paying guests here.'

'I live with my aunt and uncle,' replied Prachi. 'Their house is behind the high school here. I am gathering material from the surrounding villages on legends and folklore related to the temple.'

Maybe she could help him thought Charles, and lost no time asking her, 'It might be difficult for me to gather information from villages since I'm a foreigner. I'd be really grateful if you could help me.'

'I'll help you as best as I can,' said Prachi warmly. 'You are interested in recapturing the art and architecture of my country. To help you would be like serving my country.'

Prachi had depended from the very beginning on Vishnu Maharana, the sutradhar or narrator of many legends, and on Kushi Mausi—a depository of folklore. Now it was Charles's turn to rely on Prachi to gather first-hand information from the villages. Having found Prachi he could now relax. He liked the way she conducted research, she relied on field study and was deeply involved in every minute detail; that perhaps added to her pleasure. Charles worked the same way, going to the source for first-hand information.

They became friends. Prachi felt that since he was her guest it was her moral obligation to help him out, and Charles felt indebted to her for she offered him help without any motive.

They listened to Vishnu Maharana with rapt attention. The characters came vividly to life in the glow of the eternal fire burning in the courtyard. Charles and Prachi could sense the movements of the dancers, hear the neighing of horses, the war cries, the tinkle of bells, the devadasis dancing, the sound of chisel and mallet. The villagers believed Vishnu Maharana practised witchcraft and could command the spirits. Whatever be the cause, his oratory charmed his listeners. He had an ingenious style and would often ask Charles, 'Have you ever fallen in love, Saheb?'

'Many times,' Charles would reply cheerfully.

Vishnu Maharana would fall about laughing and then ask, 'Have you made any sacrifices for love?'

'Sacrifice, for love?? Love means happiness, pleasure, gratification—there's no room for sacrifice, sacrifice involves pain.'

Then Vishnu Maharana would become grave, 'Konark is a temple of love, an altar of supreme sacrifice, an eloquent testimony not only to the skill of the artisans of that time, but a monument to their devotion and purity. Its dignity stems from its commemoration of all this.'

'I know Konark is a temple of love,' Charles would reply, 'I have seen it in every piece of stone, the explicit panorama of love-making. Lillian adores it. But I am not aware that any sacrifices were made to render it sacred, or by those who dedicated themselves to building the monument and doing the carving.'

'Love and sacrifice are intertwined,' Vishnu Maharana would explain. 'Love is sacred. Love is not sex; it is abstinence and selfless submission. Konark is called Padma Kshetra as well as Arka Kshetra. Do you know the relationship between padma (lotus) and arka (sun)? Do you know about their love?'

'Yes, I believe it was a platonic love.'

'Each stone here has lyrics of love engraved on it. It is a pity that even after being in love so many times you still have no grasp of real love. But Konark will enlighten you,' and Vishnu Maharana would smile.

Lillian would retort sarcastically, 'Why sacrifice? Is it so difficult to find a lover? There is no dearth of potential mates when you're young—sex is not a problem. I've seen these carved depictions of sex only at Konark.'

Prachi would add humbly, 'For me Konark is simply not just a structure of unsurpassed beauty, it stands like an ascetic who has conquered his senses, his passions. I have observed the sanyas and celibacy in it.' Lillian would laugh at that and Vishnu Maharana would reiterate, 'You can know Konark only through your heart.'

Charles, seated before him like an obedient pupil would reply, 'Well I'm ready, tell me the story of Konark.' And Prachi would put her palms together, place them on her lap softly and say, 'I am ready too, Vishnu Grandpa.'

Lillian would move away, cigarette in hand, addressing herself to Charles, 'You can read about Konark even in Washington's libraries. We should be out and about, appreciating the murmuring casuarinas.'

'Sorry Lillian, I'm here for Konark. I want to get as close as I can to it. You won't have any problem finding companions, there are so many foreign tourists here.' Charles would reply, and Lillian would stalk off. And with Lillian out of sight, Vishnu Maharana would return to unfolding the story of the Sun Temple of Konark.

Vishnu Maharana was a jatismara, (one who remembers his past life). He recalled past events as though they had taken place yesterday, including those in his past life. Kushi Mausi joined him too at times. She said Vishnu was about her son's age. Her memories were even sharper. Many of their narratives were similar, and they described the events that took place nearly seven centuries ago as if they had happened yesterday. It was eerie.

Charles and Prachi noted down everything the aged duo said. Charles requested Vishnu Maharana, 'Please begin with the story of King Narasimha Deva II. I don't have much knowledge about the Ganga Dynasty and can't pursue my research without knowing about the king.'

Vishnu Maharana looked at Prachiprava with raised eyebrows. 'How much does she know either about King Narasimha Deva, despite being a student of History? History knows Narasimha Deva only as a king. History has recorded his valour, conquests, acts of welfare and administrative acumen. But I knew him as a sensitive human being, as a supreme ruler, a selfless lover, as an obedient son, as an affectionate brother—as a patriot. If anyone knew him better than I, it was Kushabhadra, the old woman. She still says whoever knew the king fell in love with him. He was an exceptional man. She openly expresses her adoration for him.'

Prachiprava said shyly, 'During my research whenever I hear about King Narasimha Deva, I feel envious of the princess of the Malava, the queen Sita Devi, the favourite queen of the king.'

Vishnu Maharana glanced at Charles, 'Was I not right? By the time I finish my story Prachi will be in love with the king.'

'I feel jealous of King Narasimha Deva too,' chuckled Vishnu Maharana and began his story. 'King Narasimha Deva, the third son of Anangabhima Deva and the grandson of King Rajaraja Deva, was a king without parallel. Only he could have constructed such a magnificent temple, left such an indelible stamp on the pages of history. Ganga rule over Odisha began with the invasion of the kingdom of Kalinga in the twelfth century by King Chodaganga Deva. Prior to that the Somavamshi[5] dynasty, also identified as the Keshari dynasty, ruled Odisha from the seventh till the tenth century AD.'

He continued, 'Chodaganga Deva was a great warrior, and during his rule the empire extended from the Ganges in the north to the River Godavari in the south, from the Bay of Bengal in the east to the Ghats in the west. He was the first Ganga monarch of Odisha. His rule also facilitated healthy cultural exchange between the Aryans in the north and the Dravidas to the south of Kalinga. The Aryans were trying to establish their supremacy in the south and had already entered into marital relations with the early Chalukyas and the Chola dynasty to advance this process.'

He looked around at his little audience and satisfied that they were listening with rapt attention he went on, 'The Gangas were great administrators, patronized art and architecture and built temples like the Lingaraja and Rajarani temples in Bhubaneswar. Yayati, a powerful Ganga king, built the Jagannath temple in Puri. But Chodaganga Deva was the last notable king of the Somavamshi dynasty. Chodaganga Deva had conquered the land of Odra or Kalinga, and in 1135 AD the Gangas built their capital at Kalinga Nagar, situated on the border of modern-day Andhra Pradesh and southern Odisha. Chodaganga Deva later shifted his capital from Kalinga Nagara, to Odisha for

---

[5]Rulers who trace their lineage to the Sun.

administrative convenience.'

Charles rapidly glanced through his notes to confirm he'd got it all down, as Vishnu Maharana paused a moment before starting up where he'd left off. 'After entering Odisha, the Ganga kings adopted its rich cultural traditions. Chodaganga Deva himself was a devotee of Lord Shiva. But by the time he conquered Odisha, he had become a worshipper of Vishnu. Anangabhima Deva III, another significant Ganga king ascended the throne in 1211 and ruled till 1238 AD. He was very powerful and maintained huge artillery. The Ganga Empire under Anangabhima Deva III extended from Ganges in the north to the river Krishna in the south. Anangabhima Deva's capital was renamed Abhinava Varanasi Katak.'

The names were tricky thought Charles, he'd have to make sure he got them right. Vishnu Maharana continued, 'Extremely handsome, Anangabhima Deva was an ardent devotee of Lord Vishnu and would present land and gold coins to Brahmans on auspicious events such as Makar Samkranti, Purnima, Amavasya, solar and lunar eclipses, etc. Being a learned man he acknowledged talent and patronized other learned men. During his reign, a large number of wonderful Hindu temples were built across Odisha along with many tanks, ponds, wells and roads.

'He also mastered the philosophy of the Vedas and the Vedanta. He revered both Lord Vishnu and Lord Shiva. But his heart rested in Lord Jagannath. Although the cult of Jagannath was very old, it was only during his reign that it became popular. Today the Jagannath cult embraces and combines in itself, elements of Buddhism, Jainism, Shaivism and Vaishnavism. By this time, the Muslim invaders had already occupied Bengal. The overpowered king of Bengal, Laxman Sen, found refuge in Odisha for some time. Anangabhima Deva, the mighty ruler, was able to thwart the attempts of the Muslim invaders. During his reign, the Kalachuris had occupied the western part of Odisha. After subjugating them, Anangabhima Deva gave his daughter in marriage to Kalachuri prince Paramardi Deva, ending the prolonged conflict between the Gangas and the Kalachuris,' concluded Vishnu Maharana looking around at the little gathering. The focus in his eyes told Charles there was more to come.

And so it did. 'Anangabhima Deva eventually declared himself as the humble "rauta" or disciple of Lord Jagannath. Recognizing his capabilities and prowess on the battlefield, the title of Purushottam was conferred upon him. Today, the king's descendants are known as rautas, for their utter submission before Lord Jagannath. He established townships, donated land and wealth among his subjects—Tulapurushadana, Danasagara, Hiranyagarbha Maadana, and others. Both his queens, Somaladevi and Kasturi Devi, were deeply religious. His daughter, Chandrika, was married to Paramardhadeva of the Heyhaja race. King Narasimha Deva I, was the son and successor of the Anangabhima Deva and Queen Kasturi Devi. He had inherited all the good qualities of his father and the heritage of his lineage. He catapulted the glory of his dynasty to its zenith. The period from 1238 to 1264 AD when Narasimha Deva ruled Odisha, is considered the Golden Era of the history of Odisha and one of the most illustrious phases of the Ganga dynasty. By the time Narasimha Deva was crowned king; his kingdom was surrounded by Muslims. They had conquered the whole of India, except for the independent Hindu kingdoms of Kalinga and Kashmir.'

He was now coming to an important turning point in his narration. 'King Anangabhima Deva had married off son

Narasimha to a princess of Kashmir, Sita Devi. The Kashmiri princess had heard a lot about the future king and had in fact worshipped Lord Shiva with one hundred thousand champak flowers to grant her desire for Narasimha Deva as her husband. He was the only eligible person in the country, as far as she was concerned. His fame, wisdom, graciousness and humanity had spread over the length and breadth of India. Many princesses were pining for his hand. But it was Sita Devi who became his favourite chief queen. The young king, however, was not so fortunate as to spend his life in the company of his beautiful wife. The gallant young man sacrificed his personal comfort, his life of entertainment and enjoyment for motherland. On their wedding night, he told his bride, "Maharani, I may have to leave for the battlefield tomorrow morning. Our kingdom is surrounded by enemies. Most of the land around us is already in the hands of the Muslim army. It is only due to the mercy of Lord Jagannath, we have not yet fallen into the hands of the Muslim enemies." Queen Sita Devi heard him quietly. Instead of words of love and endearment, she heard words of battle and of parting from her husband on her wedding night. But she spoke calmly, as though she had long prepared herself for such an eventuality, "Maharaj, I have already offered puja to goddess Gadachandi, and she has blessed this platter of sacred vermilion for your anointment. If you wish, I will bring it before you, tomorrow morning and bid you farewell for your triumph in the war." Narasimha Deva feigned hurt. "Maharani, are you not hesitant to send me to the battlefield? We have started our marital life just this night! Suppose I do not return from the battlefield?" Sita Devi replied, "One, who is named Narasimha, can never be defeated. An ardent devotee of Lord Jagannath can never be killed at the hands of his enemies. Maharaj, Kalinga is not my motherland but it is the place where I have begun my new life. I must protect her freedom. That is why I am willing to abandon my happiness as a bride. I will not hesitate in spending the rest of my life alone, without my husband, if necessary." Sita Devi's encouraging words gave the king courage and built his morale. He was determined to crush the enemies of his country.' Vishnu Maharana paused for a sip of water. Outside a thunderstorm continued unabated.

'In 1243, Narasimha Deva defeated the enemy at Katasin and attacked Lukhnor and Lukhnoti. At that time Tughan Khan, the emperor of Bengal, was looking for an opportunity to invade Kalinga. But Narasimha Deva decided not to wait for his enemy to strike; he decided to strike first. No other king had ever dared do this earlier. His father was a great warrior, but Narasimha Deva proved he was even better and planned a crushing attack. This act of courage set an example for his descendants for a long time to come. It was due to his foresight and bravery that the kingdom of Kalinga could maintain its independence despite the powerful Muslim presence. Not only did he protect his kingdom, he also occupied many of the enemy's lands. By 1243, Nasiruddin, the youngest son of Iltutmish, had been the ruler of Delhi for twenty long years. He had delegated the administration of his country to his minister, Ulugh Khan or Ghiyasuddin Balban. In 1242, Ghiyasuddin Balban was defeated by Narasimha Deva at Katasin. The next year, Narasimha Deva attacked Bengal for the second consecutive year. Tughan Khan's defeat was almost certain before the superior war plan and strategies of the king of Kalinga. Muslim general Karimuddin was killed on the battlefield and Tughan Khan was defeated without much effort. King Narasimha Deva conquered Lukhnor. By this time the monsoon had set in and the victorious king was now returning home with his army after also conquering the kingdoms of Radha and Gauda. The early monsoon rain drove away his fatigue. Lightning greeted him and his queen, Sita Devi shed tears of joy.'

Prachiprava was thrilled with the story of Narasimha Deva's victory. Charles charmed by her expression, teased her, 'How elated and thrilled the queen would have been on the return of the king! I can imagine that very vividly even now.'

'How?' Prachi asked innocently.

'By your expression!'

'And what does that mean,' Prachi inquired frostily.

'Even though your face is faultlessly sculpted, like the beautiful work at Konark, it is mostly stiff as stone. It is difficult to read your emotions, whether you are happy or sad. But after seeing your joy today, I don't think even the queen showed such delight.'

'In his victory, lies my victory, the victory of my country. Even though all this is the past, it is the glorious past of my country!' retorted Prachi.

But Charles wouldn't let go, 'It's natural to be happy! Have there been no previous incidents in your life that made you happy? Is this a special characteristic of Indian women?'

Prachi turned seriously to him. 'You misunderstand me, Charles. Indian women feel more strongly for others.'

'Excuse me, may I ask you about whom you are thinking now?'

'I think of many. Whom shall I single out?'

'If you don't mind tell me about all of them!'

'I think of our Lord Jagannath, about King Narasimha Deva, Vishnu Grandpa, Kushabhadra Mausi, Chitrotpala who sells flowers, and Dharmananda. I compare the past with the present and analyse it. I go back seven hundred years and I fall in love with events of the past.'

'Among all these people, is there no place for your wandering foreigner friend?' Charles teased.

Prachi gave him a long look and said, 'You are a guest of my country, how can I desert you? A guest is considered God here. I cannot live without God. That is why you are always here.'

'If you are so in love with the past, you should love your guest then! India has a history of hospitality. Love is implicit in hospitality!'

Prachi smiled, 'It is the same thing to love your guest and your God, for any Indian, a guest is God. From that point of view, I love you. Have you not felt that?'

Charles became emotional and reacted, 'But I am not God, Prachi! I am an ordinary mortal. Do not compel a man to stand on a pedestal; that is suffocating. Can't you simply accept your guest as a man and love him?'

Prachi stared at Charles; this wandering young man seemed deeply in torment. The slightest show of affection and he would be at her feet! But what would she do with that emotional outburst? What was her strength? And power? She knew her limits. Why should she fool him with false impressions of love for a few days? Charles had had many girlfriends in his life and there would be more in days ahead. Prachi would never be able to offer that kind of companionship to him, or to any other man. Let Charles stay with his sorrow. After all, he was here only for a few days.

'Charles,' she said calmly, 'love which does not give any sorrow is the kind of love I have for you. That is a sweet human relationship. Let India be in no way responsible for your unhappiness in life.'

Charles persevered, 'Can a guest of two days not be a friend for a lifetime?'

'I have accepted you as my friend,' Prachi replied.

Charles said, 'Then my condition is...'

Prachi stopped him mid-way, 'There are no conditions in friendship. Please do not make ours a conditional friendship.'

And Charles was forced to remain silent.

Four

~

That entire day Lillian roamed alone, while Charles accompanied Prachi and collected information from neighbouring villages on Konark, its historical antecedents, and the folklore that added to its mystery. He prized this kind of wandering, a quest for knowledge. He said he used Prachi's eyes to see, she was his Guide. To Prachi he was a guest, and therefore revered as a form of God.

Despite this mutual state of comfort, Charles privately maintained that Prachi, though quite a well-read and liberated modern woman, was still very firmly entrenched in her Indian traditions. She was conservative, shy, and gentle. And those inherent womanly qualities made her even more beautiful and attractive. To him she was the symbol of Indian culture. Compared to Lillian, Prachi was like a flame, steady and unwavering; Lillian was a source of instant joy, like lightning or a flowering bough, but Prachi was a soothing tree that spread tranquil shade. There were a few girls like Prachi in the village too, gentle and calm. While admiring them, Charles would honour her too. And Prachi would thank him shyly.

As they travelled through the villages, Prachi told him that each village though underdeveloped and deprived, had its own qualities and significance, and produced unique indigenous products. 'Would you like to buy any?' she asked.

They were returning from Hatipada and Kherang villages. Kherang boasted ten artisan families, which crafted exquisite statues out of yielding sandstone. Walking through Kherang they also came across Dhrub Kandi, a painter who made patachitras or scroll paintings. Prachi asked him, 'Would you like to buy any patachitras from here, Charles?'

'Me? I am a wandering vagabond. Even precious things become a burden. Now if you'd only fetch me a pretty woman from these villages,' he teased, 'like those depicted so beautifully in these patachitras.'

'A woman!' Prachi could not believe her ears.

'A woman of flesh and blood, but perfect like a sculpture. I like the girls over here.'

Surprised, Prachi asked, 'What will you do with a girl?'

'Marry her,' said Charles calmly.

If Charles had said murder instead of marry, she could not have been more surprised.

'But what about Lillian?'

'She is my friend. A girlfriend. There is no compulsion to marry.'

Prachi was displeased. 'But both of you live together, you love each other! Doesn't that mean anything?'

'In my country,' explained Charles, 'a relationship between a man and a woman, even if they are in love, doesn't have to end in marriage. We don't mix these two concepts, like you do and suffer.'

'But in my country, it is just the opposite,' protested Prachi. 'Complete strangers fall in love with their spouses after marriage! It is the religious conviction of our wedded life.'

'I promise that as long as I stay married, I will certainly love her.'

Prachi was irritated and shaken, 'that means your marriage is not going to last forever?'

'How is it possible? I've to return. With my lifestyle it'll be a liability to travel with a wife. I've heard so much about marital bliss here that I'm tempted to try it out, even if only for a few days!'

'In my country, marriage is the ultimate destination in a woman's life. No one would agree to such an arrangement with their eyes open—that separation is inevitable. No one experiments with marriage,' said Prachi severely.

'I am ready to pay any compensation,' Charles replied magnanimously.

'Charles! You have read a lot of Indian philosophy but you have not delved deep enough. Please do not trivialize Indian women and such a solemn matter like marriage. Not many will approve of your views. I am trying to ignore them, they are blasphemous!'

Charles was apologetic, 'I was not joking, Prachi, I was just expressing my views. You suffer because you consider matters like marriage, friendship, men and life too seriously. Please forgive me if I've offended your sentiments.'

Prachi sighed. 'Maybe you are right. Happiness and sorrow mean different things to different people. I may find happiness in what you term sorrow. There is nothing like absolute pain or absolute joy. To be able to withstand both can be enriching. The joy that is attained after sorrow is much better than happiness found easily.'

Charles thought Prachi was hiding a secret sorrow. Even though she appeared as calm and unaffected as Konark, he sensed she concealed a bleeding heart. But he dared not ask her. It is unbecoming to ask a woman her secrets.

After visiting Kheranga, Hatipada, Karamanga, Srikanthapadur, Anasara and Dalimbagaruda villages, they returned to Vishnu Maharana for another session of storytelling and Vishnu Maharana continued with the unfinished chronicle. His vivid recall and narration brought the centuries-old story back to life: 'After conquering Lukhnor, Narasimha Deva did not indulge in merrymaking or throw himself into worldly pleasures, but prepared to build a temple. "Why are you so worried?" Maharani Sita Devi asked her husband. Narasimha Deva replied, "War, conquests, bloodshed are inevitable if we are to preserve our freedom, but they don't elevate one's soul. The art and cultural heritage of our land has to be protected and nurtured. Our traditions of dance and music, art and craft are unparalleled. It is my duty to safeguard these for thousands of years to come. I want to wipe out memories of sadness and bloodshed on the battlefield by creating a monument that best exhibits the superior talents of our artistic tradition for posterity. Only then can I protect the cultural heritage that I have inherited." Maharani Sita Devi, her husband's chief adviser on crucial issues, said softly, "Maharaj! Your forefathers had worshipped the Sun God in a small temple at Konark built by King Purander Keshari. Queen mother, Kasturi Devi, was childless, and bore you after she offered puja there. The Sun God was pleased with her devotion and granted her a son. She believed that it was Mahavir himself whom she worshipped at Konark, who had granted her a son. That is why her son is so powerful and invincible today. That Sun Temple is now in ruins. The Queen Mother had promised to build a new one at the site if blessed with a son. Her wish is yet to be realized. Why do you not construct a temple which will fulfil her desire, as well as be masterpiece showcasing our art and artchitecture?" The king agreed and that same year, 1244 AD, the seed of the temple took root in his heart.'

Vishnu Maharana closed his eyes for a moment as though recalling that moment afresh. 'The king then conveyed his thoughts to his minister, Sadasiva "Sibei" Samantray. While Sibei Samantray, his minister-architect was preparing a plan for the temple, Narasimha Deva again invaded the kingdom of Gauda in 1246 AD. Ikhatiyaruddin Yujbeg, an assistant of Iltutmish, was representing the latter as the ruler of Gauda. A bloody war ensued. Prince Paramardi Deva, brother-in-law of Narasimha Deva and son-in-law of Anangabhima Deva, led the battle as Narasimha Deva's general overpowering the Muslim army with his valour and war techniques. The defeated Yujbeg lost a prized white elephant, along with the Muslim-ruled districts of Bengal such as Howrah, Bankura, Hughli and Birbhum. The king vowed to mark this victory as well, by constructing a stupendous monument dedicated to the Sun God, which would be the most beautiful work of art in the entire world. By then King Ganapati of the Kakatiya dynasty in Andhra Pradesh had also been defeated. The victory flag of King Narasimha Deva flew over the northern and southern parts of India.'

He continued, 'Meanwhile a blueprint for temple construction had already been prepared by Sibei Samantray, the chief architect. The site too had been decided upon, and decisions made on the expenditure and duration of construction. A pond called Padmatola was to be filled with sand to provide the foundation for the temple. Initially it was difficult to fill the pond as rocky boulders would disappear as soon as they were dumped into it. Seeing no way out, Sibei Samantray invoked Goddess Ramachandi. She appeared in the guise of an old woman and directed him to start filling the pond with sand from its edge, instead of throwing rocks and boulders into its centre. The local chieftain contracted the best of masons and craftsmen for the job. Finally the foundation stone of the temple of Konark was laid. When the untimely collapse of the temple occurred, only its ruins remained as testimony to Odisha's unmatched artistic heritage. This thirteenth century monument had survived in part for seven hundred years,' noted Vishnu Maharana gravely.

'When temple construction commenced, Muslim invaders were still attacking the borders of the land. Fighting them on the battlefield left the king unable to supervise temple construction on the site. It was left to the masons who worked with fervour, determined to erect a temple of unsurpassable height and exceptional artistry that would inspire worshippers and speak of their nation's glory for years to come. Narasimha Deva, revered as a hero, vanquished his enemies in a historic victory.'

He continued, 'The king was a great patron of art, literature and culture; a rare amalgamation of all the sterling qualities in one man. There was no trace of discontent among his subjects. No voice rose up against the king, ever. Both tasks—the building of an unparalleled temple to the Sun God, and defeating the enemies at the border—were accomplished with passion. As if what the king willed was an echo of what his subjects desired! His powerful persona inspired his fellow men to great heights. Narasimha Deva not only sat on the throne as a king, he also reigned in the hearts of his subjects. Although the Maharaja held supreme power, he relied on a group of sixteen trusted ministers to assist him and sought their opinion on important matters. He treated each of the sixteen with equal respect, making no distinction of caste or creed. Nevertheless, he had such a presence that no one would even think of defying him. His sister Chandrika Devi was the widow of Prince Paramardi Deva who had led Narasimha Deva's armies to victory several times. When Yujbeg became the ruler of Bengal, he was defeated by Paramardi

Deva, many a time. In the end, Yujbeg sought assistance from the Delhi Sultanate to attack Deva. This drastically changed the battlefield equation—Paramardi Deva was killed in the subsequent war, and the district of Radha slipped into the hands of the Muslim conquerors. Narasimha Deva was heartbroken at the turn of events, and with the untimely death of his brother-in-law. Nevertheless he continued the fight and kept his flag flying high until he fell. According to legend, though defeated, the Muslim soldiers shed so many tears from their kohl-lined eyes that the waters of the holy Ganga turned black and was renamed as Yamuna River! This is mentioned in some copper plate inscriptions.'

Vishnu Maharana sighed heavily and looked up. He mumbled, 'Where are those days? Where have they disappeared? A mighty king like Narasimha Deva! And his soldiers!' He continued his narrative: 'Narasimha Deva was a warrior like Arjuna, a statesman like Vrihaspati, and a patron like Karna. He was robust and well-built like Bhima, level-headed and sagacious like Yudhisthir. He was always true to his word like Bhishma, and handsome like Kandarpa, the god of love. His enemies appeared so small before him! He won many wars and had amassed huge wealth which he distributed among the poor and the needy. He was charitable and organized many events to help the needy. At the age of twenty-seven, he ascended the throne and inherited a country perpetually disturbed by invaders. In a very short time, he liberated and occupied neighbouring countries in almost all directions. His soldiers were brave, well-organized and dedicated. Despite being surrounded by enemies, his countrymen lived peacefully during his reign. His rule was punctuated by wars and also marked by his patronage of the art and culture of the land. It was the Golden Era for literature, architecture and religion. It seems like yesterday,' mumbled Vishnu Maharana, totally immersed in another world. Charles and Prachi had diligently recorded every word he uttered.

Kushi Mausi did not come to the temple for many days. Chitrotpala reported she was sick and bedridden. She visited her every morning before coming to Konark to sell her flowers. She cooked food for the old woman and attended to all her requirements. She visited her again in the afternoon. The old woman was happy with her and would bless her affectionately, 'Oh Chitrini! May you get a good husband! May you live long with your children and grandchildren. Let them have my years too. May your marriage last forever.'

Chitrotpala rolled with laughter and tried to conceal her open laugh with the edge of her cotton sari as she told the others what the old woman had said. She blushed red, as if it was the colour from her sari that was smeared on her face, then she paused and said, 'I am not even married yet and the old woman blesses me with sons and grandsons!' and would giggle again, bursting with happiness like a river in spate.

Charles, who had by now picked up enough of the language to get along, asked her, 'When are you getting married?'

Chitrotpala smiled coyly.

'Not this year. My father has not yet saved enough for my dowry.'

'What's the problem in marrying without dowry?' Charles wanted to know.

Chitrotpala looked astonished. 'Who will marry me then? Is there any good bridegroom who will marry me without a dowry?'

'Yes, of course there is!' said Charles with a naughty smile.

Chitrotpala looked sullen, 'Then he must be very old and

a widower at least thrice or four times.'

'No, not an old man. He is quite young. He may have known a hundred-odd women but he has not married any as yet.'

'Then he must be sick, ailing, ugly and a good-for-nothing fellow!' Chitrotpala grumbled.

Charles said, 'No, not a sick or ugly man. Just like me. How do I look?'

Chitrotpala was taken aback, she bit her tongue and rolling her eyes exclaimed, 'What is this? You are a Saheb!'

'Are Sahebs not human beings?' Charles asked her.

'But they are like migratory birds!' Chitrotpala replied matter-of-factly.

Charles teased, 'But do you not relish the fun of flying? Once you fly out, you won't like being tied to your caged life again.'

Chitrotpala looked at Prachi helplessly and murmured, 'Didi, I do not understand what the Saheb is talking about. Please tell him if my father hears of this he will not allow me to come here to sell flowers anymore. I have to earn enough to save for my dowry by year end.'

Prachi intervened, 'She is not a child anymore, Charles! In my country no one makes fun of girls regarding their marriage. It bewilders them We lay a lot of importance on the subject in our villages. You should be careful with your words or else you can get into a great deal of trouble.'

Charles was undeterred. 'I want danger, I want to get into that kind of trouble,' he teased.

'Why are you looking for danger? Have you gone mad?' Prachi asked.

'When I am in trouble, you come to my rescue. You offer me sympathy, shower me with affection. You rescued me once from certain death. That opportunity is yet to return.'

Prachi burst out laughing and said tenderly, 'Charles, you are interesting, you sound so romantic in everything you say. But not everybody will take you in the right spirit. Be careful.'

'But do you understand me Prachi?' Charles asked her.

'I am trying to understand you. But that is immaterial. What is important is whether Lillian understands you or not!'

Charles said off-handedly, 'Lillian has found a new companion. They are having a good time together. She doesn't need me anymore. I am free.'

Chitrotpala was listening to them intently. Prachi did not want to continue their conversation before such a young girl. She changed the topic. 'You should apologize to Chitrotpala, you have hurt her feelings.'

'I am sorry,' said Charles, catching tender hands that were putting flowers into the basket. 'Forgive me Chitrotpala. I wish you get married soon. I will dance at your wedding. Now give me some flowers, please!'

Chitrotpala handed him a garland of tuberoses. Charles said, 'I will buy flowers from you every day till you get married. I will try to help you irrespective of whether I need them or not.'

Chitrotpala was touched. 'Who knows whether you will be here till then! You are a Saheb. There is no certainty about you people.'

Charles laughed. 'I will certainly wait that long, Chitra!'

Chitrotpala was glad. She said, 'I will fetch the best flowers, Saheb! You always pay me much more for my flowers!'

Charles said lovingly, 'You do not know the real worth of your flowers. They are invaluable.'

'Sahebs are really mad. Can flowers be invaluable? We grow so many flowers in our garden. It costs a pittance.'

Charles stared at her, bemused by her innocent laughter

and her pure untouched rustic beauty. Prachi said in jest, 'Don't stare at her like that Charles, it is considered an offence here.'

Dense casuarina groves flanked the long Marine Drive between Puri and Konark. It was pleasant to walk in the shade, right up to the temple of Goddess Ramchandi. Charles and Prachi were going to meet ailing Kushi Mausi who lay bedridden in her hut behind the temple. The temple priest gave her '*prasad*' for food. They were led by Dharmananda with Chitrotpala behind him.

Prachi was worried about Kushi Mausi's failing health, and she realized that a treasure trove of folklore would vanish forever with her passing. They were still so many legends to hear from her. Charles was also worried about the same issue, plus he had a soft corner for the old woman who had called him 'son' from their first meeting on.

Lillian had not accompanied them, 'What's to see?' she wanted to know. 'The old woman is emaciated, it's natural she's sick. She's possibly dying and her suffering will end if she dies quickly. Life's to be enjoyed. When pain and suffering begin, it is better to die, instead of living in hell.'

She added curtly, 'I thought you'd come to India to research and have fun Charles. But I see you're getting enmeshed in their pain and suffering. Open your eyes, there's poverty and squalor everywhere. You don't even have to try hard to see pain and sorrow.'

And so, the little band of four minus Lillian, reached the small temple near the mouth of River Kushabhadra, where Goddess Ramchandi was worshipped. The temple was built in typical Odia style with a small hut-shaped prayer hall in the front. Inside stood a pedestal atop which the goddess was enshrined as the ten-armed Durga. A former land-owning zamindar had donated five acres of land for the daily rituals of the temple. The priest worshipped the goddess daily chanting Vanadurga shlokas.

Prachi lit a lamp, covered her head with her pallu and bowed to the goddess in reverence. Charles waited for her outside. The priest recognized Prachi, her aunt belonged to that area. She was staying with her aunt and uncle during her research work at Konark, as well as a temple of the goddess Khalkothi at Liakhia, five kilometres away where Prachi visited occasionally.

The priest put a red vermilion mark on her forehead. She returned after taking a round of the temple. Charles was surprised to see her with vermilion on her forehead.

'What are you looking at?' Prachi asked.

'I thought only married Indian women applied vermilion, why did the priest smear it on yours?'

'Vermilion, if applied to the central parting of the hair, symbolizes a married woman. If the priest was confused, I take it as a symbol of my bond with Lord Jagannath. I feel married to Him. Can anyone object?'

Chitrotpala was plucking flowers from the temple courtyard with one ear on their conversation. She laughed. 'Didi, you are always moving around with this Saheb. People think you have married him. The priest too thought like that.'

She was smiling at them, holding a bunch of oleander flowers. Prachi turned crimson with embarrassment just like the pink flowers and retorted angrily 'Chitra, why do you listen to all this nonsense? I have never heard anything like this!'

Charles interrupted lightly, 'Vermilion is the symbol of a married woman in India. Indian men must be at the top of the world to be treated like this, like God! We don't feel such pride on becoming a husband. I feel quite jealous sometimes!'

'I cannot stand proud, greedy men,' said Prachi.

'I've become greedy for many things here after coming to India. It is you who crush my ego at every step. India's really strange,' he said and walked on.

Kushi Mausi talked of strange things when they met her. 'At night,' she said, 'a young woman's ghost roams Marine Drive. It is the restless soul of a beautiful woman who wants to tell her story, but everybody is afraid of her and runs away as fast as they can. I knew her and that was why I was not scared. This woman has been deep in sleep for years together, but is now awake. Why? After so many years?' she paused and sighed.

'No one knew about her. There is no mention of her in the history of Konark. No one remembered her life, her sacrifice after the temple was completed. Her story was buried in the sands of time on the banks of River Chandrabhaga. But I knew her and that's why I was not scared.' Kushi Mausi said she knew why the young woman had woken up. It was a strange story...

'Lord Chitreshwara was once worshipped on the banks of River Kadua, about seven kilometres from Konark in Jadupur of Golaragada. Many years ago the villagers, digging a well, found a copper-plate inscription at the site. It had four letters. An old man deciphered it. But before it could be properly read, the metal was melted and converted into household utensils. The words of the inscription were never made public. Nobody believed the old man, but I believed him. It was a story that was identical to one that I had heard from my mother-in-law and her grand mother-in-law.'

The inscription apparently eulogized the sterling qualities of King Narasimha Deva and the making of the Konark Temple. She said that the villagers had also stumbled upon the stone sculpture of a woman very close to the temple, but she added, 'No one took any interest in it. There were hundreds of such sculptures scattered around the beach. They were quite used to finding them. The statue remained unnoticed for a long time. Then some children playing around the place smeared vermilion on the statue's forehead and began to worship it. The face was chiselled into the shape of a full-blown lotus flower. She had languid eyes. At the feet of the statue was engraved the name "Chandrabhaga". The woman was exquisitely beautiful.'

She continued, 'In time, the statue sank into the sand and a leaf of sacred basil grew on the site. The village women who came to bathe in the river would pour some water on it on their way home. Even today, a statue of a woman standing with folded hands can be seen at the centre of every Odia village.' She returned to her original tale about the well being dug. 'In the meantime the village priest had a dream in which he was asked to stop the digging. So they stopped and another well was dug at a distance. A strange thing happened. A skeleton was found at the spot. It was unbroken and had, with time, petrified into stone. People said the area must have been a burial ground. Some even said that the skeleton belonged to a woman. She was believed to be young and married because she wore a silver ring on one of the toes of her left foot.'

She took a sip of water and continued. 'The villagers were proved correct when a team of British archaeologists who visited the site later confirmed this fact. They had come to study the relic and concluded that it dated back to the thirteenth century and was certainly that of a young woman. They said she must have been well built and very beautiful. The statue was abandoned for many more years. Then one day it suddenly disappeared on a rainy dark night. The villagers thought the river had washed it away. But everybody was relieved they did not have to worry anymore about how to appease her soul.'

Charles and Prachi had been listening with rapt attention, but now Prachi interrupted and said in hushed tones, 'Mausi, forget about the ghost stories. Please tell us about Konark, its legends and folklore. That is much more interesting.' But Charles the wanderer liked adventure, 'How could the skeleton disappear overnight?' he wanted to know.

The old woman shook her head. 'Had it really disappeared, there would not have been any story.'

'Huh?' said Charles, perplexed.

Kushi Mausi picked up the thread again, and wove them a mesmerizing a story of love, romance, and an eternal wait.

'The skyline of Konark was dark,' she began. 'The place had been in a state of neglect and darkness for three hundred years. And in the midst of this overgrown forest a skeleton roamed the ruins on moonlit nights. It would pause at a distance and stare at the ruined temple. Then it would sigh. The echo of the sigh ruffled the leaves of the forest. People commented that the forest wept at the fate of the temple and for the artists of Konark, and for King Narasimha Deva. At times, the skeleton would bow towards the temple with its bony folded hands, then disappear into the forest along the riverbed. People were scared and avoided the place. But accidentally, if they came face to face with it, it would transform into a woman. They were struck by her ethereal beauty. She had eyes like a lotus bud, and on moonlit nights there would be tears in them sparkling like diamonds. Only a very beautiful woman could possess such eyes. She never harmed anyone. The people were so stunned by her beauty that their fear evaporated instantly.'

Kushi Mausi continued, 'It was a story of a Dark Age. Mile upon mile of dense forest stretched along the seashore at Konark. The temple had already collapsed. The idol of the

Sun God had been removed from the abandoned temple and there were no more rituals before the deity. Marine trade had stopped long before. During the next 150 years, the temple and its surroundings were deserted, except for wildlife which proliferated in the dense forest. Over time the ruins of the temple sank deeper and soon its high boundary walls were concealed by layers of sand. The Natamandir dance hall, the temple of Mayadevi, and many other structures and other holy relics were all buried. Only a portion of the porch remained visible.' Kushi Mausi shook her head sadly before resuming.

'The soul of Konark was stifled, no one heard its screams, but the desperate cries of the woman who roamed as skeleton were heard through the night, night after night. People said the skeleton cried, and along with her they said they heard the cries of the hundreds of masons and sculptors who had built the temple.'

Taking a deep breath, she continued, 'Konark remained abandoned for three hundred years as if under a curse. The skeleton remained the sole guardian of the ruined temple. When the temple was re-discovered, the skeleton disappeared into the casuarina forests. Nobody heard her cries anymore and she has been forgotten like the history of Konark. Or, has she?'

Charles and Prachi understood what Kushi Mausi was trying to say—it was the same skeleton that had been discovered on the riverbed recently. This time round it had been found because of road-building works. The construction of the road was the first step to developing the area. Konark formed part of the golden triangle on the tourism map of Odisha. Marine Drive stretched five kilometres from Chandrabhaga Square to Ramchandi Temple along the Bay of Bengal, connecting Puri, Konark and Bhubaneswar. It wound through the dense casuarina forests for about twenty-six kilometres, after which there was a fourteen-kilometre stretch connecting Chhatiana with Gopa.

Hardly a week after work on the road had begun, strange things had started to happen. There was gossip that about thirteen kilometres of the road had been washed away by heavy rain; and that fourteen-foot high sandbars along the road had vanished overnight. Some even said that because River Kushabhadra had changed course, the road to Ramchandi had suffered a setback.

But why did the river change its path all of a sudden? Some knowledgeable old men were of the opinion that the skeleton was responsible for everything. She hid in the jungle and guarded the monument.

Kushi Mausi took up the tale again, 'The construction disturbed her peace, so she created as many obstacles as she wanted to, to bring the road building to an end. She would be heard laughing so loud that it sounded like the roar of the waves, and shouting at the top her voice, "O, inheritors of Konark! The ruins continue to mesmerize the world with their matchless craftsmanship. I have been guarding the monument for over seven hundred years. The casuarina forest was my abode and sheltered me from sun, rain, storm and wind. If you cannot protect the temple, why did you disturb my meditation? Konark is collapsing, with it my soul wilts. When will my soul be released from its curse?"' and with that Kushi Mausi stared blankly at the sky and fell silent, as silent as though she had lost her voice forever.

Fact or fiction—many anecdotes and legends about Konark still remained unheard. Charles had come across many such things in India that appeared strange, but were genuine. He wondered if he could find the key to the old woman's soul and unlock the mysterious events that had taken place long ago.

Even as the thought came to him Kushi Mausi beckoned, indicating that he should untie the knot in her pallu. Charles was a little hesitant. However, Prachi stepped up and untied the knot very carefully and found a tiny box made of brass. Did this box hold the key to the old woman's soul, Charles wondered, bemused.

When Prachi opened the case, he was amazed. For there was indeed a small iron key! How could the old woman guess that he was in fact hoping for a key to her soul? She called him son. Could mothers actually read minds in India! Charles was ready to believe anything in this strange country where the past and the present intermingled. Prachi handed him the key. He was overwhelmed with emotion and looked at her surprised. 'What am I to do with this?'

Kushi Mausi pointed to an old iron trunk lying in a corner of the hut. Chitrotpala said excitedly, 'That box is full of gold coins. The king had gifted them to the sons of the old lady. They worked as artists and masons during the making of Konark. For centuries she has kept them carefully. Her ancestors belonged to a village called Begunia, near Dakshineshwar. When she left her village, she employed labourers to carry that trunk for her. She worships it daily, smears it with sandalwood paste and vermilion, burns joss sticks and lights a lamp in the evening.'

Meanwhile, Kushi Mausi was gesturing to them to open the trunk with the iron key. The trunk looked as weathered as she did, with its layers of sandalwood and vermillion paste. Charles was obviously surprised with these developments and stood still. Even if Chitrotpala were to be believed, what would he do with antique gold coins? Why should he get involved in this mess, after all, what right did he have? He wondered if Kushi Mausi contemplated bequeathing them to him. He could perhaps use them for Chitrotpala's wedding.

It would be an ideal present and a privilege for him to gift them to her on such a sacred occasion, but would his gift be accepted? He was a foreigner in this Hindu domain, not permitted to sit in on sacred rituals. But the old woman was on her deathbed; was that why she wanted to part with her treasures now? But why to me, Charles wondered.

Prachi took the key and unlocked the trunk with a great deal of difficulty, as time had corroded and rusted the lock. Once that was the done, the lid refused to yield. Ultimately, just as Charles moved to lend a hand, Prachi was able to prise open the lid.

There were no gold coins. Instead, lay something wrapped in layers of muslin cloth that had become brittle with age. It was indeed a heap of priceless treasure—immensely important palm-leaf manuscripts dating back to antiquity.

Chitrotpala's face betrayed her disgust. 'She saved these *manuscripts* with so much care and worshipped them like an idol of God with vermilion and lighted lamps! Has she gone mad?' Charles and Prachi were too baffled to respond to the turn of events.

Prachi found it strange that Kushi Mausi had handed over these invaluable objects to Charles, a foreigner. Did Mausi have so much confidence and trust in Charles, she wondered. Meanwhile, Chitrotpala was carrying on, 'Every day, Kushi Grandma wiped the trunk and told me, "Dear Chitiri, this box has only gold coins in it. I will give them to him who wins my confidence. He should not sell them. He should offer prayers daily just like I do! For these coins have a glorious past. There are numerous stories written on those gold coins!"' And Chitrotpala started giggling, 'Look, are these the gold coins?

These palm-leaf manuscripts?'

Prachi held the bundle of manuscripts carefully and lifted them to her forehead as if to offer her salutations. Charles, holding the weather-beaten hands of the dying woman and oblivious to anything around him, was comforting her, saying, 'I promise I will worship these documents like you did and keep the tradition of this country alive and honoured.'

Prachi asked him to put a bit of nirmalya (the dried rice available at the Jagannath temple; considered holy and given to dying Hindus during their last hours) and holy Gangajal (water from River Ganga) into Kushi Mausi's mouth. Chitrotpala fetched these. As Charles dripped holy water into her mouth, the old woman closed her eyes in absolute bliss and contentment, never to open them again. A teardrop fell from Charles's eyes on her forehead. He said softly, 'I will perform her last rites; does anyone have any objection?'

With tears in her eyes Prachi said, 'Kushabhadra Mausi never discriminated on the basis of caste, creed and religion. In fact, her soul would rest in peace if you performed her last rites. Odisha, the land of Lord Jagannath is indeed a confluence point of all religions.'

The pyre's flame leapt to the sky in circles of smoke and took Kushi Mausi to her eternal abode of bliss. On that bright sunny day, the smoke created a contrasting picture of light and shadow. Inside Konark Math, Vishnu Maharana sat engrossed beside the holy fire, turning the pages of the newly-discovered palm-leaf manuscripts. Prachi and Charles waited with pen and paper to gather the pearls of wisdom that lay buried.

Vishnu Maharana looked up. 'Kushabhadra's ancestors were very illustrious people. One of them wrote the history of Konark.

Since then, these manuscripts have been preserved with utmost care and are treated as a sacred object, as they symbolize God. When the manuscripts became too brittle for use, they were copied afresh on fresh leaves and the old manuscripts consigned to the river. The present manuscript is at least one hundred-years old, and was copied by Lakshman Maharana, her husband.'

He paused, and continued. 'Kushabhadra lost her husband before she reached puberty, and so became a child widow. When she came to stay with her in-laws, as was the custom, she was given these manuscripts copied by her husband as her only treasure. She possessed and worshipped them as a part of her husband. When her mother-in-law and brother-in-law died a few years later, she was all alone in the world with no husband, no children and no family for support. These manuscripts were her most important and treasured possession, a memento of her husband. She was barely seven when she was married to twenty-six year old Lakshman Maharana and two years later, when she had had just turned nine, her husband died prematurely.'

He looked at them, his eyes shimmering with unshed tears, 'Throughout her life she faced the world bravely and treated everyone as part of her family; as her own children and grandchildren. How admirably she lived her life! And she lived quite long too. I know that many researchers had come to her to buy the manuscript. She could have earned handsomely by selling them and lived comfortably thereafter. But she would say ruefully: "How can you sell something that is your very own? This is all I know and have of my husband. If I sell these, I will become powerless and lonely. How can I survive without his strength?" After her family members died of cholera, she left her village for good and came to settle in the village called Kherang. This village was established by her forefathers—and it offered her shelter.'

Charles was astounded! How could a girl of seven be married to a twenty-six-year-old! Becoming a child widow by nine, to spend one's entire life clutching the memory of a husband in the form of a few handwritten parchments that she could not even read? How could some palm-leaf manuscripts have protected her from desire, greed, attachment, anger, frustration? Charles decided it was possible only in India, mysterious, marvellous India. The land was great, he thought. He had put the old woman on a pedestal, now he wanted to worship her like a goddess.

Prachi sat quiet, pensive, as if she was re-living Kushi Mausi's lifetime of sufferings. Prachi could empathize with the pain, suffering and loneliness. She knew how many sacrifices and dedicated efforts were concealed within the folds of India's vast spirit. Prachi was an Indian. She was a woman, a symbol of creation, a symbol of motherhood and of supreme sacrifice.

After offering his prayers to the ancient manuscripts, Vishnu Maharana now began to read:

'1245 AD. The most powerful king of the Ganga dynasty, King Narasimha Deva, had just defeated the combined armed forces of the Nawab of Bengal and the Amir of Delhi in the historic battle of Laxmanavati. The king was bestowed with the titles of Hamiur Manamadana and Dillibibhanjanarana befitting his glorious success. Poets like Vidyadhar wrote epics like the *Ekavali* in praise of the king and poet Dindima Deva Acharya wrote about his valour and heroism in glowing words in *Bhakti Bhagavata Mahakavyam*.

'The victory was a milestone in his career and to commemorate the event he wanted to construct a magnificent temple on the bank of River Chandrabhaga. He wanted to invest his booty from the war, employing the best of craftsmen, masons to make it the tallest shrine as well as most artistic depiction of Odia-style temple architecture. Thus the foundation stone of the world-famous Sun Temple of Konark was laid.

'Massive stone blocks were transported from far-off mountains through river channels for the construction of the temple. Sandstone, white, blackish and bluish granite and khondolite stone was ordered from distant areas like Nilgiri in Balasore. For the massive Navagraha slab, a stone block weighing 642 quintals was specially brought to the site. The pitcher at the peak—the final stone to complete the temple building—was twenty-five feet high and fifty-six thousand tons in weight and had been brought to the site from a distance of a hundred kilometres.'

Vishnu Maharana smiled contentedly. 'Do you know, Saheb? The British could not transfer the massive Navagraha slab over a distance of two miles despite having so many modern gadgets. But centuries ago, the Odias could transfer the stone block weighing twenty tons from miles away and also lift and lodge the carved wonder at a height of twenty feet! Is that not quite an impossible feat? The Britishers had to split the slab into pieces and then carry the pieces away.'

Charles stared at Vishnu Maharana in stunned silence. How could they have transported these massive stone blocks from far-off places for the construction of the temple? It would have needed high levels of expertise. He wondered about the masons of ancient Kalinga and the indigenous techniques with which they had lifted the massive block atop the main structure and lodged it on the beam. They should be revered for their talent, he thought. These were masters. They were great!

Vishnu Maharana continued reading:

'Nearly twelve hundred artisans and masons set up hamlets

in and around Konark. The blueprint for the temple was drawn and the masons were assigned their tasks in units. Each individual task had to be completed by a definite date, as the final date for the completion of the temple was fixed on the eighth day of the Amavashya or dark fortnight of Baishakh in the year 1258.'

Charles wanted to know, 'Was it not a formidable task, for them to first carve out the smaller parts of the temple and then join them together to construct the temple? There must have been exceptional coordination and harmony among them, or how could they visualize the finished edifice right from the beginning; such dedication and unity that they even thought alike! It seems almost as if the artists were united in their souls as well. This is impossible to find in today's world.'

Vishnu Maharana said sadly, 'Saheb! You live in a small part of a divided and disintegrated modern world, which has narrowed the mind, thoughts and conscience of people. Such a world has taught us only about ego, disbelief, intolerance and lack of respect. That is why you think it impossible to have such unity and harmony among the people. But back in the thirteenth century, things were different. The land of Kalinga was bursting with joy at the victories of King Narasimha Deva, and there was able administration in the country. People lived happily and were proud of their king who was magnanimous and did a lot of good work. When the noble king thought of building the Sun Temple at Konark, the artists, masons, craftsmen, poets, dancers, singers, leaders and even ordinary people were excited and volunteered their services with enthusiasm. There was no dissent. The artists and masons came up with a brilliant master plan for the temple that was to be a timeless and peerless creation—and it was. And they committed themselves to it, dedicating in their souls, dreams, dedication and efforts to accomplish the task.'

Charles was aware of his distance from Lillian, and that he had deliberately encouraged it. But why was he not able to get any closer to Prachi in thought or soul? If Konark was a symbol of solidarity and Kalinga a sacred land of religious confluence, why could he not be united with Prachi?

Five

—

The blue waters of the Bay of Bengal were turning a deep grey and the sun, now orange-hued, was sinking into the dark liquid depths of the Bay. Lillian and Charles sat side by side on a cement bench admiring the splendid sunset. There was a small cabin from which the aroma of simmering hot tea wafted into the cool twilight air. The sea was turning cool and Lillian's drugs were beginning to act on her. As the sunlight faded, Charles became more engrossed in his thoughts. He wondered about medieval Kalinga, it must have been one of the most developed places in the entire world about seven hundred years ago. The architecture of the shrine at Konark overwhelmed him; his perception and his years of study as an architect had not prepared him for such grandeur. Having studied the maps and plans of the Sun Temple, he concluded that even an average mason would have more knowledge about construction techniques than he did—and he was regarded as an upcoming star back home!

Lillian did not like the mood Charles was in and said, 'Let's go. Let's go somewhere else. Chandrabhaga does not appeal to me anymore, let's move to Goa. Now.'

'Goa?' said Charles, surprised.

'Yes, Goa; it's the same thing. The beaches at Konark or Goa are no different!'

'Why?'

Lillian made a disgusted gesture and pointed towards the

temple. 'These amorous couples of stone that have so enraptured you are there in Goa in the flesh, alive and vibrant. No restrictions, no limitations, no rules or regulations. Lots of uninhibited women wearing scarcely any clothes on the beaches. And nowhere else in India do men and women make love openly on the beaches. And no dearth of drugs—marijuana, hashish, heroin and opium— everything is available round the clock. Why waste time here? You know what's most interesting? You don't feel lonely in Goa. Even if you are busy with your research and have no time for me, I won't feel left out. There is this "boy-girl" drug, a cocktail of cocaine and heroin, injected into the vein. Brush wants me to visit Goa. He has no objection if you come with us.'

Charles, who had not been paying attention thus far, suddenly became alert at Brush's name. Lillian could read a man's look. 'Brush is French. You could call him a hippie or even a freak. He makes a good profit selling heroin on Baga Beach, and he's happy. Tell me Charles, if we only want pleasure, why restrain passion? Why so much study and research?'

'Because it moves me to ecstasy,' Charles said quietly. 'It's the reason I am here—to seek knowledge. Our views on Konark are totally different. You look at the erotic sculptures on the temple walls and forget that it is a temple of God, of the Sun God, the source of solar energy. He is worshipped here. For the Hindus, it is one of the holiest places on earth. And I know the enormous effort and dedication that has gone into the making of this astounding twelfth century shrine. For me Konark is like a saint in deep meditation and I bow to it. Now, it's my lifelong religion, the search for ultimate happiness and bliss.'

Lillian asked sarcastically, 'All these depictions of sex, also a part of Sun worship? You bow to them too?'

Charles felt humiliated and replied coldly, 'This is just the beginning of my research work. I'm sure by the time I complete the project I'll be able give you a satisfactory reply.'

'And how many days must I wait for that?'

'I have no idea.'

'And if I cannot wait that long?' said Lillian looking Charles square in the eye.

'The wives of Konark's architects could wait sixteen years, their entire youth, for their men to return. I am an American architect, and I want my beloved to wait for me indefinitely.'

Lillian nearly fell over laughing. 'Charles! You've gone crazy, you need to see a doctor. I'm afraid you're under some spell, how can you be so absurd!'

'Really? To wait for one someone you love for sixteen long years is absurd? Is it? Were those people crazy?'

A tall young white man with long and dishevelled hair was approaching them. It was Brush, the Frenchman who had become a friend of Lillian's in just two days of his stay at Konark. Enamoured with his devil-may-care demeanour, Lillian whispered into Charles's ears, 'You look like an Indian, Charles. One who's haunted by the ghosts of Konark at that. I like Indian men, but not India. What's there in India? If you don't leave this country soon, we may not see each other again. I'm going to Goa with Brush, I'll spend the remainder of my vacation there and go back to America. If you prefer to stay in India forever, I have no objection because we respect our independence in the United States,' and with that she walked off with Brush.

Charles was in an introspective mood. Many things were not available in India, just as many things were unavailable in Western countries too; but there were many things in India which were not to be found anywhere else in the world. He truly loved his research work. Lillian had opted to leave, he did not stop her. Edward Naïve, too, had to leave his wife because of his love for India. Lillian was not even his wife, she was only a lover. Patience, waiting, sacrifice—were simply aspects of love. And could love ever become a burden?

After Lillian left with Brush, Charles quit the hotel and for some days simply wandered aimlessly. By then the monsoon was over and at night he would sleep in the open with the soft green grass as his bed, and a sparkling starlit celestial canopy above his head. The lullabies of the murmuring casuarinas in the cool fresh air lulled him to sleep. In any case, most days he was so fatigued he would fall asleep almost instantly.

The rays of the autumnal sun would gently touch him awake every morning. He would sit up, bow, and whisper, 'Mother Earth, you are so gracious, so generous. I feel a mother's touch here, even in the soil,' and he would smear a dab of soft soil on his forehead.

Every day at the Konark Math, Vishnu Maharana would read out a further portion from the brittle palm-leaf manuscripts and then explain its meaning. Prachi and Charles would jot down whatever was relevant to their research. Thereafter, Charles would go down to study the sculptures at the temple ruins and compare them with the detailed descriptions given in the palm-leaf manuscripts. Sometimes, Prachi and Charles would visit the neighbouring villages seeking ancient sculptures and artefacts.

Charles also continued to pursue the elusive female ghost who wandered the banks of the Chandrabhaga. Alone in the dark, he would search for her until he felt sleepy at which point he would just find a grassy clearing, lie down and go to sleep. Nevertheless, every morning, he tried to be there to meet Prachi at the Konark Math where Vishnu Maharana would read to them from the palm-leaf manuscripts.

The reading sessions would be postponed on days when Charles failed to turn up. Such days left Prachi anxious because by now she was sincerely attached to Charles. Charles felt like a family member, someone very close to her. She felt it was her duty to look after him ever since Lillian had left. She was appalled that Charles pursued the ghost alone in the dead of night. He needed a guardian.

When Kushi Mausi had been alive, Charles would never get wet in the rain or burn in the scorching sunshine. The old woman's protective, affectionate eyes would always look out for him. But after her death, Charles had become completely alone. What could she do? Prachi sent Dharmananda after him.

Some days, Charles would wander for miles along on the beach and sleep on the roadside, or be found in the casuarina forest, at the Ramchandi temple, or at the Chitreswari temple. Some days Dharmananda would find him at the 'burial ghat' where Kushi Mausi had been cremated. Charles appeared a different person; disoriented and sombre.

Prachi was concerned and entreated Charles earnestly, 'Since Lillian left, you have changed so drastically. You better call her back, Charles. And make some compromises so you can live with her. You are not concentrating on your research any longer. You are so carried away by Kushi Mausi's tales that you are now after that ghost almost every night. It is not proper, Charles!'

Charles replied calmly, 'The manuscript does collaborate the facts I have heard from Kushi Mausi. Believe me, I have already found that ghost! I have seen her from very close quarters on the road that runs along the coast. She was walking inside the casuarina forest very swiftly. She appeared to me like a faint bluish flame in the moonlit night. As if she was floating with the wind. She never took off her veil. But I have also never seen her in the form of a skeleton. She is shrouded in a veil. She has never blocked my path. And never scared me. She always walks at a little distance from me. But I get pulled into her world, to the thirteen century. I am sure she has a deep relationship with the temple of Konark and I am going to unravel that mystery.'

His reply upset Prachi deeply. 'It's a delusion, Charles! Are you doing drugs at night since Lillian left? This is the effect of addiction.'

'I *am* addicted, Prachi. That ghost hypnotizes me.'

Prachi became quiet. Could he be speaking the truth, she wondered. Vishnu Maharana laughed from his perch near the palm-leaf manuscripts, 'The soul never dies. It is immortal, imperishable and eternal. If you deny its existence, then all that is mentioned in these manuscripts is also not to be believed. It is her story and the Saheb is searching for her as a man possessed. This is a legend. If you believe it, it is true; otherwise it is just a story, or folklore!'

By now Charles had quit living under the open skies and moved in as a paying guest at Dinabandhu Babu's house. Dinabandhu Babu was Prachi's uncle and a school teacher by profession. His only son was in America, in Washington, pursuing higher studies after completing his Masters in Physics from Odisha. When they heard about Charles, Dinabandhu Babu and his wife Charukala gladly offered him accommodation.

While staying with Dinabandhu Babu, Charles took lessons in Odia and Sanskrit from him. He could speak a few Odia words, and this tickled Dinabandhu Babu because it made him recall his son's infancy and he would laugh. 'Dinesh also used to stumble in the same way when he was a child. Don't worry, you are mastering the language pretty well.' Charles was delighted to hear that and thanked him. Dinabandhu Babu's stature rose in the locality because he was teaching Odia to a foreigner. But his eagerness to teach was no match for Charles's determination and dedication to learn. Like his son Dinesh, Charles too was diligent, worked hard and single-mindedly at whatever he did. Dinesh had completed his diploma in French and German in a short time. The loving parents would try to find similarities between Charles and their son as it gave them comfort.

That was also why Charles was adopted into the family so quickly. Dinabandhu Babu's wife Charukala would prepare fine lace-like cakes called chakuli for him, and serve them up with fresh curd and ripe bananas for breakfast. 'This is good for your health. The food in hotels leads to many diseases. You will age prematurely. And drain all your money, no matter how much you earn; it just won't be enough.'

Charles would reply, 'Our modern lifestyle is to eat and stay in hotels. Many people actually live in hotels throughout their life. Nothing troubles them. It all depends on one's taste and habits. I am used to this kind of life, I've been living it since I was thirteen.'

Charukala would nod in sympathy, 'Alas! What poor habits you have formed from your childhood. My son Dinesh never liked hotel food. But now, in a foreign country, he too has to stay in somebody's house as a paying guest. He too eats with them. They are very nice people. They love him as a son.'

'If I go back before he returns, I will surely try to meet him in the States,' replied Charles. 'Who knows whose work will finish earlier? But he will not have any problem there. I have made arrangements for him, through correspondence with a few people. He is appreciated as being quite hardworking. His professor is happy with him, my father has written. I had given his address to my father.'

Dinabandhu Babu and Charukala became more and more attached to Charles who in turn found himself becoming increasingly appreciative of Odia cuisine and dishes like rice, roti, pithas and other delicacies. Though his landlord thought Charles was overpaying him, Charles was being compensated by the excellent food he got to eat. With time, Charles had almost become like a member of the family. It was difficult to decide whether this was due to Charles's open-hearted, straightforward disposition, or Dinabandhu Babu's affection for him. He wanted to hear about the country where his son was staying and Charles enjoyed talking to him.

Dinabandhu Babu owned two residential buildings facing each other across the main road. One was a thatched mud house he had inherited. The other, he had constructed. The old house had a spacious courtyard with a fruit and vegetable orchard in the back, and a pond. The new house was built with bricks and tiles. It had four rooms, including a bathroom. Charles was given a room in this new building. He was also provided with a fan. Another two rooms had been given on rent to students. The corner room served as Dinabandhu Babu's study-cum-drawing room. There he gave tuitions and entertained guests.

Charles could see Prachi's room across the road from his open window. Three bedrooms faced the road in the old house. Prachi stayed in one of them. She would burn her kerosene lamp late into the night. On certain days Charles would come home very late at night, but Dinabandhu Babu waited for him no matter how late it was. Charles ate outside when he was late. He was not fussy about food. He was a small eater and preferred fruits, biscuits, bread and boiled eggs, to cooked or spicy food. Fruits and biscuits were available anywhere and were good for health. But Charukala would not allow him to sleep without a glass of milk and would never allow him to sleep on an empty stomach. He would drink the milk to please Charukala. He felt that he already belonged to the family and Dinesh was almost like a relative staying abroad. He would spend a lot of time talking to the elderly couple and sometimes Prachi would join them. Prachi was soft-spoken and was more a listener than a speaker. Charles too was a little reserved, and Charukala and Dinabandhu Babu did most of the talking.

Charles had prepared a rough sketch of the Sun Temple at Konark as it would originally have looked seven hundred years ago, inspired by the description of the temple in the palm-leaf manuscripts. Attempting to describe the grandeur of the monument of that bygone era to Prachi, he felt as though he himself was involved in the building of the Konark temple—as its chief architect.

And he *had* seen the temple in its complete glory with his own eyes, whether in a vision or a dream he could not say. He was so lost in reverie, that he did not notice when Prachi left his side and lit the lamp in her own study across the road.

Charles kept searching for detailed information about the temple in the palm-leaf manuscripts—the architectural style, the building materials, the craftsmanship. He made a critical analysis based on the data. He was intrigued by King Narasimha Deva and the work done by his subordinates.

The night deepened. A faint ray of light came from Prachi's room and merged with the glow of the electric lamp in Charles's room. Charles's fair skin gleamed and a luminous lustre highlighted Prachi's pink and peach complexion beautifully. Charles was tired after a day's hectic study and prepared to sleep. Prachi's serenely attractive face lulled him to sleep. He switched off his lamp. Prachi snuffed hers as well... only darkness prevailed. Normally sleep would claim him as soon as he hit the pillow, but that night he was dreaming. This was strange, as he had never dreamt before. A damsel in distress haunted him. Who was she? Someone from his past? Or was she yet to come in his life?

Charles's mind slipped back seven hundred years and events began to vividly unfold before his eyes. In the middle of a township stood the temple of Konark, a majestic, colossal chariot driven by seven imperial horses cast in black stone. There were two structures, the 'Vimana' or main temple, where the idol was worshipped, and another structure in front called 'Jagamohana' where the worshippers congregated.

The monument was built on a raised podium—a chariot about to take off. It had twelve pairs of intricately-carved giant wheels. The main temple was built in 'Rekha' style (where the sanctum is surmounted by a curvilinear spire), and the audience hall in 'Pidha Deul' style (a square hall called 'mandap', roofed with a pyramidal horizontal design), in keeping with the prevalent Kalingan temple architect's rural designs. At a little distance, to the east, was the Natamandir dancing hall, intricately carved with motifs of people, birds, animals, flowers and other images that made it delightfully picturesque.

In the south-west corner at a furlong's distance, was a temple for Goddess Chhaya Devi, the consort of the Sun God. Samba Pith was located in the north-west corner, while the south-west corner had a kitchen with several other structures inside the courtyard. There was a site for a sacred fire, and huts to house the masons and architects involved with the making of the temple and there were some huts for visitors as well. There were two wells, one for the use of the divinity and the other for the public. An elevated masonry boundary ran round the complex.

The Simha Dwara or Lion's Gate was the entrance facing the east. Visitors, irrespective of their caste, creed, colour or religion could enter the temple premises. The temple was open to all, just as sunlight was free for everybody. Konark represented the confluence of all religious sects and made no distinction whatsoever.

Charles walked in through the Lion's Gate and scrutinized the foundation structure of the enormous shrine with the trained eye of an expert architect. To the west, was a rectangular construction. There were beautiful sculptures, the guardian angels, over the walls and enshrined as 'Mitra', 'Pushpa', and 'Haridashwa' respectively in separate small cubicles called 'Nisha Deuls'. Charles instinctively knew all this; though how or why he did he did not know.

There were wide entry points to the temple on all sides except from the west. Charles, as if in a trance, slowly went down the steps. There were impressive carved pillars flanking the flight of stairs. On the eastern entrance, the pillars were crowned with colossal 'Gaja-Simha' images of lions pouncing on elephants. On the southern entrance, were dynamic war-horses perched on top of the pillars, while on the pillars to the north were fully caparisoned war elephants. Charles had seen them several times in earlier dreams too.

Finally, he stood before the Natamandir facing Aruna Stambha, an enormous monumental iron column, installed on a six-foot-high carved pedestal. The column had six sides. On its summit was Aruna, Lord Surya's charioteer, seated with folded hands. Charles sensed someone's presence behind him and turned. It was Prachi, smiling at him as if she was the one he was destined for. He did not speak and they walked silently, hand in hand like a pair of wheels of a chariot, in perfect tandem. They stopped before the Aruna-Varuna doorway near the Nandyavarta staircase. There were many people entering and exiting the Hall of Audience. Each entry door was carved exquisitely and lavishly, much to the wonder of all those who saw it.

Charles was awestruck by the intricacies of the motifs. Suddenly he felt as if the temple of Konark had bloomed like a divine scented lotus flower, and he was inhaling its fragrance! Upon the pedestal carved with lotus flowers, the Sun Temple appeared as a divine manifestation. Lotus flowers were braided all along the immense pedestal rising and falling as they followed the figure. There were honeycomb carvings all over, unsurpassed in beauty and craftsmanship. Lotuses abounded, making a pedestal for the feet of the Sun God.

Charles entered the sanctum sanctorum and was overwhelmed by the rich embellishments inside. The ornate pillars on which the massive Navagraha slab stood, indicating the presence of the nine planets that orbit the sun, was richly embellished with flowers and creepers in decorative motifs. Each planet on the slab had a separate niche. Charles walked in slowly. He stopped at the mukhashala, the porch that admitted visitors inside. It was a massive fourteen-foot long, seven-foot wide structure carved of black chlorite. There was a drain for the holy water to flow after the completion of the puja in the inner chamber.

Charles was being led by his dream. There was no one at the door to stop him. He stood before the ratnavedi, the intricately-carved diamond throne. It was a small replica of the temple itself, eleven feet long and eight inches wide. In the middle of the throne was the altar of the Sun God, embedded with precious stones and gems. Behind it, was an arch—a headrest for the deity. A polished and ornate set of stone steps led up to the altar for the offering of prayers. The entire structure was fitted with five richly-carved stone wheels.

Charles bowed to the artists in reverence for having accomplished this unsurpassable piece of craftsmanship. He was oblivious of the divinity to whom the temple was dedicated. Two elephants flanked the pedestal at the base.

The sides of the throne were filled with ornately-carved motifs of animals, birds, vines, flowers and other designs depicting spring, with deer, rabbits and elephants roaming in the forests. Charles felt as though they were greeting him.

In front of the throne was a beautiful image of the king, clad in regal apparel with a sword tucked under his arm, kneeling on the floor along with Queen Sita Devi, worshipping the Sun God. Seven attendants stood behind them and another attendant held a garland to offer the king after he completed the morning ritual of worshipping the Sun God. Female attendants stood with plates bearing joss sticks, earthen lamps; and holding cymbals and the mridang drums. They were perhaps dancers and musicians and were extremely good-looking. Charles watched them admiringly.

In front of the throne were two lions rearing, in a typical Odissi posture known as Olata Simha—lions depicted with their heads flung backwards. There were two elephants crouching under the lions. The lions looked ferocious and they bent in a curve so that their tails touched their heads. There were two more Olata Simha images behind the throne, seen crushing elephants. There was ample use of brass to hold the stone slab firmly in place. Elephants with riders added to the beauty of the throne.

Charles admired King Narasimha Deva, who had constructed such a magnificent temple. But he wondered why the king carried his sword when he was worshipping the deity. He felt as if someone answered in a deep voice, 'O foreigner! I am removing your doubts. At that time the Muslims surrounded Kalinga and there were continual threats from them. The king worshipped the Sun God as his Ista Deva and he was committed to guarding the sovereignty of his kingdom at any cost. He was worshipping his God asking for valour and strength to fight the enemy and protect his motherland.' By then Charles too was kneeling on the ground. But he was kneeling before the noble King instead of the Sun God. He was overwhelmed by Narasimha Deva, the king and his devout nature.

In the morning, Charles was found sleeping in front of the stone image of King Narasimha Deva. Dharmananda woke him up and said, 'Didi is waiting for you at Konark Math. You are getting late for the reading session.' Charles opened his eyes and asked 'Who is it? Dharmapada?' Charles addressed Dharmananda as Dharmapada.

'Yes, Dharmananda. Didi has sent me to fetch you.'

Charles said wistfully, 'Not you. I was searching for Dharmapada last night, in the temple courtyard and around the boundary walls. When the entrance door in the east was unlocked at daybreak, I went inside the temple and I do not know when I fell asleep.'

Taken aback, Dharmananda asked him, 'Who is Dharmapada?'

'Dharmapada,' explained Vishnu Maharana, after they reached him at the temple, 'was an ordinary boy, an architect-in-the-making not included in the legends of Konark. Nevertheless, his artistry is indelibly embedded in each lotus petal of the Konark Temple. He is not to be forgotten. There were masons like Vishnu Maharana, Nila Maharana, Dhabala Maharana and Kamala Maharana who remained in the memory of people down the generations. It was due to their individual dedication and talent that the final capstone could be lodged at the crown to mark the completion of the temple. In each of those masons, Dharmapada survived like a legend. Sadasiva "Sibei" Samantray, the Minister for Developmental Works, was also an engineer and a proficient draftsman. He had been instrumental in preparing the blueprint of the temple and also setting a time-frame for the completion of the monument.'

Vishnu Maharana continued, 'Preparing the plan took two long years. Sibei Samantray put his entire experience, knowledge and intellect into the task and worked without rest. He had decided that the temple would take at least twelve years to build and twelve hundred masons were to be employed for the job. The masons had to work in harmony and with absolute concentration. They had to forgo their families, children, wives, parents and all personal comforts for twelve long years. They had to sacrifice their personal joy, happiness, comfort, love, marriage and all worldly desires for the noble mission of temple building. It was not an easy assignment.' He looked up, 'and now the manuscript refers to Kamala Maharana.'

He picked up the palm-leaf and began reading, 'Kamala Maharana was twenty-two years old, handsome, well-built, a fair and tall man with curly dark hair and an aquiline nose. His eyes were those of an artist, doe-shaped and poetic. He was prominent among the twelve hundred masons, and in charge of the Rupashagada unit. He headed a team of hundred masons. The Dalabehera or chieftain of Rupashagada was put in charge of the administration of the project. He was assigned the job of recruiting suitable masons and artists and extracting the best out of them. The king's men went in every direction declaring the king's intention to build an outstanding temple for the Sun God, which would be peerless in beauty and would last till eternity. Expert artists and masons gathered in large contingents for the job. They left behind their families, wailing children and wives, lamenting young brides, and helpless aged parents in their twilight years.'

Vishnu Maharana looked up at them but seemed as though looking at something beyond time and space. 'Would they ever see their sons again? Twelve years seemed an age to them. Would their sons be able to perform their last rites when they died? Would they put nirmalya, (sacred dried rice) from the temple of Lord Jagannath into their mouth when they were dying, or light the funeral pyre? Could they do that? The inspiring words echoed everywhere. "Go son! Do not hesitate to give your life for your motherland. Let there be no obstacles like desire, greed, lust, attachment in your noble path. Put your soul into building a monument that will speak for years about your talent and imagination. Let the land of Kalinga be known the world over!" Kamala Maharana had come as one of the twelve hundred masons. He too was determined not to go back till his task was accomplished and the final crowning pitcher placed atop the temple spire. These incidents had become folklore, handed down the generations—stories of adventure and valour.'

There was no doubt in Charles's mind that Kamala Maharana was the hero of the story that was told in the palm-leaf manuscripts. Kamala Maharana, the ancestor of Lakshman Maharana of Begunia village, had written his own history in that manuscript.

Vishnu Maharana picked up his narrative where he'd left it off. 'Kamala Maharana was born to an artisan family near the Khandagiri hills and married to a nine-year old girl, Chandrabhaga from the neighbouring village. He wrote the story of his bride Chandrabhaga, based on his imagination and the information he received from his brother, Dhabala Maharana, and others.'

Vishnu Maharana noted that Kamala Maharana described his bride as, 'being more beautiful than he had imagined. Had she been with him, he could bring life to his creation. But exquisite and perfect Chandrabhaga was the creation of God Himself. Everyone who had seen Chandrabhaga agreed. Kamala Maharana could never match God's creation! He would dream about her, and carve his sculptures based on the image in his mind about his beloved wife. People would wonder if one day Kamala Maharana's handiwork would compete in terms of perfection with God's creation. Thoughts of his bride, who would have turned twelve that year, were always on his mind and he would blush like a pink lotus flower, whenever he thought of her.'

Vishnu Maharana picked up the next palm-leaf and continued reading aloud, 'The sound of her jingling anklets throbbed in his heart. She was to have reached his home dressed as a lovely bride at the onset of the monsoon, just two months after he left. His mother had been preparing for her arrival. His Chandrabhaga would enter his house as an embodiment of prosperity, happiness, fame, good health, bringing with her the promise of a long and happy married life. An auspicious time had been decided upon for her homecoming. But it was two months too late,' said Vishnu Maharana.

Sixty days too late, to be exact. 'Kamala Maharana desperately longed to see his beloved. After becoming a bride, Chandrabhaga would no longer be a waif, a childlike soul. She would be like the River Chandrabhaga, deep, quiet and flowing slowly. She would epitomize the earth, an ever-patient and forbearing woman. The fragrance of her innocent charm would be in the air, and be a magnet drawing Kamala Maharana to her.'

The deepening pathos of Kamala Maharana's narrative touched every heart. Vishnu Maharana continued. 'That day Kamala Maharana had been returning from a far-off village and was passing by her village. Perhaps he deliberately chose that route and walked through the paddy fields and the hills for a fleeting glance of her. Something made him walk away from his group and enter her village that day. There was a lotus pond at the outskirts, where women bathed. The artist in him was drawn instinctively in that direction. But he could not recognize any face among the lotus flowers. He was accompanied by his friend, Brajabandhu. They were walking along the edge of the pond. It was a pleasant and sunny afternoon with a soft orange hue. There were three maidens frolicking gaily in the lotus pond. And one of them was lean, slender and wore a red sari. She stood rooted to the spot in the water, like a lotus stalk and had drawn her veil so as to cover her face before the strangers. She resembled a lotus flower and her two lovely eyes seemed like two black bees on her face.'

'Then,' said Vishnu Maharana, 'Brajabandhu whispered, "Look, Kamala! That beautiful girl in the red sari is your bride. My aunt lives next to her house and I know her." Just then, another girl screamed excitedly at the girl, "Look, my friend! The one for whom you are waiting so anxiously is right in front of you! Your husband is here! Quickly finish your bath and worship him!" The giggles of the young maidens sounded like the notes of the jalataranga[6] as they teased their friend. Kamala Maharana meanwhile, desperately tried to catch a glimpse of his bride. His heart beat fast, but being warned by her friends about the onlookers, she plunged into the water. In her place

---

[6]A musical instrument that uses bowls filled with different levels of water.

was a lotus flower smiling at him!'

There was a collective sigh of disappointment from the little audience, at the fact that this meeting had been thwarted—seven hundred years ago.

Vishnu Maharana continued, 'She was shy and would not come out of the water again! Only a ripple circled the lotus stalk. Kamala Maharana was heartbroken and left quickly. He was scared that if he did not leave as soon as possible, she would drown. He was upset at the girls for teasing her. It was only a matter of a few days when she would adorn his neck like a wreath of flowers, but then she was so shy that she preferred to stay under water and risk death. Before moving away from the pond he turned back for a fleeting second. And there she was, the girl in a wet sari, staring at him. As soon as their eyes met, she again hid in the pond like a flash of lightning! Kamala Maharana did not dare look back again. He vowed to be patient for a few more days and wait for his bride. Every time he tried to recall his wife's beautiful face, which he had momentarily seen from a distance, he would be reminded of a lotus flower. He decided he would rename her Padmini or Komalika instead of Chandrabhaga, when she stepped into their house.'

The narrative now turned to that momentous period when Chandrabhaga left her parent home for good. 'At the predetermined auspicious hour, Chandrabhaga came to her in-law's house, dressed as a beautiful bride. But by then Kamala Maharana's house had become empty and desolate! He had left home, family, and village to join the king's retinue to construct a unique temple for Lord Surya at Konark. And he would be gone for twelve long years. The day the Dalabehera of Rupashgada had selected a team of expert masons from his village, Kamala Maharana was included. He was a brilliant stone mason but he wanted another glimpse of his lotus-faced bride before leaving for Konark! This would inspire him to excel as an artist, he felt. He could at least live with her memory and could recreate her face on stone! But he could not speak about his despair to anyone. For he was not the only one, nearly twelve hundred masons like him had left their homes and families for the noble cause. Some had even left wives on the wedding night, while some had to leave behind their wives at the altar of marriage itself! No one displayed any sadness, no one grumbled. It was not only the king's command; it was a call of their motherland and the wish of Lord Jagannath! The king, the obedient servant of lord Jagannath, was merely carrying out instructions! To obey the Creator would benefit the entire world. Kamala Maharana too abandoned his personal happiness and sorrow for the greater welfare of his motherland,' said Vishnu Maharana.

'That day he visited his bride's village deliberately and walked again to the pond. But there was not a single lotus flower in it. As if the lotus buds too were grieving! They stood quietly in the pond, in distress. They made no accusations, but their tears glistened on the petals! Every time he witnessed the sun rise and set, Kamala Maharana was reminded of his bride Chandrabhaga and how she would have spent her first night in an empty room! She would be looking after his aged parents and his fourteen year-old brother, Dhabala Maharana, who was two years older to her. She would be cleaning and plastering his house, and painting lovely chita motifs on the mud-plastered walls. She would be doing the cooking in his house and pouring water on the basil plant after bathing. It had been planted by Kamala himself! It grieved him to know that his bride would suffer, glowing like an earthen lamp, trying to be an ideal daughter-in-law, toiling with daily chores. Then she would wait for him.'

Vishnu Maharana looked around, everybody was listening raptly. 'Well,' he continued, 'Chandrabhaga was doing exactly that. She burned like an earthen lamp in the darkness of Kamala's room, illumining it and scattering the darkness with her radiant beauty. She was like a lovely statue living in his house, resembling the images he was sculpting at Konark. Perhaps she would turn into stone. Alas she was a human being too, and suffered her share of sorrow and longing. No one bothered much that she waited and pined for him in her loneliness, longing to see him. She did not reveal her heart to anyone. What was the use of sharing her pain? Who could solve her problems? It was not a matter of a day, or a month, or even a year! It was for years together. Twelve long years of waiting!' It was not to be thought of, felt Charles—yet this spirit of sacrifice permeated the fabric even today, he sensed.

Vishnu Maharana intoned, 'That was the will of the king, the command of Lord Jagannath. Kamala Maharana had chosen to put duty ahead of his beloved wife. There were rows of sculptures of beautiful maidens, which he had sculpted with care and dexterity. He sought to depict his beloved wife's loveliness on the walls of Konark. He felt as though the lifelike friezes were asking him, "When are you going to put life into us? When will our wait be over?" Kamala Maharana would murmur, "If I were to put life into you, you would be subject to all human ailments like old age, disease and death. I want to take you away from the world of life and death. You should remain eternally youthful. You will outlive the stones! I too will grow into a stone one day and with the strength of a stone I will be able to bloom stone lotuses."' And with that Vishnu Maharana closed the manuscript for the day, wrapping the leaves reverently in the cloth that encased the manuscripts.

Six

The story was picking up pace, and the next morning the little group eagerly wound its way to where Vishnnu Maharana was waiting.

With greetings out of the way, he began, 'The artist Kamala bowed to the Nrityacharya, the dance master, Somya Sridatta who blessed him: "Long live the artists! You are the pride of Kalinga. Let your statues represent the tradition of dance, music and song of the land. I can hear the jingling anklets echoing everywhere on the deserted banks of the River Chandrabhaga. I can also hear their melodic voices! It is as if that resonance comes from your stone figurines! You are a great artist. You are to be worshipped for your talent." Kamala Maharana folded his hands in humility. "Nrityacharya! It is you who is the mastermind behind all these models and their carving. It is only because of your teaching that each stone has such vibrancy that it is able to reverberate with music, to sing and dance. Your ingenious way of describing the nuances of dance and music inspired us to chisel the images on stone. Without you, how could we gain such proficiency?" Somya Sridatta smiled benevolently and went on to inspect each sculpture.'

Vishnu Maharana continued, 'The work went on in full swing. The masons and the artists were as though in a trance or in deep meditation, as if concentrating to accomplish the noble work. After they finished their individual tasks, they would join the pieces together in perfect coordination for the final piece to emerge. There were six animated *Bhairava* images, which were to be installed atop the ears of the *Jagamohana*. The carvings were near completion. There were images of guardian angels on the eastern, northern and southern sides to protect the monument from catastrophe, be it vandals or the vagaries of nature. They were endowed with weapons like the dambaru, knives, as well as a garland of rudrakshya, fire-spitting tridents, and cups of poison. The dancing Bhairava image had faces on the four sides. These images were powerful and demonstrated the best specimens of dance poses as mentioned in the Nritya Shastras. Somya Sridatta was satisfied with the outcome. He was confident that the sculptures would survive the onslaught of time and survive till eternity. At the top of the Jagamohana, were two rows of dancing women playing the mardala, manjira, karatala, kahali, veena and the flute. They were to be depicted as if they were alive! The work had just begun.'

Thereafter, said Vishnu Maharana, some specific directions were given. He began reading: 'Nrityacharya Somya Sridatta said, "You have to chisel very tender images from hard rock. These women are to be embellished heavily with ornaments and should manifest as celestial beauties. They will possess vibrant, youthful bodies and are to be draped with fine muslin and their hairstyles are to be elaborate and ornamental. They will have extremely feminine and graceful postures. The art will speak volumes about the dexterous chiselling and exquisite carvings by Odian artists and it should remain unparalleled in the world." Kamala silently obeyed the commands of the king conveyed through Somya Sridatta, who said again in a heavy tone, "Maharaj has recruited a hundred sanas (court dancers) for the temple of Nrishinghanath in the southern part of Kalinga. The king is a great devotee. Konark is his masterpiece and it will be a centre of art and culture. There will be elaborate dance and song performances for the Sun God at dawn and also at nightfall in the Natamandir. It will constitute an important part of the daily temple rituals. The king has ordered that the devadasis here, be ravishingly beautiful and highly skilled in music and dance but he wants the statues of women at Konark to surpass them and represent the captivating celestial angels!"' Well the king should have been pleased, they'd certainly succeeded, thought Charles.

Vishnu Maharana carried on reading, 'Kamala Maharana replied with veneration, "All the masons employed here are well versed with the traditional dance forms of Kalinga. We have had to learn the rudiments of dance and music even before we are taught painting and sculpture. It is impossible to carve and chisel out dance poses perfectly without considerable knowledge. We will carry out our king's orders with our heart and soul." The Nrityacharya was relieved to hear that. "I have complete confidence in all of you. I also have ample faith in the masons. I will leave it to you to supervise the overall activities and the statues of Konark. There is no doubt that you have considerable depth, knowledge and acumen in the art and craft of Kalinga. And you are also well-versed in the dancing techniques of Kalinga. Nevertheless, let me tell you once more about the dance forms of Odisha. In the Natapravarda my instructions are to be completely carried out. You have to ensure that." Kamala Maharana noted every instruction carefully.'

The next section of the manuscript revealed a fascinating glimpse of the dance and musical forms present in that bygone era.

'The basic dance pose,' read Vishnu Maharana, 'was the Bilashapurna Lalita Abasthiti, which is termed Bhangi, a dance pose. A Bhangi was possible only after synchronization of every limb in the body. The head was tilted and the hips thrust out in the opposite direction. The dancer stood with her feet crossed. Kamala Maharana bowed and said, "Your Grace, I have decided to sculpt the statues in the Natamandir in distinct shapes and poses in the Odissi dance form. We will sculpt them in traditional postures like Alasha, Pranata, Parswa Mardala, Archana, Biraja, Abhimana, and others. The sculptures will live up to your expectations. I promise." The Nrityacharya was elated with the depth of knowledge of Kamala Maharana. Like an examiner he asked, "What about the accompanying musical instruments? Have you thought about them?"

'And,' said Vishnu Maharana, 'Kamala Maharana described the imagery he had envisaged in minute detail.

'Kamala Maharana began, "The accompanying musical instruments will be that of the Odissi dancer—the tala, mardala and flute. Depending upon the distinctive situation and the pose of the dance the veena, karatala, kahali and cymbals will be used. In dance poses like the tribhanga, the chauka forms will be frequently depicted. The dancers will be adorned with headgear that has elaborate tassels and feathers as mentioned in the treatises on dance. There will be ardhapataka, arala, anjali, kapitatha and pushaputa poses too for the dancing nymphs. With all these, the statues will look well adorned and vibrantly beautiful. Their facial expressions, head and hand movements will portray our dance style." The delighted Nrityacharya replied with great conviction, "My students will be dead and forgotten with time but their creations will remain on stone for years to come. The exquisite dancing maidens on stone poses will inspire dancers all over the world, they will become timeless. Nrityacharya Somya Sridatta will no longer be there, but Kamala Maharana will survive the onslaught of time and will be remembered for his images on the stone walls of the Sun Temple. Konark will not only be a temple of God, it will also be an epitome of love and culture. A unique monument dedicated to painting, music, dance and craftsmanship; a treasure house of all these put together! Centuries later scholars drawn to Konark to learn about ancient Odisha, will also be fascinated by the dance poses which will not only portray classical Odissi dance forms, but will also be a repository of folk dances too. There will be specimens of martial dance forms. The Paik foot-soldiers will be seen wielding swords and shields, and moving in rows. There will be tribal men and women, dancing to the beats of the Ghoomooras, the tribal drum-like musical instrument. Konark will be enriched with all types of Odian dancing traditions. Can you achieve that, dear artist?" And Kamala responded humbly, "Master! Before that, I will try to carve your image on the walls of the Natamandir. I will put your image at the highest niche, to guide and choreograph the dance and music programmes. The Ganga king has honoured you by bestowing a kundala (earring) and padaka (medal) upon you, and he has acknowledged your merit and expertise and conferred the title of 'Acharya' on you as per the Nritya Sashtra. You have been conferred with the title 'Somya' too for your excellence in the field. You have been patronized by the king and you have been instrumental in including the immortal dance poses of Odisha in the Konark Temple. Without your statue, the embellishment of the temple will not be complete. And my craftsmanship too will not reach its zenith. It is the king's command that your image be sculpted on stone here." The Nrityacharya said calmly: "This is another example of the king's greatness. Let the king be ever prosperous. But…'"

Here Vishnu Maharana paused and looked around at the

expectant faces before continuing, 'Kamala Maharana looked at him with surprise. The word "but" conveyed a sadness that emanated from the heart of the master. Immediately Kamala Maharana replied, "There is no space for 'but' in the making of the Konark Temple. Master, please have faith in the artists of Kalinga." Nrityacharya responded gravely, "Remember, there should be no trace of obscenity in the sculptures at the Natamandir. The devadasis will be sculpted as divine nymphs, their facial expression and movements of limbs—all should reflect their ecstasy, joy and devotion to God, for whom they perform their dance. For that you need a model to depict the expressions accurately. Without a model, the dancer's poses, postures and expressions will never be complete or perfect. Which devadasi should I assign to you? Will they be able to overcome their passion and yearning when they work with a handsome youth like you?" To which Kamala Maharana humbly replied, "I believe every artist here is aware that he has to resist all sorts of temptations and has to treat the model only as an inspiration. We have shut the door on all our passions. I give you my word that we will not deviate from that vow. It is possible for a man and woman to share a platonic love. There is this symbolic relationship between the sun and the lotus. It will not be any different in the sacred Padma Kshetra. But, Your Grace, there is no need for any model here. The inspiration of the Konark already exists in the hearts of every artist here. Konark has put music in our souls and in the stones as well. When I close my eyes, I am inspired. My muse is everywhere. She is the beloved of my imagination," Kamala Maharana said humbly,' and Vishnu Maharana put down the palm-leaf that had just read.

Charles analysed the carvings of Konark with the eyes of a

researcher. Prachi had seen them many times. But ever since they had begun comparing the images with the descriptions in the palm-leaf manuscripts, the temple of Konark looked even more ethereal and beautiful to them. Charles had seen them many times arm-in-arm with Lillian. But with Prachi, the feeling was entirely different. Even the lovely couples in erotic embrace looked more divine to him!

He bowed his head to Kamala Maharana and his determination. But Prachi was all praises for Kamala Maharana's muse Chandrabhaga, her dedication and her indefinite patient wait for her husband.

The Natamandir was built in the form of a Pancha Ratha Deul. The platform was divided into three parts. The first part was two feet and four inches high, decorated with lotus flowers. The second section was nine feet and seven inches high and decorated with miniature Pidha Deuls on all sides. There were scenes of lovely damsels, dancing women, Lord Shiva in the Tandav dance posture. The entire platform was richly embellished with dancing girls and musicians accompanying them. The uppermost portion was carved with lotus flowers, creepers and dancers.

They stepped into the Natamandir. There were entrance doors on the eastern, western and southern sides. None of the entrances had any doorframe. The entry doors were carved to synchronize with the Sun God's movement through the seasons of the year. In every season, the first ray of the sun would enter through the Natamandir and touch the Ratnavedi inside the main Deul. The sun's rays would enter the Natamandir at all hours of the day.

Charles was wonderstruck at the architecture of the Natamandir. But Prachi was completely lost in the quality and calibre of dancing depicted so lavishly everywhere at Konark.

She felt like falling at the feet of Nrityacharya Somya Sridatta in gratitude. But that was not to be.

There was an inscription, a rare feature, at the foot of a statue of a male dancer at the northern side of the eastern entrance. On it was written 'Somaechey' in Kalinga Nagari script; the guides said it was 'Somei Visnav' or 'Som Gupta'. Prachi had never come across such an inscription on any other statue of Konark. The dancer depicted was Nrityacharya Somya Sridatta.

It was an outstanding sculpture. Kamala Maharana had poured his soul into it. He had mentioned the name of the dance master at the bottom of the statue. It was a standing statue, one foot and nine inches high and nine inches wide. The dance master was draped from neck to feet and wore a turban on his head. He wore kundals in his ears and a necklace with a diamond medallion as a royal insignia of honour to his artistic merits. He was shown choreographing dance poses and playing cymbals. To Prachi, it seemed as though the statues were coming to life right before her eyes. She wondered who was greater, Kamala Maharana or the dance master Somya Sridatta?

Charles took photographs of the carvings and once again realized that the art and architecture of the temple had no parallel. The brilliant carving of each statue was a theme for study and research. Charles had travelled all over the world. But nowhere else had he come across such a superb example of art and architecture. From any angle, the Natamandir looked perfect; each minute part carved with precision.

Charles and Prachi descended the stone steps that led to the northern and southern sides of the Natamandir. Charles walked briskly, but Prachi was slow and walked with the gait of a dancer; she appeared to Charles like one of the lovely dancing damsels of Konark. He wondered if it was Prachi, so ethereally beautiful, who inspired Kamala Maharana years ago! Prachi smiled, 'Come, Charles! We will enter the ruins of the Natamandir now. Have you turned a philosopher after coming to Konark?'

Charles following, said, 'Not Konark. It's the divine dancers here who look so real. They look like they are about to spring to life; they entice me and I feel helpless.'

Prachi glanced at him with a smile. She had reached the scattered ruins of the Natamandir and went in to the sanctum sanctorum. It had a circular pedestal richly embellished with lotus flowers and a diameter of five feet. Charles came and stood behind her.

With the main temple, the upper portion of the dance hall had collapsed too. But the two rows of lotus petals revealed its grand plinth; it was a magnificent lotus flower in full bloom, with sixteen petals. Each petal was enriched further with dancing nymphs.

Charles imagined those sixteen dancers to be the replicas of Prachi in the shimmering sunshine of the golden afternoon. There was a small lotus flower in the middle with an image of the Sun God holding lotus flowers in each hand. The guide was narrating, 'Even if the Sun God was not visible on some cloudy days, the lotus flowers would still be waiting patiently for Him. But the Sun God never descends to the earth. He moves round the earth on his orbit along with his wives, Chhaya and Sangya. This is a supreme example of divine love. Women in India always wait for their men. No matter if he is a saint or a devil, the wife looks devotedly forward to his homecoming. Konark symbolizes that kind of devotion and love. The wives of the twelve hundred masons waited for their husbands patiently for over twelve long years.'

Prachi was a little unmindful. She sighed. Charles thought that this devotion was indeed unnecessary. What was the meaning of such waiting and suffering? 'Besides,' he muttered to himself, 'This Konark, in ruins today, this lotus flower, which lies abandoned—Kamala Maharana, I sympathize with you. Is this the price of your sacrifice and suffering?'

There were two gigantic lions and elephant images flanking the staircase to the eastern side of the Natamandir, the main entrance to the temple. Near the statue to the north stood a smiling Chitrotpala with her basket of flowers. She handed over a bunch of fresh flowers to Charles. Thanking her, Charles gave her a five rupee note. Chitrotpala was counting the coins to return the balance to him when Charles said, 'Leave it. Today's flowers are priceless. They are worth a lot more than five rupees.'

Chitrotpala's eyes went wide as she said, 'No Saheb, it is not proper to take more money than the actual cost. We are in the business to earn our livelihood. That does not mean I will cheat my customers. At this seat of justice at Konark, God sees everything; I'll not be able to benefit from the extra amount.'

Charles was taken aback to hear this from a simple rustic girl like Chitrotpala. 'Who taught you all this,' he asked.

'Am I a child that someone will teach me this? My father is saving money for my wedding. If I cheat at my work, I may get cheated in life!' Her lotus-like eyes trembled in fear and anxiety. She closed her eyes for a second. Dharmananda, leaning on a Gaja-Simha image at the southern wall with a packet of photographs for sale, burst into laughter.

Annoyed Chitrotpala, chided him, 'What makes you laugh?'

Dharmananda said, still laughing, 'Why shouldn't I laugh? Who ever survived by sticking to such principles? Survival of the fittest, that's what is. An elephant tramples man because man is weaker. And the lion attacks the elephant because the lion is stronger. In this world, the strong always dominate the weak. The mightier always exploits the helpless. Do you know who is strong and mighty in this world?'

'Who?' asked Chitrotpala earnestly.

Dharmananda became grave and replied like a man of experience: 'Those who have wealth and power. The poor are weak in every respect. People who commit injustices, crimes, become rich and powerful. With wealth comes power and respectability. Poor people who act like you and give importance to justice, religion and upright living only go hungry and become old trying to save for their dowry. Do you know how much money is needed for a watch, cycle, radio and other expenses? Have you any idea, how many years it will take you to save that amount?'

Chitrotpala became pensive. But the next moment she said brightly, 'The poor may always remain weak, but God helps and protects them. Look at this image of Gaja-Simha. The lion is rescuing a man from being trampled by an elephant. "Ill got-ill spent", have not you heard the saying? I will also see how rich you can become in such a business,' and Chitrotpala frowned at Dharmananda.

Charles was surprised to hear Dharmananda's philosophy of life. Prachi wondered who had filled his young mind with such thoughts. She noticed he had grown up in the last few months and that his demeanour had changed as well. She was upset with the developments.

Dharmananda did not answer Chitrotpala, but muttered looking at the others, 'I was only teasing her. Can you not see how desperately she is saving up for her wedding,' and moved away quickly. Prachi was worried about Dharmananda. She had no means to alleviate his poverty; to make him strong enough to include principles into his survival kit.

The gigantic statue of Gaja-Simha had three images entwined in it. A lion crouched upon a huge elephant, which in turn was crushing a soldier underfoot. The lion looked realistic and menacing rearing on its uplifted hind legs. It had been carved from a single piece of stone.

Prachi explained its meaning to Charles. According to the Silpa Sashtra, an image of Gaja-Simha is mandatory at the entry point of all Hindu temples. That is why the main entrance is called Simha Dwara, or 'Lion's Gate'.

They returned to Vishnu Maharana after lunch. He reverently extracted the next stash of palm leaves and began narrating what he read.

'It was dawn. The Sun God was yet to rise from his slumber. Kamala Maharana was at the Natamandir searching for his perfect woman, and wondering whether he should give prime consideration to a shapely body or to her attire and ornaments. Any decoration would look good on a well-formed figure and if she was also endowed with womanly charm and grace she would look like a celestial maiden. This would inspire wonder and bliss. She would be a superb epitome of artistry. Kamala Maharana had already thought of the ornaments to adorn her with. But it was the model that had to capture his soul first. Who could be his inspiration? He heard the tinkling sound of ghungroos. Someone was coming towards him, her rhythmic steps echoing in the air. Who was she? Devadasi Bhadra? Or was she Sweta? Or Mugdha? Who but those devadasis could model for the dance poses of the Natamandir? Only those devadasis could emote divine expressions or add divinity to their gestures.'

Vishnu Maharana continued, 'A dancing girl was slowly

walking towards the artist, lithe and graceful as if she had just descended from heaven, swaying like a wave from the sea. Kamala Maharana gazed at her, bewitched as if she was a stone statue come to life. Who was this celestial maiden? No, she could not be Bhadra, Sweta or Mugdha as her posture was outstandingly beautiful. Was she a nymph from heaven? He looked at her feet and saw two half blown lotus buds there. As if the red vermilion of the rising sun had painted a thin red-hued line of alata on her lovely feet. He watched her with cautious attention and finally his gaze rested on her faultlessly sculpted face. His heart missed a beat. Could he really carve a replica of this exquisitely beautiful ethereal maiden? She had a delicate and shapely body and a heavenly face. Kamala Maharana tried to capture her beauty in his imagination so that he could depict her and her graceful postures in his creation.' Vishnu Maharana paused to take a sip of water and carried on reading and narrating.

'Kamala Maharana tried to put a rein on the passionate, youthful longings that welled up within him. He had decided to think and behave like an ascetic at Konark, and he had to keep that sacred pledge for twelve long years. He had to abstain from any amorous thoughts at the altar of the Sun God. He would rein in his passion and make thousands of lotuses bloom in stone. The work he had started had to be completed at any cost. If he could not control himself it would lead to disaster and tarnish his image as an artist. Besides, his beloved lovelorn wife would be loyally waiting for his return. And yet why was he so restless, incapable of subduing his turbulent soul? Kamala Maharana gazed fixedly at the lovely eyes of the maiden and tried to steady his excited heart. He asked calmly, "Who are you, young woman? Who has asked you to become a devadasi and offer yourself as a tender lotus flower at the feet of a God of stone?" The damsel did not answer. Was she dumb? He felt sad for her. Alas! A devadasi! Her entire life dedicated to a God of stone! The institution of devadasi or temple dancer had been introduced during the reign of King Chodaganga Deva for his Ista Deva, Lord Jagannath at Puri.'

Turning to Charles, Vishnu Maharana said that the next section highlighted stipulations governing the lives of devadasis in the twelfth and thirteenth centuries. Charles aware, but always eager to learn more, nodded at what Vishnu Maharana had to say.

'Physical happiness, joy, desire, love, marriage and motherhood—were all forbidden to her by the dictates of society. She was the dasi of God, his chambermaid. She was the temple dancer, who danced for God. But she too had a heart, a soul! She too had desires for love and motherhood, had aspirations for a home to call her own! Yet, it was considered a sin for her to even think of them! Was she only a body? All her needs were taken care of by the temple authorities. Did she have no other wants? The Maharaja provided for all her physical needs. She owned a lot of property. This tempted poor parents to surrender their young daughters at the feet of God and they lived off her life of dedication! But who was this devadasi, wondered Kamala Maharana? The beautiful maiden stood silently in a captivating pose. Her champak-hued skin was tinged blushing red with the rays of the rising sun. Her face was illuminated with a divine brightness. "Who are you? Are you a devadasi? Of which temple? To whom have you surrendered yourself?" Kamala Maharana asked softly, gently, tenderly. In the calm breeze of the morning the flower petals shook a little. She replied in a musical tone, like the notes of the veena, "I am the daughter of Nrityacharya Somya Sridatta. I am dedicated to serve the Sun God." Kamala Maharana's young throbbing heart subsided at once. He became suspicious about the girl. Firmly, he asked her, "Has your father asked you to pose as a model? This will be a difficult job. It needs concentration, patience, dedication and involvement to keep standing still for long hours. Can you do it, young lady?" Silpa smiled and said, "I can, Artist! I certainly can. I have come of my own free will to pose as a model for the Natamandir. Even my father does not know that I have offered myself up as a devadasi to the Sun God. If I can contribute even a little to the completion of the Konark temple, I would be honoured." Kamala Maharana's throbbing heart quivered again. He said, "It is not proper to come here to pose as a model without your father's permission."' Vishnu Maharana looked around at the small group. Prachi was nodding sagely, yes it was not proper.

He looked down and began reading again, '"But I too want to outlive my mortal years in the carved stones of Konark. Oh Artist, please accept me as your model! If the king's wishes are to be honoured, Lord Jagannath will be pleased too. I have sincerely surrendered myself before Lord Jagannath!" Kamala Maharana was elated. "But young lady, do you have any knowledge of the classical dance styles?" he asked. She replied sweetly, "It is true that I have not formally learnt classical Odissi dance. But when my father was teaching others, I watched him closely and practised on my own. I am sure I can be a befitting model for the dancing statues of Konark. Please have faith in me," and she looked at him with beseeching eyes. "I have no qualms believing you, young lady! But won't your father object?" Silpa said softly, "I am the soul of the 'art of dance' for my father, Nrityaguru Somya Sridatta. He forgets about dance if he does not see me before him. My face, eyes and the rhythmic movement of my feet inspire the muse in him. He calls me Kala meaning art. He says, if I disappear from his sight, his art too will vanish. After I was born, he achieved excellence in the art of dance. I am his inspiration. How can he live without me? That is why I have surrendered myself before the lotus feet of the Sun God. After the temple is completed, I will live life as a devadasi. My father will remain my teacher forever and I will be his inspiration. Once I have dedicated myself to the Sun God, my father will not try to bring me back."'

Kamala Maharana was a trifle unnerved, narrated Vishnu Maharana. Kamala Maharana had written next, 'This innocent maiden is blindly devoted to her father. Yet, this same maiden is eager to dance. When the torrential rains of passion excite her, how will she manage to live a solitary life; stay away from home for so long? The innocent girl has not understood as yet that passion can drive one wild. It is wrong to commit oneself emotionally on such a major issue as becoming a devadasi. He spoke to her like a guardian, "Young lady, you have not yet heard the song of life. That song will devastate this vow of yours. Without understanding the meaning of life don't take such a serious decision solely on faith." Silpa smiled. Her sweet, shy smile illuminated her entire face with an unspeakable ethereal beauty, like the red hue of the sun slowly lighting up the blue sky in the eastern horizon. Young Kamala Maharana was no longer in control of his emotions. He was oblivious to everything around him. His past, future, duty, work, the orders of the king, the instructions of the dance master, his bride at home—everything. Even the sky, fields, trees and creepers, were slowly becoming obscure. Thousands of images of Silpa appeared before him. He stood mute in dazed amazement. His eyes were still. And his heart trembled. His face was calm but his soul was in turbulence.' Vishnu Maharana paused, and Charles felt a kinship with Kamala Maharana. He too was dealing with an ethereally beautiful and sweet but unattainable someone.

Vishnu Maharana resumed. 'Silpa said a little cautiously, "I do not know whether you are married or not. But of the twelve hundred masons, many are married young men who have left their young wives behind for the sake of the country. Some have not even seen their wives. They will work for twelve long years without distraction. By the time they go back home, they will be deprived of youth in body and soul. Life's most beautiful period will be over by then. If they and their wives can sacrifice so much, then why can't I? Kalinga is a land of sacrifice, dedication and sacred submission. Am I not a daughter of Kalinga?" Kamala Maharana, hypnotized by her argument, was thrilled. He felt that without her Konark would never reach its zenith. And it would be impossible to chisel artistic carvings. If she were not before his eyes, his chisel could never move again. He said, in a tone of gratitude, "Young lady, Kalinga is blessed to have given birth to you. Your beauty and noble persona are difficult to define." Silpa smiled. And with her pious smile, sparkling sunshine filled the universe. Kamala Maharana murmured to himself he would be blessed if he could capture her perfect innocent loveliness on the stones of Konark. "The artists of Kalinga will be honoured too," he added, as she continued to gaze at him. "I will always remain indebted to you," he said. "If you could judge your perfectly-moulded body and faultless features, your delicate bearing, divine beauty and absolutely captivating expression, only then can you understand your real worth."' And with that Vishnu Maharana set the palm-leaf down with the others. The day's reading was over.

Seven

~

Seven hundred years ago Kamala Maharana had written his life on a palm-leaf manuscript, documented the history of Konark, and stated that no other dreams had any relevance before the making of the temple itself. Kamala Maharana and the twelve hundred masons sacrificed their youth, and in some cases their lives, so that the shrine to love survived.

Seven hundred years later, another young man very close in age to Kamala Maharana when he had written the manuscript, was deeply engaged with the minutae of not only the narrative but was also studying the temple complex in detail in light of what he was learning. Charles was driven to compare Oriental and Western lifestyles. Charles was beginning to fall in love with India, influenced by its great cultural legacy and was almost equally impressed by Prachi.

When Prachi recited couplets of Jayadeva's *Gita Govinda* in her lovely voice, Charles could now understand some of the Sanskrit verses and was charmed by her poetic recitals. He would forget all his pain, despondency and loneliness. Her melodious voice flourished as a flowering creeper of spring in his arid life. It was as if Prachi's magical voice that made everything simpler and more meaningful.

The deities Jagannath, Balabhadra and Subhadra were worshipped in Charukala's puja room. Charles was prohibited from entering this room. He would listen to Prachi's recital from outside. She would be immersed in devotion, soulfully singing verses from the *Gita Govinda,* tears of joy streaming down her face. Charukala and Dinabandhu too were involved in the puja, completely cut off from the mundane world. Charles wondered why Prachi was so sad, why she cried before Lord Jagannath. He asked her about it. She replied, 'Not in sorrow. These are tears of ecstasy. You won't understand the joy of singing from the *Gita Govinda* if you are not able to appreciate these verses. You are so accustomed to western music.' Charles could not understand how a young woman could weep while singing the verses of *Gita Govinda* before Lord Jagannath every day.

He felt that girls of Prachi's age should be in love with a man; instead here she was very inexplicably in love with Lord Jagannath, the Universal Lord of Amity. She would say, 'Jagannath Swami is my Lord, my Ista Deva.' Charles was taken aback at such intense philosophical words from Prachi.

She would tell him, 'Music is happiness. This happiness transports one from the superficial to the profound depths of supreme joy and eternal bliss. Music calms and steadies the unstable mind and brings one closer to divinity. God is identified with music. Satchidananda, that is the most joyous path to reach God. And that is why I sing.' Charles wondered if Prachi was actually a devadasi dedicated to Lord Jagannath? Were pleasures like desire, love and romance forbidden to her? Was the practice of the devadasi cult still prevalent in the temple of Jagannath? Meanwhile, Prachi was still holding forth, 'Lord Jagannath is Omnipotent. He does not lack anything. When you have him, you have everything. I seek salvation by surrendering myself to Him.'

Had he been in his own country, Charles would have taken Prachi to a psychiatrist. Prachi pontificating about the concept of supreme love seemed absurd to him. Sometimes Charles felt that she was clutching Lord Jagannath to redeem her soul, to fill the void with such strong emotions.

On the walls of Konark was an image of Lord Jagannath, an idol of Lord Shiva, along with an image of Mahishashusmardini. Lord Jagannath was installed on the southern wall of the Mukhashala and the Goddess on an intricately carved pedestal nearby. King Narasimha Deva was depicted worshipping Lord Jagannath and receiving a garland from the priest. Prachi stood before them staring intently at the sculpture; stood like a statue before the chlorite images of Shiva-Jagannath-Durga. It was difficult to understand whether she was lost in her own world or immersed in Lord Jagannath, as though Lord Jagannath was bonded to Prachi by some mysterious link from time immemorial. Charles asked her, 'Why do you become so absent-minded when you look at Lord Jagannath?'

'I told you, he is my husband.' Prachi replied laughingly and moved ahead. Charles moved with her too, to study the lifestyle of ancient Odisha depicted on the walls of Konark. The exquisite carvings captivated him. He no longer remembered when he had left his home for good. It was because he had never known what home was. The day his mother divorced his father and left for Washington, he became cut off from his home, family and relatives. He always felt like an intruder at his mother and her new husband's home. The day he left his mother to live independently, he became absolutely free, a wanderer without any bindings.

Dinabandhu Babu and his wife Charukala were still worried and anxious for their twenty-six-year old, financially independent son. Prachiprava was not their daughter; she was the daughter of Charukala's elder sister. But they were affectionate people, and were worried and extremely anxious for Prachi. This intrigued

Charles. He stopped before a sculpture carved on the southern wall of the main temple. It depicted a scene where a son returned home to his old parents, wife and son after spending years away—the aging mother embracing him, the wife touching his feet and the young child crying for attention. That beautiful picture of reunion on the walls of Konark looked like a perfect family. It depicted the greatness of Indian family life.

Charles thought about his own home. Only loneliness would greet him there. Even Lillian would not be at the airport to receive him. She had written that she was having an absolutely fantastic life on the beaches of Goa with Brush, her new boyfriend. That she was very happy. If Charles would consider coming to Goa, she would not mind his company, too. Charles did not respond to the letter. She was so engrossed in her unbridled pursuit of pleasure in Goa, that Charles's letter would not excite her.

Prachi stood before another sculpture, that of a labourer couple. The man was carrying a large hoe on his shoulder and his wife had a bundle on her head. She carried her infant who was shown suckling blissfully. Prachi sighed. Let no one listen to her heart, and no one see the mystery of her soul. But her secret sigh had reached Charles. He was standing just behind her. 'Is there anything special in this picture?' Charles asked. Prachi replied, 'One may live in the most developed country, be highly cultured, but this is his basic requirement. To call a home one's own, have a companion to walk with along the difficult journey of life, to share its burdens and to have a child of one's own flesh and blood. This is life indeed, the continuation of one's lineage, and living through one's descendants.'

'If you want all that you can get it too. Home, husband and child—it's not beyond your reach. Why worry?' Charles asked earnestly.

'I am a nomad like you, Charles! There is no home, no bondage, and no responsibility for me. Sometimes it feels like a burden even to keep myself going...'

Charles was taken aback. Prachi had divulged something hitherto hidden deep within her. Even though he longed to, Charles knew she had not granted him the right to probe further. What was her sorrow? What did she lack in life? How intense were her problems? Could he actually be of any help? All those queries remained unasked, unanswered. Prachi was now standing before an image of King Narasimha Deva, carved on the southern wall of the porch. She seemed an infinite question mark to Charles. The events described in the brittle palm-leaf manuscript seemed to be coming to life, turning the clock back seven hundred years.

King Narasimha Deva was resplendent on the stone carvings of Konark. Each stone declared his valour, his generosity, his ability to rule his country firmly and ably, his benevolent soul and his excellence. At several places the masons had mentioned their beloved king in their craftsmanship. The king was depicted with his queen. At some places he was shown worshipping Lord Surya with absolute reverence; in battle regalia in a war scene; in a relaxed moment seated on a swing with his queen. The artist who had worked so hard to make his king timeless had himself become immortal. Recording the king's greatness, he unknowingly acknowledged his own greatness too; yet, he remained anonymous. He never wrote his name anywhere on the stones. All those artists, separated from their homes and families for so long, actually depicted their own magnanimity while glorifying the king's greatness.

Vishnu Maharana continued to read and explain from the manuscripts. Continuous fights went on with the Gouda ruler Ikhatiyaruddin Yujbeg whose army had marched up to Amardan Fort at the northern tip of Odisha. Yujbeg had also sought assistance from Delhi as he was facing a formidable counter-attack from the dedicated soldiers of Kalinga led by King Narasimha Deva. The king could not leave the fate of his country to the mercy of his enemies for a life of comfort and enjoyment, with his favourite queen, Sita Devi.

At the same time, the construction of the Konark temple was on in full swing. The devoted foot-soldiers, the spirited Paika foot-soldiers, were on the battlefield. Twelve hundred masons and many more people had put in their soul into the country. The king would visit them from the battlefield and take note of their progress. When the night became deep and desolate, he would visit them in disguise to gather first-hand information about the well-being of his devoted countrymen. Sometimes, he would come as a policeman, a chowkidar, a rustic villager, a soldier or as an unknown wayfarer. He would gather information and solve their problems. That is why no one suffered in his country. At times, the Muslim army would cross the boundaries of the land and create problems. But the alert guards, soldiers and police foiled their attempts. People had enormous faith in the king and his Paika foot-soldiers. They lived without fear.

Vishnu Maharana settled himself comfortably and began the narration, transporting all of them seven hundred years into the past.

'It was a luminous moonlit night. Even the colourful flowers were distinctly noticeable in the bright moonlight, standing out from the green foliage. The king was patrolling the city in the guise of a priest. Where there were villages or habitations along the way, he tethered his horse beneath a tree outside the village and entered the village barefoot. The scented flowers were in bloom everywhere as though in celebration. He walked slowly, relaxing his tired mind.'

'Soon the king came upon an old man chanting God's name sitting on the verandah. The priest stood there for a while. When the old man opened his eyes, the priest asked him, "Noble Sir, is everything all right in this village?" The old man stared at him and asked politely, "Which village do you belong to? I have never seen you before, I can't see properly these days, son." The priest smiled and said, "My village wants to have an alliance with this village. That is why I have come. I am a servant of Lord Jagannath. Is all well in this village?" The old man replied with a beaming smile, "By the King's grace everything is all right. People are able to live in peace and happiness. There can never be problems in a country where the king himself remains alert to all the needs of his subjects."'

The king was deeply touched and responded with an innate humility, which was what made him so great. Vishnu Maharana resumed, 'The priest folded his hands and offered prayers to the Almighty and then said calmly, "Noble Sir, it is not the king's grace. Please attribute it to Lord Jagannath's grace. Who is the king? He is merely a servant of Lord Jagannath. He only carries out his orders as a 'routa'. Without Lord Jagannath, the king has no existence." The old man smiled and said, "For us they are the same, the king is the same as our Lord Jagannath. Lord Jagannath is looking after us through our king. He is a part of Jagannath. Otherwise there could not be so much peace and contentment in this land."'

Vishnu Maharana continued: 'The priest asked, "I heard that a temple for the Sun God is being constructed in Konark. How many masons and artists have joined in the job?" The old man made a rough calculation and said, "A total of twenty-six youths have joined up from the village. Why do you need this information, son?" he asked. The priest smiled "We are planning to build a temple for Lord Vishnu in our village. We need some expert artisans. I heard this village is known for temple building. When will your artisans return?" The old man looked at him in surprise, "You do not know about this, priest? None of them will come back soon. They are gone for sixteen years. The main temple will engage them for twelve years. The other temples, wells, swings, pandals, boundary walls of the temple complex will take another four years. Do not wait for them. Search for other artisans for your job."

'The priest looked astonished, "The artists will labour for sixteen years, away from their homes and families, for the construction of the Konark Temple? That is injustice by the king!" The old man bit his tongue. With folded hands he pleaded, "Do not talk like that! Our king can never commit injustice! And especially King Narasimha Deva! What does he gain from temple building? He is not building a grand palace for himself; it is a befitting abode for our presiding deity."

'The priest appeared to be mulling something over, and then said, "Yes, the temple is being built on the king's orders. The God of Justice will establish himself on earth. There will be justice on earth. But what about the artisans' families who have had to sacrifice their happiness?"

'The old man lost his temper, "You may be a priest, but you are young and immature. That is why you have no idea about the king. The king has taken up all the responsibility of the families of these artists and soldiers. He has made special allowances and granted them landed property. They are living quite comfortably and singing the glories of the king."

'Satisfied that his people were truly not suffering in this village King Narasima Deva bowed and humbly said, "Thank you Noble Sir. Let Jagannath bless all! Let this village prosper," and so saying walked on his way in the moonlit night.'

Vishnu Maharana set down the palm leaf, picked up the next one and began: 'In the middle of the village stood a temple. Just outside the boundary walls was a well. In the dead of night he could see a female form approaching the well. As she came closer the king saw she had covered her face with her veil and was walking as though in a stupor. She carried a brass pitcher. The king wondered if the large vessel was too heavy for her; how would she carry it back filled with water, wouldn't that crush her young and delicate body? The king watched her, standing under the shade of a bakul tree.

'The maiden put down the pitcher near the wall with obvious pain. Her forehead now visible in the moonlight showed drops of perspiration as she leaned onto the boundary wall exhausted... like a creeper... too tender to stand on its own. Perhaps she was mustering strength to be able to pull water from the well and carry it home. It looked like she was waiting for someone to arrive. It was a desolate place to be in at night, and she had to fetch water from the well. But who was she waiting for the king wondered, and waited too with baited breath. She appeared anxious and tense and peered through the dark repeatedly in one direction. Her face, though veiled by her pallu falling low over her forehead, glowed like a lustrous moon. There was a diamond nose bud on her aquiline nose, sparkling like a star. Her closed lips resembled a pale pink flower, quivering softly. She was guarded and watchful. Was she a damsel in love?'

Vishnu Maharana paused for a sip of water before continuing.

'The king became increasingly apprehensive. He wondered

about this simple girl who had ventured out in the dead of night to fetch water from the well, unaware of false promises heartless lovers make, and oblivious of the defamation that would ensue if she were caught. At a distance someone's footsteps were heard faintly. She became agitated. As if she could not stand another moment of separation; as though, in a moment, the secret union of two lovers would take place. Whom should he punish? His conscience pricked him. He felt reluctant to punish the girl. She was dove-like, innocent, and tender... like the moonlight. Possibly, he thought, her lover was betraying her with false promises. But she looked as if nothing could defile her. Her face was still under the veil and he could not see her eyes. Only her breathing was heavy and her heart heaved with some unknown emotion. The footsteps came closer. She stood straight and wrapped the pallu of her sari firmly around her waist and went up to the well to draw water. Then she made a noose with the rope, tied it to the neck of the pitcher and lowered it into the well. With a splatter the pitcher went down and struck the water.'

They could almost hear that splash in the dead of night seven hundred years ago.

'The king continued to observe everything standing quietly under the bakul tree. The activities of the maiden amused him. She was demonstrating her temper to her lover! She had been waiting for so long, pretending to draw water, knowing well that her lover was late but on his way. But such a large pitcher when filled with water would be impossible for her to lift. She might slip into the well with the weight! As if she had chosen to commit suicide in an emotional outburst against her lover for being late! Or she thought her lover would be filled with compassion at her helpless condition and would take the rope from her hand and gallantly draw the pitcher out of the well with a single pull! Every woman wanted her chosen man to be fearless, brave and powerful. The king was to be the witness of her lover's strength that night.

'The pitcher was filled with water. The woman would crane her neck to peer into the dark from where the footfalls were heard, and then bend into the well with the weight of the water-filled pitcher. Where was her saviour? The footsteps were fading. She was mistaken. It was not her lover. It was some wayfarer crossing the road. What could she do? Who would save her from the great danger she was in? She couldn't hold on to the heavy filled pitcher inside the well, nor could she haul it up on her own. In fact even now just trying to hold on to the rope with the heavy pitcher at the other end was pulling her in. By the time her lover came, she would have long since fallen into the well and drowned. Within seconds her strength failed and she could no longer hold on. She was about to fall into the well and a desperate cry of despair slipped from her lips.'

Vishnu Maharana looked up, and the small group looked back at him horrified at the tragedy that was unfolding. He turned back to the manuscript with a small smile. 'And,' he said dramatically, 'at that moment two long and strong arms firmly grasped her waif-like body from behind and pulled her back to safety. Holding the semi-conscious and frightened damsel on one arm, the man pulled up the water-filled pitcher from the well with the other hand. Her noble and chivalrous saviour had saved her life. Her veil slipped from her face and she lay like the crescent moon in the arms of the king.'

Vishnu Maharana's listeners heaved a collective sigh of relief. He continued, 'Her beautiful face lit up the surroundings. Her tears shone like dewdrops under closed eyelids. She was quivering in fear, shame and grief. A few teardrops trickled onto the king's palm. The tiny triangle-shaped nose pin glittered on her lovely nose. Her dishevelled hair tumbled down like the sea on the vast shore of the king's chest. He froze, as his conscience alerted him "You are the king; you are the provider, the saviour. You have abandoned your personal happiness, the luxury of royal pleasure, for safeguarding the art and culture of the country. It is the sacred duty of the king to protect the honour of women. If he cannot keep the honour of the women how can he safeguard the honour of his motherland! He is then bound to be defeated."

'Narasimha Deva assured the maiden, "Do not fear, young lady. You are now out of danger, keep calm. Compose yourself." She steadied herself and stood up. The king released her and stood at a distance. The moonlight fell on her hazily like a veil, as if the moon was jealous of her unveiled beauty before a stranger. When she saw him she blushed. Only a few moments ago, this man had saved her life! She instantly drew the folds of her sari to hide her face. In her blue sari she appeared like the moon in the sky, now shadowed by the clouds. The king wondered if the clouds had concealed the moon and spread shadows around!

'Restraining his senses and recalling his duty, he asked calmly, "Who are you? Who is your father? Who is your lover?"

'She was too shocked to react, then a soft, musical voice replied, "I am not a girl, I am someone's wife. I do not have any lover. You have dishonoured me by asking such questions."

'The king was astonished at her fearless reply. He felt honoured to be a king of a land where a young woman could speak her mind so boldly. He said with remorse in his voice, "Please forgive me, lady. I am an outsider. Who are you? Who is your husband? Who were you expecting here at the temple in the moonlit night?"

'She replied simply, "A wife waits only for her husband. Ages pass waiting. But the women of this land are determined to wait till the very end."

'The king was elated, impressed by her. And he asked again, "But does anyone wait by the roadside? I am apprehensive, lady. Please remove my doubts."

'She glanced at him and asked, "Who are you, stranger? You have saved me from sure death tonight like an angel. But without knowing who you are how can I reveal everything about myself?"

'The king answered politely, "I am a servant of Lord Jagannath. I serve him as a routa. I have come from a distant village to meet a relative."

'The young woman sighed and said, "Then I have nothing to fear. You have saved me from death and you are a great man. My mother-in-law would have mistreated me for you have touched my body, but I am saved because you are a servant of Lord Jagannath. It is not you, but almighty Jagannath who has rescued me. How else could you enter the scene at the right time?" The king at once responded, "Who am I to do anything, I am only an ordinary mortal. Whatever good is being accomplished is due to the wishes of the large-hearted Lord Jagannath. Only He saves people. Lady, you are innocent. But for whom were you waiting here alone in the night?"

'"I had come to fetch water. Our home is to be plastered."

'"You will plaster your home with water from the well?"

'"Yes. Those are my mother-in-law's instructions."

'"You will carry this large pitcher filled with water?"

'"My mother-in-law asked me to. I do this every night."

' "Strange!" the king muttered in disbelief.

'The young woman understood and then said, "That is why I was waiting for my brother-in-law to come. Every night he pulls the water for me. It is he who actually carries the pitcher and puts it on the verandah. I plaster our home with that. My mother-in-law knows nothing about this. She is happy believing that I am suffering. Tonight I thought my brother-in-law was nearby and I dropped the pitcher into the well. I would not have let it go even if I had to fall into the well with the heavy pitcher. By coincidence you arrived. Otherwise my torment would have ended tonight."

'The king was incredulous and exclaimed, "But your life is much more precious than that pitcher!"

'The maiden smiled sadly, "For my mother-in-law, it is just the other way round."

'The king wanted to know more. "Why does your mother-in-law torture a young woman like you?" he asked. "What is your fault? Is there no cure? Tell me lady, I will try to do something," he said.

'The maiden sighed, "It is not my mother-in-law who torments me."

'The king was now ready to battle anybody torturing the gentle maiden, "Who is that heartless man who tortures you like this?" he asked.

' "What will you do to him?" she wanted to know.

' "I will punish him," the king replied firmly.

' "Do you have the power to punish him?"

'The king swiftly replied, "I will punish him through Lord Jagannath. I am a priest. It is my job to inform Lord Jagannath about everybody's sorrow and suffering and to provide justice to all."

'The maiden's answer stunned him. "Well it is the king himself who is the cause of my sorrow. The ruler of this country is responsible for my miserable fate. What will you do about him? The king is very close to Lord Jagannath."

'The king was stupefied. He had rescued the beautiful damsel in distress just a few moments ago. How confidently she had taken shelter in his arms! And now, she was blaming him, though unknowingly, for her misfortune!

'The woman continued, "Can't you understand? He is responsible for the sorrow that we the wives of the twelve hundred artisans have to undergo. Only twelve days remained for my homecoming to my in-laws' place when the king took my husband away for temple construction. By the time I stepped into my in-laws' house my husband was already lost in the world of the stone maidens of Konark. I have not seen my husband. That is why my mother-in-law says I am not virtuous. Because of my sin, my mother-in-law will have to die without seeing her grandchildren. It is a reality. She is already sick and may die soon."

'The king was mystified, "But how are you to blame for this?" he asked in surprise.

'She replied, "There may be some reason. The destiny and affluence of a house depends on the virtues of the woman."

'The king said calmly, "Your husband is the artist of the Sun temple of Konark. Are you not proud of him?"

'She replied, "I am proud, but that does not lessen my sorrow. With every passing day my mother-in-law's tortures increase. I cannot bear it any longer."

'The king became thoughtful. He asked softly, "Lady, you want your husband to come home leaving the temple work unfinished? Should I plead your case before Lord Jagannath?"

'The young woman turned apprehensive and protested, "No my lord, I do not want that. If all twelve hundred wives desire this, how will the temple be completed? When the Sun Temple is completed, it will establish the genius of the gifted Odia artists and their hard work will survive for many years to come. My husband's contributions will remain engraved on the walls of Konark till eternity. He will survive in the hearts of the people of Kalinga. Every wife wishes for her husband's longevity and his well-being. How can I be any different? My happiness lies in his noble purpose in life."

'The king was not happy with her answer. "What about your sufferings and torments?" he wanted to know. She smiled through her veil and said sweetly, "I will endure everything. When my husband has suffered so much, why can't I?"'

And Vishnu Maharana stopped to clear his throat, moved by the purity of sentiment expressed by this young Odia girl to her king seven hundred years ago.

He took a sip of water and picked up the manuscript again.

'The ruler of the great Ganga kingdom was stupefied. This simple maiden was repeatedly provoking him, had wounded his ego though he was an able ruler, a good administrator. He, who had never been defeated in battle, was being humiliated by a village woman's reasoning!

'The king asked gently, "Who said that your husband is going through difficult times? The king has made provisions for their food, clothing, habitation and health. They have nothing lacking in their lives. Shri Balai Nayak is in charge of all expenditures. Allalu Nayak looks after the store and Gangei Nayak takes care of the treasury accounts. All are carrying out their responsibility efficiently. Bhramarabara Harichandan of Bayalishi Mouja is keeping accounts. The king has ordered them to look after the comforts of every artisan. The Dalabehera of Rupashagad is handling everything perfectly."

'The maiden at once became suspicious, "How do you know all these details?"

'The king replied, "I am the priest of the royal household. It is my job to know about everybody's welfare."

'"But you said you came from a far-off village?"

'"No matter which village I belong to, that is a part of this kingdom. Though I am a priest of that village, my king is Narasimha Deva. For the welfare of his country, I serve Lord Jagannath and keep track of the happenings in his country. That is the instruction of Lord Jagannath and is the duty of every priest."

'Her doubts disappeared. She said without fear, "You have kept track of all the good news about the artists, but are not aware of their sorrow."'

'Once again the maiden had surprised the king. "What sorrow? The king himself looks after them. Queen Sita Devi has discarded the comforts of her palace to also look after their problems. She knows their hunger like a mother," the king replied.

'The maiden said sullenly, "The king and the queen have knowledge of their hunger but not their hearts. That is the crux of our sorrow."

'The king turned thoughtful, "The king sometimes roams through his kingdom in disguise to gather direct experience about his countrymen. I have heard that there is peace in his country. The artists are very content and busy in the temple construction. Their families are very comfortable."

'The maiden replied, "The king has seen only the hunger of his countrymen during his visits in disguise. He has ensured that the families of the artists and the Paika foot-soldiers do not face any problem or want. But he has not understood the pain their wives and beloveds have to undergo. He has not realized the yearnings of those artists."

'The king was taken aback, then he gently asked, "What is their pain?" The maiden remained silent for a moment. And then she mustered strength and said, "You are a priest. A servant of Lord Jagannath. You are my saviour. That is why I consider you as my God. Or else you know how immoral it is for a young wife of a person to bare one's soul before a stranger, alone on a lonely night."

'The king was quick to reassure her, "Have no fear lady; it lessens your pain to speak it out. Is there anything possible that I can do?" He looked at her intently.

' "Can the king remove the pangs of separation of the twelve hundred masons from their wives by giving them food, clothing, land and allowances?"

'The king was stunned. Such a question had never crossed his mind before. He had no answer. Still, he had to find a response. He replied in a benevolent tone, "We sacrifice personal comforts for the greater good of the country. There are many tales of the sacred sacrifices made by the men behind many immortal monuments in the world. You do not know about them, that is why you are so affected. At Konark, the temple is being built for the Lord of Justice. It will become a blessed destination for sanyasis[7], jitendriyas[8], and a place of sacrifice and dedication. The masons and artists will construct the temple at Padma

---

[7]Monks.
[8]Those who have attained mastery over the six senses and the body and its wants.

Kshetra, which will be a temple of the divine love of the sun and lotus. That is why these artists have to observe abstinence from earthly pleasures. They will create immortal works of art. Their wives will wait for them to return after twelve years with the devotion of the lotus flower. Abstinence from worldly pleasures strengthens a man, sharpens his talents. The artists have to be strong to make the Konark temple immortal. The king expects that much control, dedication and moral strength from the artists of Kalinga," he said firmly.

'The maiden threw yet another challenge at him. "The king is the role model for his subjects. Can the king observe abstinence in his own life and will he be able to pour all his strength and talent into the sacred soil of Konark for twelve long years? Can he mingle his soul with their souls? Can the king make this sacrifice to strengthen the souls of the artists who are pining for their beloveds? If not, how can he expect the artists to do so? What the king himself cannot do, how can he expect his subjects to do? Is not an artist a human being? Is he not made of flesh and blood? Have all his desires died before the command of the king? You are a wise and considerate priest. What do you think?" she boldly asked.

'Narasimha Deva was dumbstruck and immensely saddened. Until this moment he had seen an artist as solely a creator, whose only desire and passion in life would be to create and to nurture. It had never occurred to him that the artist was also a human being with attachments, aspirations, desires, and passions. As a servitor of Lord Jagannath, the king had ordered his Paika foot-soldiers to fight for Kalinga on the battlefield, and his young masons, artisans and artists to go to Arka Kshetra to build the temple. They had devoted their lives to their motherland, and toiled hard to leave behind a glorious cultural tradition, while the king himself lived happily with his wife and children. This village woman, a rustic, had reminded the king about his own injustice. She had pricked his conscience.

'It had such a chastening effect upon his whole character and the viewpoints he had held, that all at once he realized she was his guide, his conscience keeper, his counsellor and his source of strength. She transformed into an all-powerful image of Goddess Durga herself before the king! He knelt and bowed to her, "Lady, accept my respects! Even though you are a young woman, you are honourable. I will surely convey your resentment before Lord Jagannath. Whatever God will command, the king will definitely comply." The woman was startled to hear this and stepped back.

'In very humble and plaintive tones she said, "Please forgive me, Sir. I have no complaints against the noble king. I revere him for his illustrious and heroic achievements. But I also feel the pangs of separation, the humiliation, and torture of the wives and beloveds of the twelve hundred masons. I have only revealed my feelings before your kind-hearted soul. You will pray for the health, wealth, happiness, fame and longevity of the king's life before Lord Jagannath. You will ask for my husband's name and fame, long life, and also for his dedication, concentration and for the completion of the temple of Konark. I pray for that every day." Her voice became suffused with tears as she continued, "As soon as the temple is completed, my husband will return home. If the temple is not completed he will never return."

'The king was deeply touched and said, "I will pray for his well-being. Tell me his name!"

'She gasped, "How can I utter his name? My name is Chandrabhaga. There is a lotus pond at the end of our village. He is fond of lotuses. And he has left behind a lotus carved in stone for my sake at the bathing ghat. I have made myself strong like that stone and wait for him as devotedly as a lotus; if you can, please tell him that."

'The king was deeply touched and gently said, "Chandrabhaga try to be happy; gain strength from the stone. May Lord Jagannath bless you. I will come again. I regularly move through the villages. I offer you my regards. Goodbye!"

'Thus did King Narasimha Deva frequently leave his palace in disguise to gather firsthand impressions that his citizens had about the running of the country and to learn their misery and grievances, and treasure them as his own; and remove them with his powers as king.

'His young queen, Sita Devi, would stay awake waiting for her husband late into the night. Towards the last quarter of the night, her enchantingly beautiful face resembled that of the serene pale moon in the sky and even that looked hauntingly fresh against the fresh flower petals. She would rush to greet her husband with elaborate ceremonial paraphernalia before leading him to the ante chamber to eagerly seek his response about the well-being of their subjects. Seeing him worried, she would ask if everything was all right in his kingdom. "By the grace of Lord Jagannath, all are well. The people are living in peace," he would answer with a smile. Today the reply was the same, but he looked grave. "Then why is the king so worried?" she asked softly. He failed to give her a direct reply, saying instead, "You have been waiting up for long. I ask for your forgiveness for my delay;" he replied.

'The queen said softly, "I won't feel weary even if I have to wait for you my entire life. You are not only my master; you are responsible for the entire nation as well! Your duty towards your subjects is as important as my desire for your attention as a wife."

'The king's heart felt lighter at her words and he said, "My Queen, I am indeed honoured to have you in my life."

' "Do not embarrass me, Maharaj, I am fortunate to be the queen of Kalinga," she said humbly.

'Nevertheless, the king remained troubled. "My mission is not complete as yet! Without the temple at Konark I cannot attain fulfilment in life! If I remain imperfect myself, how can you become complete?" he asked.

' "It would be the greatest honour and privilege, and Maharaj would oblige me greatly if he could instruct me on anyway that I could serve Konark," she replied gracefully.

'The king was deeply appreciative, and spoke his mind, but in a manner that would not disturb his queen more than was absolutely necessary—"Although I criss-cross the land night and day, month and year to ensure the well-being of my subjects, and am personally looking after the well-being of our masons and artists, the Sun Temple at Konark still demands more!"

'The queen stood with folded hands, "Command me, Maharaj!"

'He replied quietly, "I had a dream. And till the temple is completed, I have to observe a vow."

' "What manner of vow Maharaj? Tell me. I will consult the priest and arrange for the Yagna, for sacrifice or worship if necessary!"

'The king turned to her, "I beg of you to grant me twelve years of celibacy in married life. Samba, the son of Sri Krishna, also worshipped the Sun God for twelve years and abstained from worldly pleasures. Since then Arka Kshetra is a holy site for the Jitendriya, who are unmoved by pleasure, and I am their king too. I want to be the example for my twelve hundred masons or else the Konark temple will never be complete! It will remain a stigma in the glorious history of the Ganga Dynasty," the king said.

'The queen did not fail him. "Is that all Maharaj? The Konark Sun Temple will be completed, and your vow will be observed without any hindrance. I, too, share the pain of the pining hearts of the wives of the twelve hundred masons. Bhanu Deva was born as a boon from Sun God. When the temple is completed, it will bring prosperity for my son. Let not an ordinary woman like me stand between you and your duty. Let not my desires and longings obstruct you in any manner! Will Maharaj excuse me for a moment, I shall return shortly."

'And with his permission she withdrew, returning shortly garbed in the spiritual garments of an ascetic having shed the exquisite royal robes and jewels that had adorned her just moments ago. Her unadorned and flame-like beauty glowed before the king, almost blinding him with its purity. Overwhelmed with emotion, he spoke, "Accept my reverence, my goddess! Let your sacrifice, dedication and devotion be the inspiration for the artists!" And so saying he bowed and moved out of the queen's chambers towards his own.

'As he walked along the long palace corridors he saw a flame flickering in the darkness of the night. It was a shadowy woman who had lit a lamp at this unearthly hour of the night. For whom was she waiting? Who was she, standing in the path of the construction of the temple of Konark? The king stopped to find out.

'It was none other than his sister Chandra Devi. She stood there alone in the moonlit night looking like the silhouette of a statue with a lamp in hand. The king realized she was talking to the memory of her late husband Paramardhi Deva, who had but recently made the supreme sacrifice on the battlefield.

'"The Muslim invaders will be defeated, Konark's victory monument too will be complete, Kalinga's independence will continue for years to come, and the names of the brave soldiers and artisans who are engaged in creating an artistic wonder will always be remembered." Loath to disturb her, her brother vowed under his breath, "Like Paramardhi Deva, there will be thousands of brave soldiers who will give their lives fighting for their motherland. Their valour, skill and victorious tales will be engraved on the stones of the temple of Konark as well, immortalizing those brave souls. Dear sister Chandra! Konark will be a memorial to their sacrifice and their victory—an abode of the Sun God revered for his energy and strength."'

And with that Vishnu Maharan placed the palm-leaf along with the others that had already been read.

SECTION ENDS

SECTION BEGINS

'Strange! What a strange country; unbelievable faith and unbelievable sacrifice. The land of great traditions and heritage. Its history is marvellous,' Charles admitted to himself. Prachiprava sat before the statue of King Narasimha Deva, bowing to the great soul depicted seated in meditation.

'Was it not sheer foolishness for a king to stay celibate and, abstain from worldly pleasures for twelve long years, just because of a young woman? I find it hard to believe,' said Charles.

'Have you read the Ramayana, Charles? Have you understood the benevolence and compassion of the benign King Ram for his subjects? He valued the opinion of a washerman and banished his beloved wife Sita! Queen Sita had to prove her fidelity in public! Ram who is worshipped as a god did know the truth. But he valued the opinion of every subject that he ruled. It was an exemplary action when he abandoned his own wife to establish the truth, because in a nation everybody is equal. So what is so strange about King Narasimha Deva heeding the opinion of the beloved wife of an artist and observing celibacy for twelve years?'

Charles had meanwhile descended the stone staircase on the western side. He observed the sculpture once again and was walking atop a large stone block of the ruined main temple. Prachi followed a little way behind. It was difficult for her to walk fast in a sari. She climbed up carefully and reached the idol of the Sun God on the north wall on her way to join Charles on the western side, stepping carefully on the stones with unsteady steps.

Down below Charles, waiting for her, stretched out his hand. Without a second thought she held her hand out to him. There was a little distance still to be covered between the two seeking hands. If she bent forward a little, she could hold Charles's hand or if Charles leant across he could catch hers. His hand looked like a lotus stem, shapely and long. His palm was pink like a lotus petal. Prachi's tender hand paled before his, but looked lovely nevertheless. Prachi admired Charles's handsome hand. Then she noticed that it was trembling slightly. She quickly withdrew her hand and climbed down, cautiously leaning on the stones. She said smilingly, 'Look! I can climb down all by myself, without your help! It is not good to think that women are weak in every sphere!'

Charles withdrew his trembling hand reluctantly and said sharply, 'What is the harm in holding my hand to climb down? Does this also go against your customs?'

'Yes! The left hand of a girl is exclusively reserved for a particular person. No one else has any right over it!'

'Do you remember, that day you dragged me away by your left hand and saved me from catastrophe?'

Prachi became serious, 'That was the hand of God. Not mine. God's hands alone can save a man.'

Charles was offended and said gravely, 'There is a soul in me too Prachi. There is God, too. My hand, too, is the hand of God!'

'The God in you is not aware of Indian customs and culture and there lies the trouble,' came the tart reply.

Charles followed Prachi as she walked on. He thought that Prachi was walking very fast.

Eight

~

Charles hurried across to where they were to meet Vishnu Maharana early next morning, and was happy to see he had reached before Prachi. She arrived just as he was getting out his note-pad and pencil. Vishnu Maharana was still unfolding the cloth wrappings that held the next set of palm-leaf manuscripts. By the time Prachi had organized herself, he was ready too and began reading.

' "O Artist!"

' "Yes, Silpa?"

' "Why is your mallet quiet today? I've been holding this pose for such a long time."

'Kamala Maharana looked at her. Silpa had been posing for the artist in the darkness of the night every day since they had met. Since then Kamala Maharana had given shape to thousands of celestial maidens on stone, depicting them as dancers or musicians. He had chiselled the beauty of woman—in her different moods, roles, costumes, and adornments, her everyday routine life as a cook and as a wife sharing her husband's chores, as a mother feeding her child, tying her hair, decorating it, trying to enhance her beauty before a mirror, waiting for her lover—as a devotee.

'From birth to death every stage was being given form by the skill and deftness of the artist. But that day Kamala Maharana looked sad and despondent. His chisel did not move and his mallet lay still. "What happened? What is today's command for my pose, dress, my expression? Why is there no direction today? Should Silpa go back? But Konark temple is not yet complete! Order me, O artist!" Silpa said plaintively.

'Kamala Maharana finally spoke, "Last night Nila Maharana died. Bhakta Maharana has already taken his place and will complete Nila Maharana's unfinished tasks."

'Silpa said quietly, "This is life. Nothing remains incomplete in the absence of anyone. Konark will be completed on time."

'Kamala Maharana sighed, "Of course the temple will be completed. The job left behind by Nila Maharana will be carried through by Bhakta Maharana. After Krushna Maharana, there will be Shiva Maharana. But the many yearnings, longings and desires of Nila Maharana will remain unfulfilled. If he had not died, he would have got married on his return. His betrothed must be counting the days to his homecoming."

'"I am sorry. Despite every effort of the royal physician, Nila Maharana did not survive. May his soul rest in peace," and Silpa closed her eyes and prayed silently.

'Kamala Maharana brooded. "Silpa, the unfulfilled soul never attains salvation. It will now traverse the universe as a restless spirit looking for rebirth. Who knows how many of the twelve hundred masons will die in these twelve years! May be Kamala Maharana too will be one of them, to die with unrealized hopes and desires. And then will you pray for his soul silently with your eyes closed?"

'Silpa replied calmly, "Nila Maharana was an artist. When the temple of Konark is completed, his soul too will be fulfilled."

'Kamala Maharana sighed again, "Silpa the artist is also a human being, of flesh and blood. Like food, thirst and sleep, sex is one of the primary needs in his life. Nila Maharana had taken a vow to observe celibacy for twelve years. But he was not a monk! How could he suppress his desires and longings? The artist carves out lotus on stone, but is not a piece of stone himself."

'Silpa stared at him, like a steady flame in the dark. How could she help him? A symbol of single-minded dedication, the artist of Kalinga, Kamala Maharana looked visibly disturbed that night! His eyes looked different. He was staring at the beautiful daughter of his master without blinking. A restless throbbing was pounding his soul. Yet, the maiden Silpa could not decipher its meaning. In what pose did Kamala want to see her?

'He was talking to himself, "The soul of Nila Maharana has to be redeemed. Or else there will be many more souls like Nila Maharana whose despairing sighs and inauspicious presence will destroy the holy temple of Konark. They will pose threats to the many worshipping, and to the rituals taking place at the shrine. It is now the prime duty of the artists to protect the temple from such ill omens."

'He turned to Silpa and said, "Silpa, till now you have posed at different angles as mentioned in the Silpa Sastra. But there have to be a few more models for protection against the inauspicious presence of the ungratified spirits of the dead artists. We have to carve special sculptures on the walls of Konark."

'"Command me artist! I am ready."

'"No, for this I have no instructions for you. Real models are not available for all kinds of sculptures. The artist visualizes them in his imagination. I request you to only be my muse. You will be ever present before my eyes. Your eyes, face, perfect body, beauty and grace will bloom through the nayika of my dreams."

'"What will be the image?"

'Kamala Maharana, as if in a dream, said, "The image of men and women in blissful moments of togetherness. Their cosmic union has to be depicted faultlessly on the walls of Konark. The ghosts, imps and demons will be thrilled to see them. All their unfulfilled desires will be released seeing those arousing, erotic sculptures. The spirit of Nila Maharana will also be appeased. He must have dreamt a lot about his beloved after leaving her behind to come to Konark!"

'"But artist, if you carve these erotic images on the walls of a temple, it will also disgrace the artists of Kalinga. Future generations will think the artists of Kalinga left behind their own erotic, lusty thoughts on the temple walls! The king who erected this temple will also get a bad name. The future may also say that artisans were made to carve erotic images on temple walls to please a debauched king. It is not impossible. Konark will not belong to Kalinga only. It will be revered by the world and will be world renowned. It should be your duty to portray positive images and of course, the generosity of the king before the world. This is my request; let there be no stigma in the twelve years of dedicated efforts and creativity in building the outstanding temple."

'Kamala Maharana said excitedly, "In the land where a maiden has boldly come forward to pose as a model for the Konark temple and is not afraid for her reputation, the art of that land can never be disgraced. The erotic couples on the temple walls are sanctioned by the Silpa Sastra treatise. It says the Gods are pleased with the depictions of worship, meditation and religious discourse. Fairies are pleased with the art of dance and music, demons with frightening images of yakshas which resemble their own reflections, while kinnaras want to see images of creatures that are half men and half animal. Human beings like to see the king and his activities, and animals are represented in bands like Ashwabandha (bands with a row of horses) and Gajabandhas (bands with a row of elephants), birds are represented in bands called Pakshibandha and Nagas or serpents love to see the images of the Nagabandha garland on the front entrance," he said listing all that the Silpa Sastra laid out.

' "But," he continued, "ghosts, gnomes and demons are happy to see sculptures of copulation and erotic postures on the walls of temples. If they are not appeased, their insatiate souls disrupt the peace of the temple and create many problems in the rituals. The Silpa Sastra mentions that images that please all are to be engraved on the temple walls. Every soul is fond of beauty and Konark will be the epitome of beauty and happiness in heaven, earth, as well as in hell! Those who practise tantric rituals, do so completely naked. The evil spirits therefore pay no attention to them. The erotic nude images carved on the temple walls are only symbols of the art of sex. These are also important aspects of temple rituals."

'Talking of tantric rituals, Kamala got carried away and passionately looked at Silpa's tender face. Before his eyes, a blurred vision of a lotus face bloomed. The face belonged to his beloved Chandrabhaga. Nila Maharana's untimely death had reminded him after many years of his child bride. Would he ever see his Chandrabhaga in this life? What if something happened to him as had happened with Nila Maharana? Then the souls of Kamala Maharana and Chandrabhaga would soar in the sky of Konark, but could their spirits ever meet?

'Kamala Maharana, restrained his wandering mind and became busy carving indescribably beautiful fine needlework designs. He draped his models with minutely designed attire and intricately crafted ornaments like a skilled goldsmith. It was as if he was adorning his beloved with those ornaments and clothes! Facing him was Silpa, the daughter of his master. He got totally immersed in his beautiful world of fantasy.

'The artist was now carving the gigantic wheels of Konark, and the fine carvings on it depicted the lifecycle, and the circles of time and creation. There were twenty-four wheels, twelve wheels each on the north and south sides of the chariot-shaped temple. There would be six wheels each on the sides of the main temple, four each on the sides of the porch and two wheels on the sides of the staircase. The entire monument would thus look like a well-adorned chariot. Seven horses appearing to fly would be fixed to the chariot. The artist decorated the wheels in minute detail. The clogs and spokes were carved with fine fretwork. The twelve pairs of wheels of the chariot of the Sun God represented the twelve months of the year. The eight spokes in them symbolized the eight praharas that make up a day and the seven horses epitomized the seven days in a week. The chariot upheld the eternal nature of life, time and the wheel of creation.

'The mystery of the universe and the riddles of life were carved on the wheels. On the south, the wheels depicted the bright fortnight and were carved with images depicting spirituality, such as the incarnations of Lord Vishnu, Gaja Laxmi and other Gods and Goddesses, the elephant rider, the horse rider, scenes of worship, and more. The north side depicted the dark fortnight and the dark side of life. On the northern wheels were indolent maidens, dancers with their lovely headdresses and women were busy with household chores.

'Finally, the artist depicted the mystery of the universe on stone, like a lyrical poem. There was a lifelike representation of a nuptial cot and scenes of love-making. The Sun, the source of light, the symbol of strength and virility, reveals the eternal truth. The artists of Konark, too, revealed and magnified the absolute truth of life on the stone walls of Konark. Everything seemed to pulsate with life, open to warmth and excitement of passion.

'Yet, the inspiration of the artist, the beautiful Silpa was absolutely calm and unmoved, and so was Kamala Maharana. A young artist who could so faultlessly depict the absolute truths of life in stone, and one who remained undisturbed, unaffected, and highly focused on his art was truly a Jitendriya, a great soul.

'In the deepening darkness a blue flame suddenly illuminated the carved "cycle of creation". The artist looked to the source of the light. It was the widow of the legendary hero Paramardhi Deva who had so recently fallen in battle—Princess Chandrika Devi—and she was looking at his latest carvings, murmuring, "You are a great artist. Your concentration and dedication are marvellous, as is your control over your mind and emotions. Had you been angry and suffering from pangs of separation or repressed sexual desire while carving, your sculptures could never have reflected such perfect craftsmanship. Konark would have remained incomplete, you would have been redundant as an artist, and your work mundane, not awe-inspiring. A temple of Lord Surya, a temple symbolizing the cultural traditions of a great race, could never be completed by the hands of a lustful artist." The princess turned to him and said, "You have come out with flying colours in one of the toughest tests, one that even an aspiring Jitendriya would balk at."

'After her husband fell in battle, Chandrika Devi had abandoned the luxuries of the palace life and chosen to live a life of austerity and was now looking to the completion of the sacred monument of Konark. She was worthy of worship. Kamala Maharana bowed to her and touched her feet with respect. Blessing him she moved on, showing the light to other artists nearby working through the night. Then, setting the torch down beside them, she walked further to inspire artisans inscribing tales from her husband's heroic life on stone in the form of verses.

'Silpa meanwhile had disappeared like a dream. Sometimes he wasn't sure if she was real or just another figment of his imagination.'

And with that Vishnu Maharana set the palm leaf down and began pulling the cloth wrappings together.

Charles was examining the carvings of men and women on the top of the porch and wondering if granite and not khondolite could have been used; granite would have added further grandeur. Any way you saw it, its amazing sculptures had rendered Konark immortal and was still bringing its artists acclaim even after seven hundred years. How could they have sculpted such amorous couples without being distracted by passion, wondered Charles—were they made of stone?

Dharmanada had come up to him unbeknownst and was now showing him a packet of photographs and whispering, 'These pictures are very interesting, Saheb! They sell well. These are to be treasured. A thing of beauty is a joy forever.' Charles felt a little embarrassed. Prachi was smiling innocently at him from a distance. Charles said, 'Let it be, Dharmananda, Lillian has taken many photographs already. You give them to your Didi.'

Dharmananda bit his lips and said, 'My God! She will wring my ears. Let my photos be with me. When you go back to your country, you can take as many as you wish. There is a great demand for these photographs in your land.' Hearing giggles like a spring gurgling by, Charles turned to see Chitrotpala, flower basket in hand and the edge of her pallu caught between her teeth to hide her laughter.

'Didi,' she sang out, 'Saheb has reached this far.' Then she turned to Charles and Dharmananda and asked, 'What are you both looking at?'

Charles left them to sort it out and went to where Prachi was standing. She was looking at the granite images, thoroughly engrossed. The statues were chiselled with such intensity that they looked almost lifelike, so vibrant and perfect, as though artists Kamala Maharana, Harita Maharana, Dhruba Maharana, Krushna Maharana and Shiva Maharana had just laid down their chisels and gone for lunch. As though seven hundred years had not passed by.

'You are immortal O artist,' murmured Prachi. 'I surrender all my earthly desires, my errors and illusions before your noble soul.'

All those gathered there, looked as though gathered to pay homage to those long-gone artisans and their creation. As though Konark had drawn them because it was the unified throbbing soul of all artists of Kalinga; drawn them because it signified the acme of achievement in an epoch, in the eternal history of a great culture.

Chandrabhaga, Silpa, Prachiprava, Chitrotpala; the past, the present, the future, and eternal time itself—lay at the feet of these Kalingan artists much like the flower petals that Prachiprava offered to God. As Prachi's eyes met Charles's, she came back to reality and with a smile asked, 'What took you so long?'

Charles's handsome face had turned pink like a lotus flower. He glanced at Prachi and said in a hushed voice, 'Those nude pictures were extremely erotic.' He could not say more. He turned his eyes to the blue expanse of the casuarina forest at a distance.

Prachi smiled softly and said, 'All these images adhere to

the treatise on temple architecture. The palm-leaf manuscripts mentioned the tantric cult.'

'But they have no scientific justification,' argued Charles.

'Seven hundred years ago,' said Prachi, 'temple construction texts defined the rules. They were meaningful at that time, and held a scientific logic for the artists of Kalinga.'

'But these images must have polluted the sanctity of the temples! Many visitors from abroad don't approve of scenes of sex and copulation on temple architecture,' he protested, before realizing he was expressing his displeasure to thin air. Prachi had left Charles behind.

A guide had sidled up to Charles in the meanwhile and said, 'Observe these sculptures carefully, Saheb! Do not make such offensive comments about them. They have such divine faces and ethereal expressions. Had the art and architecture of ancient Kalinga, and the lifestyle of its people been so ignominious, or had the artists chiselled these images motivated by their own unfulfilled desires, they could not have carved such aesthetic sculptures with divine and spiritual expressions. How could they work on these sculptures for twelve long years with such dedication? Had they been immoral, the sacred devadasis would have perished in the fire of their sexuality and the art and culture of Kalinga would never have existed today.'

'Strange... this country is really very strange,' murmured Charles to himself, 'but the masons of Kalinga and Konark were exceptional.'

The guide who was leading them continued, 'A man's life experiences nine rasas or emotions, and love is the prime emotion. When the artists decorated the exteriors of the temple reflecting these nine rasas could they leave out love? Konark was designed to express all the nine or Nav rasas, we call it

"Navarasa". The lifecycles depicted here would have remained incomplete. So the artists have depicted each emotional urge, each predominant mood that drives life, and through that paid homage to the Divine. Don't you feel they have carved a niche for themselves, proving their greatness?'

'Perhaps you are right,' Charles replied, now having caught up with Prachi, 'It is a fact that Konark displays all human sentiment.'

Walking on, Prachi said, 'The Brihat Samhita states that bird, coconut palm, swastika, water-filled pitcher, leaves, men and women, as well as couples are symbols of prosperity. Each has been depicted at Konark. When the artist has not left any feature of life untouched, how could he ignore couples expressing passion?'

The guide said, 'Did you notice another thing here, Saheb? You lagged behind while viewing these couples, but Didi moved ahead. Do you understand?' Charles stared at the guide, not comprehending. Prachi smiled, 'That is the difference between us. You are a foreigner from the Western world, and I am Prachiprava...' she did not end her comment.

The guide continued, 'The exteriors of a temple are often carved with erotic images to test the earnestness, devotion, dedication and self-control of devotees. Those who are distracted and give way to passion cannot reach God. Even if they enter the temple, they do so only physically, but their mind wanders. Those who are not influenced by these scenes move ahead on the path of devotion, and attain freedom from the troubles of mundane life. Just like Didi. Have you noticed, Saheb? She has such a divinely serene expression.'

'Of course,' retorted Charles. 'Your Didi is a sanyasini. She is a maha yogini, great devotee or perhaps one of those stone sculptures! But I am a human being, a very ordinary man. I sometimes get blinded by anger, greed, attachment and love. I am a normal being. But she is...' Charles stopped, it was hopeless...

Prachi feigned anger and said, 'Charles! You have every right to speak about your own life. But not about anybody else!'

'I am sorry, Prachiprava. Sometimes one tends to forget one's limits. Forgive me.'

Prachi smiled enchantingly and Chitrotpala was just behind her, laughing uncontrollably. She was amused by the Saheb asking for forgiveness from Prachi. Charles laughed too, 'To laugh through life is a lovely art, nobody can beat Chitrotpala at it; only a daughter of India can laugh so wholeheartedly.'

That afternoon they gathered again at Vishnu Maahrana's feet and he began reading.

'Queen Sita Devi was staying in the makeshift capital at Padma Kshetra near Konark. The king after many years of peace was now away fighting the Muslim army of Bengal. She used to come down often from Cuttack, the capital, to stay at Konark and supervise the temple construction. This was one such visit. Chandra Devi, Narasimha Deva's sister, too stayed here. After the death of her husband she had put her heart and soul into the temple construction.

'The king, unbeknownst to the queen had returned from the battlefront to see how his people were getting on. As he approached the entrance of the palace he thought longingly of his queen. He had not met her for a long time. If Konark was to be a pedestal of self-negation, then the king too had to observe the sacred rites of an ascetic. Perhaps, she was deliberately staying away from him to let him observe his vows unhindered. She had forsaken all royal trappings, all marital joys to honour his commitment, and had become a mendicant herself. He knew if his queen was not at the palace she would be at the temple site. He had learnt that she actively interacted with the artisans, supervising their progress in his absence. As a mother, she went down to their tents to check on their well-being. So now that he had returned exhausted from battle, how could he put his feet up and rest?

'When his queen Sita Devi had quit the palace and its comforts to stay at the temple site to support the artists and help her husband accomplish the sacred work of temple construction, relaxation was far from his mind. The enemies roared at the frontiers of his country, and within it the young masons and artisans worked with warrior-like determination at great speed and tremendous dedication to build the temple. The king was one among them, the greatest warrior.

'Now his main concern was to move out incognito to check how safe his countrymen were feeling. He would reassure them, in village after village that the invading Muslim army was being given a fight they would never forget, prior to their complete defeat. The simple villagers trembled with the fear of attack at any moment. They had to be reassured that while the king and his sons and grandsons were alive the sun of Kalinga would never set.

'Having bathed, eaten and donned his chosen disguise, the king rode his favourite horse out into the dark night. The guard was astonished to see the Mahadandapasha (Inspector General of Police) disappear into the dark so swiftly.

'Sandy beaches, entangled creepers, dense forests, miles of rocky terrain, small patches of thorny scrubland and vast plains, his horse left them all behind. Though the hamlets, villages, and cities were fast asleep, their guards were awake and alert and wondered, "Who is this? Is it an enemy Muslim soldier? Is it possible to intrude into our land guarded by the alert brave and valiant sentinels of King Narasimha Deva? How can enemies even contemplate invading our land when it is almost suicidal to do so?" And so they would yell "Halt!" and the king would quickly dismount in the guise of the Mahadandapasha.

'He would collect information from the village guards and assure them, "By dawn, let the villagers be informed that they are protected by the king. Let normal life be restored. Let everybody live without any fear. It is impossible for the enemy to cross our borders, with the Ganga Dynasty reigning. Deliver this message of the king through the drum beaters to reach every village." So saying he would turn his horse and gallop away, taking his message to the next village, and then the village after that...

'Nevertheless, the pounding of the king's horse's hooves scared the simple villagers in the quiet night. Mothers hushed their wailing children saying, "Be quiet, go to sleep, the Muslims are coming!" They were very scared of the Muslim soldiers and the very thought of them sent a cold shiver down their spine. The rumours of their brutal carnage, though heavily concocted, had created shock waves among the citizens. Doors were bolted by twilight in fear of the Muslim army. The women got alarmed at the faintest noise.

'The king rode on thus, through the night, through village, hamlet and town, until he reached a village where in the depths of the night, a light but brisk footstep was heard. Someone was awake and in a hurry, running through the jungle. The king had left the guard at his post at the gates of the village, and he decided to see to the matter himself. Going by the rapid footfalls on the fallen leaves—at times quick, and then stopping and continuing—he seemed in a hurry to escape, afraid and uncertain in the face of some imminent danger. The king followed the sound on horseback. Soon he heard many footsteps, and a muffled voice. Then a shadowy figure emerged, silhouetted by the moon that had just come out from behind the clouds.

'It was a woman. She seemed about to jump into the lotus pond. He rode across just in time to grab her tender lotus stem-like arm, lift her on to the horse, and gallop off into the dark. There were a few more shadows ahead. Who were they? Muslim soldiers? Were they planning to abduct the maiden? Why was she was trying to jump into the lotus pond?

'The woman he had rescued had fainted in his arms. He rode away with her and the footsteps chasing them melted into the distance. Soon everything was quiet, still and calm—the hamlets, villages, habitations were all left far behind. He pulled the horse to a stop. The woman's hands and feet were turning cold. She had to be attended to first, or else her rescue would be futile. The king looked around. The horse stood near a ruined temple in a desolate area in the midst of a dense forest, with a few derelict, abandoned huts still standing. There was also a small silted pond, and an obviously unused well.

'The king dismounted and laid the unconscious woman gently down on the temple courtyard. He bound some wild creepers together, tied his scarf to them and slowly lowered it into the well. Fortunately, there was a trickle of water inside. The king pulled out the dripping scarf and shook some cold water onto the woman's face. Then he looked around and found a flowering bough, which he snapped off to fan the woman's face. A streak of moonlight found its way through the darkness and caressed her closed eyelids.

'The king was bewildered. He had seen her pious face somewhere before. But where? A familiar scent of lotuses emanated from her. Who was this woman with a lotus scent? Her beautiful, shapely hands were lying lifeless. She had picture tattooed on one of her hands. Below it was inscribed "Radha-Krishna". The king despaired, "Ah!" at the inhuman act by the tattoo artist who could inflict such pain on such delicate arms. Meanwhile the woman had regained consciousness.

' "Who are you?" the king asked.'

' "Who are you?" she asked in return. "Why did you save me?"

' "Suicide is a crime."

' "There was no other option for a sinner," her voice was choked with emotion.

' "What is your sin?"

' "While constructing the Sun temple at Konark, my husband…" she could not complete her sentence and sobbed uncontrollably.

'The king grieved too and wondered if she was the wife of Nila Maharana? He composed himself and said, "Although Nila Maharana was not married, he was betrothed long ago. Are you…?" He paused for her answer.

' "I don't know who Nila Maharana is."

' "Only Nila Maharana is dead among the artisans of Konark. The others are fine! They are busy with their auspicious job."

' "But somebody came and informed my mother-in-law about my husband's death! My Lord, who are you? Do you know my husband? Is he alive?" Her voice throbbed with a welter of emotions, and the king heard anxiety, euphoria, happiness and sorrow. The king, kneeling, said, "I am the Mahadandapasha of the city of Konark. It is my duty to maintain law and order in the country. I am a servant of King Narasimha Deva. The king is the servant of this country and of Lord Jagannath and that is why I too am his servant. Lady! This servant of Lord Jagannath does not lie. The sad news of the death of Nila Maharana has been conveyed to his family by a special messenger. The inauspicious news that your husband is dead is baseless and a lie. Did a messenger carry this news?"

'"No. No messenger came with this news. It was hearsay, but my mother-in-law believed it."

'"One should not believe such things. Whoever be your husband, he is carrying on his job for the country. Now let us go, and I will take you to your home."

'She raised her hands to the sky and prayed to Lord Jagannath, thanking him, "Jagannath Swami! I don't care what happens to me, but protect my husband. His period of ill-omen has passed. Lord your kindness has no limits."

'King Narasimha Deva too raised his hands in reverence. He whispered to himself, "Lord Purushottam! Let the soul of Nila Maharana rest in peace! Please grant long lives to the rest of the twelve hundred artists. Let your wishes be fulfilled!"

'The young woman's heart melted with sympathy for the noble man. He whose heart cried for others, he was worthy of honour, he was the Purushottam, noblest among men. The king said humbly, "Lady! Permit me to take you to your home and complete my duty. The morning star will appear in the sky within a few minutes. I have to go back to the capital before daybreak."

'The veiled woman's face, which had brightened like a flower in full bloom hearing that her husband was alive, now fell as though drained of life. She implored him, "My Lord! Return to your capital. Let God bless you. Leave me alone to die. My husband is alive, and he is busy for the country. After knowing this I do not have any more sorrow."

'The king was perturbed. Even after learning the good news she still wanted to end her life? She should have gone back home happily and provided comfort to her distraught mother-in-law, but she did not want to go home. Something was amiss. The king said gravely, "I am the Mahadandapasha of this country. It is beyond me to leave a person so heartbroken to commit suicide. Let us go, I will reach you home and will explain everything to your mother-in-law."

'The young woman said dispassionately, "I left my in-law's home long ago; they barred their doors to me. They believe I am impure and a sinner." She was in tears now.

'"But what is your sin?" he asked, concerned.

'"My brother-in-law's affection and sympathy for me. My mother-in-law considers me inauspicious because my husband had to leave home for temple-building shortly before I was brought to his house as a bride. She ill-treats me for losing her son. But my brother-in-law defends me. He used to pull water from the deep well of the temple and carry it back for me every night. He helped me in so many ways, but there were many who could not stand this. They spread the rumour that we were having an illegitimate relationship, meeting under the bakul tree near the temple."

'She became too distressed to continue. She sobbed hiding her face and then said, "Oh God! My brother-in-law, who is like God, was defamed for helping an unfortunate woman like me. I am ill-fated, my destiny is uncertain. Is it a crime to pity a sufferer?"

'The king in the meanwhile had recognized the familiar lotus smell and those delicate features, and was now astounded hearing the plight of innocent Chandrabhaga. He was stunned. There would be so many young women like her who suffered separation from their husbands, and would have to undergo similar painful experiences. It had never crossed his mind before!

'Chandrabhaga continued, "When my mother-in-law drove me out, I came to stay at my parents'. She told my father I was a fallen woman and ordered that her son should not see my face on his return. The lies about my character deprived me of everybody's love and affection. Nevertheless I have still survived. I was waiting for my husband, like the lotus flower awaits union with the Sun. I hoped that one day my husband would return and meet me at least once. That he would understand me when he looked into my eyes. Then came the news that he had died. My mother-in-law thinks I am to be blamed for it, and if I live her entire family will be wiped out. To respect her wishes, I left my parental home too and decided to end my life in my favourite lotus pond. I saw my beloved only once, and it was at that lotus pond, but from a distance, hazily. That is why the pond is very dear to me. But then you interfered."

'The king became sombre, "You should go back to your father's house. Your husband is alive and will definitely accept you. His artist's eyes will surely recognize your unblemished tender soul."

'Chandrabhaga sobbed uncontrollably, "My father is no more. I am a burden to my brother's family. Now with my scandal, he cannot live with dignity in our village. Besides, after spending the entire night outside the village, how can I go back? I do not have the courage. I do not know how far I have come. If I go back, let alone my brother, my entire village will discard me. All roads have been closed to me after tonight. Leave me here and go back to your capital."

'From time immemorial, women have suffered such injustice thought King Narasimha Deva. He was absolutely certain of her unblemished character and innocence. Although she had left home the night before, she was pure and unsullied; he knew it in his heart. And yet, it was beyond his capacity to procure justice for her in the eyes of society. Although a king, he found himself helpless. Virtuous Sita too had to be banished from Ayodhya bearing just such a stigma. But how could he leave her behind? Alone, and on the doorstep of death? He pondered the next course of action. The sky was changing colour and when it was a little brighter, he would find his way.

'Soon the benevolent sky spilt some of its brightness into the world. It was as though a lotus flower was unfurling its petals. The beautiful face of the young woman was visible now, tinted with a pink and red glow. The king had seen that face only once, on a moonlit night seven years ago and had been besotted by her; the same face mesmerized him in the sunlight. She was the epitome of virtue, not a shadow of a sin could ever besmear her divine face. And yet she was considered unchaste and inauspicious, a whore! The woman, whom he had supposed in the dark of night to be young girl, had grown into a mature woman. Seven years had passed. The temple construction at Konark was half way through. The years wives, families and beloveds had waited for the masons and artisans would also come to an end. But where did Chandrabhaga's end lie?

'The king said gravely and softly, "Lady! There is still time for daybreak. I will take you to your lotus pond near your village. You will return after bathing in the pond. Nobody will know because no one would have left their bed!"

'Chandrabhaga stared at the noble and considerate man. The young Mahadandapasha's broad chest, high forehead, sharp nose, expressive eyes and graceful features filled her with a sentiment of deep reverence and poignant feelings. Seven years ago on another moonlit night too a tall and handsome young man had rescued her. It was the same nose, the same eyes, and the same soft soothing voice. That day she was glad to be alive, but today there was no alternative to death. That was the difference. He wanted to take her back with him. Didn't he know that life was more difficult to bear than death?

'Chandrabhaga spoke, "Sir, as a married woman it would be improper for me to go back with you on the horse. You proceed first, collect information from the village and let me know. If no one is aware of my absence, I will surely return and wait for my husband."

'"But it is nearly daybreak. If the night ends you cannot go back. The news of your absence will become known."

'Chandrabhaga said calmly, "No matter what happens, it is impossible for me to ride on the horse with you. If I do so there will be another mark of disgrace added to my name in the village. Please leave. Do not waste time. May be if you can return quickly, I will be able to reach the border of my village."

'Like an obedient child, he agreed. "But there is a condition. If I come back with bad news, I will take you with me to the capital city of Konark. Your husband is busy building the temple. You will become his inspiration, and the temple of Konark will become a masterpiece of peerless beauty."

'Chandrabhaga was surprised to hear this and said, "In that case, the king will order for my husband's head to be severed as punishment, and he will punish me as well. For him, stone is more precious than man. He has turned human emotion into stone and tries to put soul into the stone."

'King Narasimha Deva was once again stumped. A simple rustic beauty repeatedly forced him to question his strength as a powerful ruler. Seven years ago it was she who had led him to take a vow to abstain from earthy pleasures for twelve long years, and yet she never acknowledged the other noble deeds he had done. She refused to love him as a man! This pained him tremendously.

' "Lady, the king is an ordinary mortal. There is kindness, forgiveness, affection, love, devotion and pity in his heart. I know King Narasimha Deva personally. His heart bleeds for his people. The fact that you are not even aware of this will hurt him immensely."

' "The king suffers!" Chandrabhaga smiled sarcastically. Narasimha Deva thought to himself, "Everybody thinks the king has nothing to feel sad about. That is the sore point." Man accuses God of being stone-hearted, when his sufferings are too intense to bear; and the king is only a servant of God. So if Chandrabhaga accused him of being stone-hearted there was nothing surprising about it. Besides, this ill-fated woman's burden of sorrow was so deep that it did not allow anybody else's sadness to reach her. She had no other means to keep herself alive, except her pain.

'Before mounting his horse, he asked, "Won't you be afraid alone in this dense forest?" Like a pale star in the morning sky, Chandrabhaga gave a wan smile and said, "One who is ready to give up her life, can she be afraid of anything?" The king climbed the horse and assured her, "Do not be afraid, Lady. I will return soon. Let Lord Jagannath protect you," and he rode away.

'Chandrabhaga bowed to him and said to herself, "Oh young horseman, whoever you may be, you are worthy of my respect. You have time and again rescued Chandrabhaga from death, like an angel appearing from nowhere. But she has no other path other than death. I will remember you at the moment of death. Because I met you I learnt to recognize a true man—his appearance, his strength, his personality—just by seeing you. You appeared as the man in my life; a man I can adore because I've never seen even my husband at such close quarters."

'At the edge of the village, the king stopped. The village had awoken very early that morning and people had gathered in groups, discussing something with sombre faces. The king asked the guard, "Is everything all right?"

'"No sir. A Muslim soldier on horseback abducted a young woman last night. But she was considered a stigma for the village! Death is better for her."

'The king said gravely, "Maybe she will return, and no Muslim soldier ever entered this village!"

'The guard said modestly, "You are the Mahadandapasha. That is why I am telling you frankly. I have seen him with my own eyes. The Muslim soldier fled on his horse with the woman. Many people of this village also saw them. In case she escapes by some ill-luck and comes back, the village won't accept her. Her grief and humiliation will be far more difficult for her to bear than death. In the land of King Narasimha Deva, there is no scope for any crime. No one steals or abducts anyone. Who else but a Muslim soldier can do such a thing! Who else can be so barbaric in this land?"

'The early rays of the morning sun touched the earth. The Ganga monarch turned his face away and vanished into the forest. The night was over and he would have to shed his disguise soon. But his heart was agitated. What should he do about Chandrabhaga? If she could be sent to her husband, maybe her plight would improve. But it would disturb the process of temple construction. Her appearance would pose problems for the concentration of all the builders of Konark, and they would be distracted from their duty.

'Konark was a sacred seat of self-discipline and austerity. What on earth was her role there? What was the solution? Before he could find a solution, the king arrived at the ruined temple. The courtyard where he had left her standing was bright with sunlight and filled with the scent of lotus flowers. But the lotus had vanished.

'The Ganga king searched for Chandrabhaga like a bee maddened by the scent of a lotus flower. On the footsteps of the courtyard were flowers carved in stone and on those flowers he spotted her sad tears fallen like drops of dew. The noble Sun God was even now wiping them away. But where was Chandrabhaga? Had she gone beyond all sorrow? The king bent and looked into the well. There was no trace of her. Had she vanished of her own accord, or was she was dragged away by wild animals? He looked around. No. There had been no such mishap. Peace reigned in the forest where nature had spread her beautiful and colourful veil. The creepers, bushes, flowers and leaves were all in place. There was no sign of any accident or disturbance.

'The fear of Chandrabhaga's having met with a mishap receded, only to be replaced with anguish. He had been unable to rescue a woman in distress. Chandrabhaga's indifference had crushed his valour, heroism, success and fortitude. This defeat would not be recorded in the history of the Ganga dynasty, but it would be inscribed in his heart till his death. Chandrabhaga's name would not be mentioned in the history of the building of the Sun Temple at Konark, but her soul would eternally drift in the sky, looking for her artist husband.

'The Ganga king's unsettled emotions searched for a glimpse of Chandrabhaga's soul in the forests, in the sky. As his restless eyes scanned the horizon he saw far into the distance the Patitapabana[9] flag flying high above the blue-wheel of the Nilachakra[10]. All sadness and remorse vanished in a moment. King Narasimha Deva felt he had his answer—the "God of the Fallen One" had indeed wiped away the sorrows of Chandrabhaga, considered as a fallen woman in her society. She had attained her freedom. One who takes shelter in Lord Jagannath, finds his way like a ray of light in the dark.

'The Ganga King hands aloft, bowed to the flag and pleaded, "My Lord! If it was your wish that Chandrabhaga should leave this mortal world, then she should have drowned herself last night in the lotus pond. Why did you rescue her through me and again call her back to you? Was this a test for both of us? Is it your desire to vanquish my pride in remaining unconquered by defeating me at the hands of an innocent woman? This Ganga king stands defeated now. Is this what you wanted? What is this mysterious game you are playing with this servitor of yours my Lord?"'

And with that Vishnu Maharana too bowed, placed the palm leaf on the pile of read manuscripts and pulled the cloth wrappings over it.

Despite all his research, Lord Jagannath remained a mystery to Charles. Invisible and enigmatic just like Prachi, just like mystic Konark. Charles could not understand Lord Jagannath, could not fathom the mystery of Konark, nor comprehend Prachi either.

---

[9]Help of the helpless, refers to a flag flying over a temple.
[10]The blue wheel, again representative of God—the blue indicating the sky, and the wheel the 'wheel of life', a reminder of the Divine force that lies behind the wheel of life and the blue sky above.

When he looked at the unfinished idols of Lord Jagannath and his siblings, Prachi said serenely, 'Lord Jagannath can never be incomplete. He is manifest everywhere and He is the Lord of the Universe. He reaches out to our needs, with his invisible hands and legs. He embraces us when we need Him.'

Prachi was enchanted by the deity. She would cry out, 'Oh God, how beautiful you are!' and Charles's eyes would dwell upon the large-barrel shape of this peculiar idol, the enormous wide-open eyes and smile that spread unbounded, the arms which seemed never-ending. Charles wondered if Jagannath could appear so attractive in the eyes of a good-looking girl like Prachi, then Charles's good looks ought to surpass all. But Prachi never complimented him on his looks. She never mentioned his looks. Perhaps she did not see beauty through her eyes, he consoled himself. She had enshrined Lord Jagannath in her heart, and there was no space for any mortal man.

Not just Prachi, but Dinabandhu Babu and Charukala too, were enchanted with Lord Jagannath. At the entrance of every door in their house, a painting of Lord Jagannath hung on the wall. Before the visitor entered, he bowed to it as if entering a shrine and removed his or her footwear. Everyone entered a house barefoot here. Charles obeyed each rule set by Dinabandhu Babu's. This pleased Dinabandhu Babu, and Charukala too became close to Charles.

Lots of rituals were observed at Dinabandhu Babu's household. Though he often wondered about them, he was happy to be part of them nevertheless. During some rituals, Charukala did not touch even a drop of water and would fast rigorously. Odia women observed many fasts and rituals for the well-being of their children and husbands. Simple people like Charukala felt God existed in images of stone, in the winnowing fan, broom, grinding stone, betel, coconut, trees, ghosts, cobras, cows, bullocks, kites, jackal and almost everywhere. Charles was amazed. In a world that had become so complex, such simple people nevertheless existed!

Women like Charukala suffered unhesitatingly for the health and prosperity of their family. Observing the joy of sacrifice on her face, Charles would wonder why he never noticed such an expression on the face of his own mother. According to him, she remained an embodiment of dissatisfaction and displeasure, though living in the lap of luxury.

He was also offered many types of sweets and got to taste Odia cuisines. Though a small eater, he loved the food. Charukala would come to him with a plate full of sweets; he would eat only one or two pieces. Then Charukala would be reminded of her son and chide Charles, 'You are just like my son. Do I toil so much, preparing these sweets just for myself? Your stomach is full with just one or two sweets? Tell me, which mother will like that? Dinu went away ages ago. He does not get a chance to savour his favourite cakes.' By this time she would be in tears and coax Charles to take at least one more sweet. Watching her affectionate motherly face, Charles would eat some more sweets. And he would wonder why Charukala took so much trouble preparing these delicacies after all.

On many occasions, he saw Charukala painting beautiful white motifs on the floor with a paste of rice powder, using her fingers. She worked swiftly putting skilled artists to shame. In fact, not just Charukala, he had seen many Odia women do this exquisite alapana artwork in minutes. He spotted Prachi too painting the tulsi chowra in the courtyard with ground rice powder one day. Though she was a modern girl, she was a favourite of Charukala as she was also very traditional. She was drawing motifs with a lot of concentration and was lost in her own world. She drew faces of Lord Jagannath and added coloured powder to beautify her designs. Interrupting her, Charles asked, 'Weren't supposed to search for Chandrabhaga today?'

Prachi asked astonished, 'What does that mean?'

Charles sounded disturbed, 'I was thinking about her throughout the night. Where did she disappear in the dense forest? We have to trace her from the palm-leaf manuscripts today.'

'What if we can't find her?' asked Prachi while she washed her hands and got ready. Charles followed her as they left the house. 'It is the king's job to find her,' she added as she entered the temple complex. 'If it was not done, then it was a grave injustice to her. But if Chandrabhaga were to be found, her pain would have become more intense. Poor girl, she must have vanished and her soul, soaring into the vast sky, must have finally dissolved at the feet of Lord Jagannath. All problems and sorrows end at His feet,' she said quietly, her head bent.

'Why so hopeless, Prachi? You are so ruthlessly dispassionate about everything. But you are only causing yourself more harm.'

'Ruthlessness is the most pronounced emotion among people and animals. It overpowers compassion, expectations and love. If you are soft hearted, you become weak and will be exploited. Can't you see even the lion dominates the elephant here! Tenderness is always weak, helpless and exploited.'

Charles stared blindly at the Gaja-Simha statue, but his mind was searching for a trace of beloved Chandrabhaga through the centuries of a seven-hundred year old history.

Nine

~

That morning everyone was on time, even Charles. Vishnu Maharana had the next set of palm leaves opened and ready when Charles and Prachi arrived together. The mystery over the fate of a girl lost seven hundred years ago, had everybody in its grip seven hundred years later. Nobody had had the time to even glance at the newspaper that morning. News about Chandrabhaga was all that they wanted.

Vishnu Maharana, who had nobly resisted casting an eye over the manuscript in their absence, now picked up the palm-leaf with anxious anticipation and began reading.

'The supreme King, Narasimha Deva, residing at present in his palace at the capital, was in deep thought. Queen Sita Devi was equally anxious. Why was the King so worried? What could be the cause of his distress? What did he lack in life? What could be the reason for his discontent? It was unlikely there could be any discontent or anxiety in the Fort of Barabati in Cuttack, the capital of Kalinga!

'To the north of the fort, flowed the rivers of Mahanadi and Birupa. The Fort of Choudwar stood at a distance, made impregnable by the rivers that surrounded it on either side. To the west, were the Mahanadi and Kathajodi rivers, flowing turbulently along the Fort of Bidanashi. The Kathajodi flowed to the south and beyond it was the Fort of Sarangagada, which protected the Fort of Barabati in Cuttack. The armed soldiers of Kalinga were ever alert as they patrolled the ramparts at each fort, ready to thwart any enemy attack. Outside the Fort of Barabati, was a wide moat and a high masonry wall. There were parallel boundary walls for defending the fort from inside. The fort was thus doubly protected.

'The watchmen and the Paika foot-soldiers were always on guard, clad in armour round the clock. They wore iron helmets, donned tiger skins, smeared turmeric paste and oil on their bodies and put large vermilion marks on their forehead, which made their appearance even more menacing. When those within the Fort of Barabati lay asleep, these sentinels would become even more alert. Their eyes, reddened like that of a hunter, would glow in the dark warning off any intruder. In the dark nights their sharp and shining swords flashed like flame. They carried large shields with wooden frames covered with tiger skin held in place by iron rivets.

'And yet, despite all this, the mighty king could not rest in peace. Why? What was the reason? Sleep evaded Queen Sita Devi, too. How many years more? For how many years would the king observe his vow? Had he turned into stone with his dedication to the construction of the temple at Konark? The queen suppressed her longings and led an austere life so devotedly that she could no longer feel the throbbing of her flesh. It was her duty to follow in the footsteps of her husband. What did she lack in life? By the grace of Lord Surya, she was blessed with a son like Bhanu Deva, a copy of King Narasimha Deva. He was growing up fast, gifted with strength, valour, knowledge, and all the noble qualities that he had inherited from his father. She had no reason to complain about anything, no reason to be unhappy.

'Despite possessing a great deal in life, the heart sometimes aches because of an acute void. Though she was the Queen of

Kalinga, today she was just a woman in distress at the throne of King Narasimha Deva. Her wishes remained ungratified, as she could not conquer the heart of her husband. The king looked pensive, wistful, and distant. For whom? What troubled him?

'The victorious king had conquered Bidar and Kalabarga in the south-west. He had returned from Bengal, amassing wealth and fortune. The Udra soldiers, well trained in warfare, were led by the King and reinforced by allied forces from neighbouring countries. They had defeated their Muslim enemies repeatedly. Though there was still a constant threat from the Muslim army, there was absolutely no fear inside the country.

'The army of Dhenkia Paikas was alert and well prepared with their swords and bows and arrows to safeguard peace inside the land and defend it against invaders. The Banua Paikas, fully armed, were ready to fight at the borders. They were prepared to join in the war in case of any eventuality, though engaged in farming. While they raised crops they also practised martial skills, so that when the clarion call came to defend their motherland, they could jump into the battlefield. Throughout the country, Paikas were busy improvising new techniques of war. In different cantonments, group leaders trained batches of Paika foot-soldiers. During the Golden Era of the Ganga dynasty, peace, happiness, bravery, and valour ran powerfully through the length and breadth of the country. And yet there was no peace for King Narasimha Deva. No trace of happiness at all!'

'The king never rested at Barabati Fort to recoup from fatigue in war. He never indulged in worldly pleasures. He had discarded his desire to spend time with his beloved queen, Sita Devi, and preferred to rest at the Fort Palace of Konark. Every night he would leave it in disguise and collect information about the welfare of his subjects. Was he looking for someone in particular? When the queen asked him about it, he smiled and explained, "What man does not get, he searches for throughout his life. The hardship of that pursuit affords the most desirable gratification on earth."

'The queen would ask, "What is it you have not got and are searching for?"

' "The soul of the artist. The soul of Konark. I am searching for it. Is it possible to find it among the stones?"

'The queen sighed, "Yes. It can be found among the stones. I'm looking for it there as well, I am searching for myself in you. I know I will never be disappointed. The completion of Konark will create a soul in the stones and I will find myself in you. I have that confidence."

'The king would relapse again into thought: how could he find her? The soul he was pining for could already have left the earth to mingle with the floating clouds, sailing in the sky, or have merged with the fragrance of the forests or even the waves lapping at the sea shore!'

Vishnu Maharana too sighed deeply and took a sip of water before setting down the palm leaf he had read and picking up the next and reading aloud.

'Kamala Maharana worked without a break. He had worked on a sculpture on the southern side of the Natamandir and was it giving the final touches, making the fine design even more intricate. It was a wonderful image of a woman in waiting. Who was she? She was depicted leaning over a half open door, eagerly waiting for someone's arrival. Her veil had slipped from her face. Her heart-shaped visage looked bright, innocent and eager in anticipation.

'In the scorching sun, Kamala Maharana's strong body was sweating heavily. The sevaks stood with a royal umbrella shading him while others fanned him. Drops of sweat fell from the king's forehead, too, as he watched the mason silently. He thought how small he was before the master craftsman. Who was greater, the king or the artist? In the protective care of Lord Jagannath, both were mere servants of God.

'The artist was now giving finishing touches to the statue, putting life into it. Kamala Maharana's chisel could not have moved more gently. He touched the lips of the stone statue as though he were touching the petals of a flower and he whispered into her ears, "Chandrabhaga! You can feel my touch over there, I am certain. Because I can sense your breathing. I know you will wait for me till eternity. That is why I am leaving your image here in a posture of waiting. This waiting, my beloved, will immortalize the temple of Konark. One day the whole world will know about it. Stay well, Chandrabhaga, our days of waiting are about to come to an end."

'The king standing spellbound watching him work, froze when he heard Kamala Maharana utter "Chandrabhaga". Almost without meaning to, he asked, "Chandrabhaga?" The artist's concentration broke. He turned and found King Narasimha Deva standing behind him staring at the stone woman in waiting. The harsh sun had reddened his fair face.

' "Forgive me, Majesty! This humble servant could not sense your presence," said Kamala Maharana, distressed and apologetic. The king looked at him affectionately and said in a deep voice, "One who sits on a throne becomes a king. But the artist becomes a king even without a throne. The artist is worthy of salute by all. Mine as well."

'Overwhelmed with emotion, Kamala Maharana said, "There is no limit to the King's graciousness."

' "But artist…!" the king stopped midway.

' "Command me, Maharaj!"

' "I want you to tell me something about this woman in waiting."

' "If you find any fault, I will immediately rectify it, your Highness."

' "Can an artist of Kalinga ever make a mistake? You all have travelled all over the world and are revered for your superb artistic talents in countries like Sri Lanka, Java, Sumatra, Bali, Borneo and the Malaysian islands. These eyes may have defects, but it is not possible to find fault in the work of the artist."

' "Then?" the artist asked confused.

' "Is this woman only a creation of your imagination?" the king asked him, eyes downcast.

' "Partly real, part imagination."

' "Who is she?"

' "Chandrabhaga, the beloved wife of the artist!" '

'The king hung his head with secret guilt, and wondered how devastated the smitten husband would be upon returning to his village. Whom would he curse, the king or Chandrabhaga?

'Chandrabhaga, who was like a sacred river; the two brief encounters with her had left him feeling like he had been touched by splashes of holy water. She remained in the deep recess of his heart. And her memories were as fragrant as the jasmine blossoms. When those memories rushed in like flood waters they would completely distract him. Her scented braids as she lay motionless in his arms sent ripples through his throbbing soul, making him devastatingly weak. Did Kamala Maharana know that? Did he know that his wife, whom he had not seen properly even once, was rescued by the king himself, and that she had fainted in his arms? How would he react if he knew?

'The king asked him cautiously, "Do you believe in such

waiting?"

' "We cherish that hope, my Lord. If that faith is in doubt, we would feel lost and powerless. But our saviour is aware of this; he understands our innermost thoughts…" said Kamala Maharana and bowed to the king.

'Narasimha Deva watched the faith shining brightly on the face of the artist who stood with his head slightly bent. Remorseful, he said inaudibly, "Oh artist, let your faith live long. Only then can the tales of your sacrifice and greatness be written in indelible letters in the history of Konark. The shrine will be immortal and so will be its artisans!"

'The king preceded to the next scene. It was an exquisitely engraved piece of art on the southern wall of the Natamandir. A lovely maiden bathing in a pond with her long braid floating in the water. Drops of water fell from her hair and a swan stretched its long neck to drink from her wet braid. What fantastic imagination! The artists of Kalinga were so imaginative that they would not let even the water from the hair of a lovely maiden fall on the ground and become soiled!

'But who could the woman be? She did not resemble Chandrabhaga. Her eyes; nose and the face were different. She did not look as if she was someone's wife either. She was depicted as an unmarried maiden at a bathing ghat. The artist was so protective about this beauty that he made her wear shoes even when she was in the water bathing, so that her lovely feet did not become dirty! This puzzled the king enormously. Who was she, really?

'Nrityacharya Somya Sridatta, who was accompanying the king, too paused before the bathing beauty, stunned. Who was the maiden? Well, how was he to say it? How could she have been portrayed in this manner by the artist? And how could she pose before the artist while bathing! She was certainly not a devadasi; she was his very own beloved daughter. Had she then posed before Kamala Maharana without his knowledge? But Kamala Maharana had repeatedly refused to allow any devadasis to be his models when he was working on his sculptures... He maintained that the devadasi belonged to God, not to the artist, and said, "The artist of Konark visualizes his models through his imagination. A flesh and blood devadasi can distract an artist, but the image formed in the imagination helps the artist to attain self-control on himself and also makes him stronger."

'But what was Somya Sridatta witnessing here? His darling daughter Silpa sculpted in various poses and attire, looking divine and poetic, carved by the chisel of Kamala Maharana! He said in a whisper, "The imagination of the artist is great. Let the glory of Kamala Maharana triumph!" and the King proceeded to the main temple. The Nrityacharya was still confused. Silpa was his only daughter. She could not have become a devadasi!

'King Narasimha Deva wondered whether he was responsible for Chandrabhaga's disappearance. Was it justified for a king to cause her husband inconsolable distress at the end of his single-minded devotion to the construction of the temple?'

'On the southern face of the temple, there was another image of Chandrabhaga waiting anxiously at a half-open door for her beloved to return. It seems as if the woman of stone was mocking the king from behind her veil: "When does this waiting end?" By orders of the king, the Kalingan artist had developed a heart of stone and made his beloved a statue of stone as well. There were several such portrayals of waiting depicted on the walls of the stupendous shrine. This waiting was to continue for years to come. Kamala Maharana would never be able to see his beloved wife again in the flesh. He would have to look for her in stone images. He would be able to complete his task at the temple but would himself remain incomplete forever.

'The king turned away from the statue. His eyes travelled to another sculpture. Nrityacharya said, "Here too, Kamala Maharana's proficiency is outstanding."

'"What incredible imagination," agreed the king.

'"This artist," continued the Nrityacharya, "can even read his beloved's mind. At times, she must be craving motherhood. But that does not mean that she will deviate from her path. Then what can she do? How is she to endure the unfulfilled desire of not becoming a mother? She escapes into the world of her pet birds and offers her breasts to them to gratify her maternal longings. And this is how she would satisfy her urge."

'Memories of Chandrabhaga flashed before his eyes, as the king wondered how Chandrabhaga's tender heart pined for her pet parrot, which she had left behind when she wandered into the forest to end her life. He remembered her grief and anger. How deeply Kamala Maharana had understood the soul of his beloved, thought the king.

'On the walls of the main temple, Kamala Maharana had depicted a beautiful image of the king and queen. Some foreigners were gifting a strange animal—an exotic giraffe—to the royal couple. A hunting scene was engraved on the stone slab nearby. The artist of Kalinga was not only lost in thoughts of his beloved, he also kept track of the happenings of his country! He had recorded everything on the pages of stone at Konark, be it scenes of hunting, trade, war, or the everyday mundane lives of people. Konark was a diary of the kingdom of Kalinga, with all activities on record! The king murmured to himself, "You are great! Great is the Kalingan artist. You are the master, and you will be worshipped all over the world!"

'The king stood motionless at the west side of the main temple while Nrityacharya Somya Sridatta explained the thought behind each sculpture. "Here is the narrative of a young man who left his wife behind to trade in far-off lands or to participate in war. His grief-stricken wife is in pain over the separation. If someone took advantage and forced an illegitimate relationship with her in the meantime, what would be her punishment?" The king was stunned, how could Kamala Maharana have visualized everything that had happened in the life of his beloved Chandrabhaga? Was he clairvoyant? Somya Sridatta continued, "Here there is a scene where the husband returns and shaves off the long hair of the sinner. That is her punishment for adultery."

'Narasimha Deva was inwardly defending himself, "But I did not touch her deliberately! I rescued Chandrabhaga from drowning, and only acted as her saviour. That was Lord Jagannath's will! This act of chivalry cannot be labelled adultery!" With this judgment on himself, he turned away and wondered if anyone else could fathom his inner turmoil.

'Kamala Maharana had depicted Chandrabhaga's daily life in a sequence on the walls of Konark. In one scene, a woman was whispering in another's ears. They were probably gossiping about Chandrabhaga, and thus lies about her spread, and the entire village was set against her. The next was a scene where the mother-in-law, obviously in a very foul mood, was abusing her daughter-in-law. The innocent bride was listening to the cruel words with a pale face. "How could Kamala Maharana visualize all those painful incidents in his beloved's life when he was so far away from her! Were their souls connected so intensely?" thought the king.

'A man who carried a mist of worry in his soul even while

braving the constant threats of enemies on the borders, the king now became pensive. His able commanders, Senapati Tulashi, Senapati Ramagovinda, and Senapati Vishnudeva were defending the east, west, north and south of the country with their frontier foot-soldiers, the brave Paikas.

'Never could an enemy attack suddenly. But how could he shake off this sudden onslaught of gloomy thoughts? It was not enough to entertain the king with the dances of devadasis, as they danced exclusively for God. The royal court poet Bidyadhara, and the priest Sadasiva, tried to involve the king in their discourses on religion, literature and music, but to no avail.

'Maybe the king feared the Sun Temple would not be completed; that could be the reason behind his worry. But why did he doubt that the temple would not be completed? Moreover, Nrityacharya Somya Sridatta had also been constantly assuring the queen. "At the pre-ordained time, the filial pitcher will be placed at the peak of the sacred temple. There will be no deviation. Let the Maharaja be at peace!"

'But that day, even Somya Sridatta was quiet and lost in deep contemplation. With the twelfth year of temple construction in progress, an auspicious date to consecrate the temple was finalized. Instead of the pre-decided date on Baisakh Krushna Astami, the pundits had suggested Magha Sukla Saptami. That year it would fall on a Sunday, and Sunday happened to be the day of the Sun God's birth. It was a great coincidence. But was it possible to complete temple construction three months ahead of schedule to match the new day decided for the consecration?

'Was that doubt assailing the king?

'Subconsciously the king wished the construction of the temple to go indefinitely on. Because, when the temple was completed, it would also mark the end of the artists' dedicated efforts. The artists would then go back to their village where their beloved wives would be waiting for them anxiously. But what fate awaited Kamala Maharana then?

'Was the king really responsible for Chandrabhaga's tragedy?

'How could his queen know what tormented the king! She had offered ornaments—kundala (earrings) and a jewelled crown—at Lord Jagannath's feet, praying for the early completion of the temple. She had also offered ornaments such as strings of pearls, a three-tiered necklace of rubies with a pendant, a diamond necklace, a choker, amulets, bracelets, clothes, scarves, and much more. Sahasha Mulla, one of the king's allies, had offered 103 gold coins and fifty cows while praying for the completion of the temple. Senapati Ramgovinda and Srikarna Suru Senapati had also made many offerings to Lord Jagannath, desiring the king's good health and happiness.

'But the king remained despondent. He apparently lacked nothing but no one could fathom why he was worried. Was he worried for the temple, or was it Chandrabhaga who haunted him?

'The Konark temple could be completed with the sacrifice, self-control, dedicated devotion of the queen, and with the whole-hearted goodwill of the subordinate rulers, senapatis and royal preists. But without Chandrabhaga, Kamala Maharana's life would never be complete.

'Rajguru Bhaba Sadasiva kept assuring the king, "By the virtue of the king's devotion, even the impossible will be achieved. His soul's desire will definitely be fulfilled."

'Meanwhile, the king's generosity and godliness had drawn many tormented mendicants of Bengal to the sacred land of Kalinga in search of shelter. Arrangements were made for them to stay at Bhubaneswar's Sadasiva Matha. Several neighbouring villages were assigned to provide them food and fuel wood. The holy souls remained deeply immersed in their worship, praying for the fulfilment of the king's noble desires. And yet, despite all the rites and rituals, King Narasimha Deva remained crestfallen and despondent.

'A poetry meet was arranged to distract the king. The royal court poet recited Bidyadhara's Ekabali's anthology on the figure of speech or Alankara in the presence of many eminent poets of the country. Bardhamana Mahapatra, Raghubira Mahapatra, Govinda Bhanja, poet Harihara and Raghunatha Parichha recited the 364 stanzas of the volume and discussed them in detail. Another volume of verses, *Keli Rahashya*, written by Bidyadhara was recited and analysed at the poets' meet. It received tremendous praise from the king who felicitated the poet with a silk sari and a medal.

'King Narasimha Deva was a great patron of literature. War and literature moved him in the same way. He listened quietly to the literary discussions among the poets with a serious demeanour. Out of the 364 stanzas, 314 stanzas were devoted to his noble deeds. They described him as powerful, wise, and daring and a consummate military genius as well as a great lover of art. Subsequently, the poets eulogized the king and his deeds even more. But that added to the agony of the king; the more he heard himself being praised, the more he drowned in his secret sorrow.

'Where was his masculine strength, his valour and fortitude? A rustic maiden had jeered at his prowess and then vanished into the abyss! Despite being the king, he had been unable to grant her the fundamental rights of life, protection or justice! It was his minimum responsibility as a ruler. If he could not even accomplish that, he had failed in his mission. The praise and the glory being described in the *Ekabali Shasta* only humiliated him further. He felt it was Chandrabhaga who had robbed him of his happiness; honour, self-confidence and the ability to feel joy in his own success. The king's listlessness left all the poets feeling ignored, rejected and dejected. Bidyadhara felt if his creation did not please the king and cheer him up, it had no value.

'Poet Raghunath Parichha had written the Sanskrit drama, "Gopinatha Ballav", based on Krishna and his Gopis and was to be enacted that evening in Konark. The ships that sailed from Sri Lanka and Suvarnadwip had anchored at the Port of Charitra. Merchants visiting from abroad were also present. They were to watch the drama in the open-air auditorium. Jayadeva's *Gita Govinda*, dealing with the sacred love dalliance of Radha and Krishna was also enacted with such passion that it seemed like a stream of love.

'The king exhausted by the constant wars became engrossed in the play and lost himself in the mystic charm of Lord Jagannath and Krishna Leela. It transported him from the mundane to spiritual bliss. And he recalled how Lord Jagannath's Holy Leela had been revealed to his ancestor in a dream—the Ganga king Raghava Deva in the twelfth century.

'Jayadeva was born in Kendubilwa village near the sacred River Prachi in Puri district during his reign. Destined to become the greatest devotional poet of Kalinga, Jayadeva spent his entire life in Srikshetra Puri. His sole immortal creation, *Gita Govinda*, was dedicated to Lord Jagannath. The Mahari dancers at the Puri temple would sing stanzas from the epic every evening. The temple's ambience reverberated with their melodious renderings and graceful dance movements. *Gita Govinda* was dear to Lord Jagannath.

'One day Lord Jagannath became so enchanted by a gardener

girl singing *Gita Govinda* that he visited her home in disguise to listen to her sing. She was plucking brinjals from her back garden and singing to herself. The Lord of the Universe followed her wherever she went. The next morning, the temple priest discovered bruise marks on the limbs of the deity and His silk dress was also torn at several places. But God was smiling benignly.

'King Raghava Deva received the message from the priests and other servitors and became worried, too. That night he had a dream which revealed to him the entire episode. The next morning, he sent for the gardener girl and ordered that she should sing the *Gita Govinda* every day at the temple. The king also donated some property to her family. Since then the descendants of that girl have been known as Maharis and they alone sing the *Gita Govinda* before Lord Jagannath.'

Deeply moved, Vishnu Maharana touched the palm-leaf reverently to his forehead before placing it with the palm-leaf manuscripts that had been read.

The mystery of Chandrabhaga was yet to be solved, but the way matters had played out day after day seven hundred years ago, taught Charles more about Konark and the culture and traditions that prevailed even today than any academic tome on the period would have.

The birth place of Jayadeva is today known as Kenduli Sashana. Prachi, too, was born in the same village, which made her feel blessed. She too felt overwhelmed while explaining about Jayadeva and tears of love streamed down her eyes when she sang the *Gita Govinda*. She became emotional and said, 'Charles! Sri *Gita Govinda* is an endless treasure-house of the divine love between Radha and Krishna. One who realizes this can easily charm Lord Jagannath. Lord Jagannath has always surrendered to the love and devotion of his devotees.'

Charles joked, 'In this country, it is far easier to win over Lord Jagannath with love and devotion, than people. Hearing a couplet of *Gita Govinda*, a celestial god leaves a diamond throne and pursues a gardener girl; but to win over Prachiprava in love with Lord Jagannath, one has to meditate at least for seven years!'

This startled her. Charles added, with sincerity, 'I have told you everything about my life. But you have not revealed anything about yourself. Like Lord Jagannath, you too are a mystery to me.'

'It is men who surrender before women, as did Lord Jagannath.'

Charles smiled, 'I had come here to study the art and architecture of Odisha. But I find I will go back to my country a Vaishnavite, after listening to your preaching on Lord Jagannath and the love lyrics of Radha Krishna and *Gita Govinda*.'

Prachi ignored his jest and continued describing Jayadeva's life, 'That small shrine of Madhava in the village of Kendubilwa. Jayadeva was living in a small hut near the temple with his beautiful wife, Padmavati. The couple was devoted to the service of Sri Radha Madhava. It was here that Jayadeva had written his immortal song, Sri *Gita Govinda*. According to the text, Sri Krishna had begged for Radha's love by touching her feet! But the very thought that Lord Jagannath would touch Sri Radha's feet and beg for her love, did not appeal to Jayadeva's male ego. His pen would not move further. He was in deep meditation wondering how to describe the love of Radha and Krishna. Soon, with a heavy heart, he closed the palm-leaf manuscript and went for a bath in nearby Prachi River, praying to the

Lord: "Oh, all knowing God! How can I let my hands write of Sri Radha's feet in your hands? How incongruous it seems for a man to touch a woman's feet!"

'Upon learning about the pain of his devotee Lord Jagannath took the form of Jayadeva and asked his wife Padmavati for the manuscript. He told her he had thought of how to complete the half-finished stanza and had come back to jot down his thoughts before he forgot. Lord Jagannath completed the couplet with his own hand, "Dehi Pada Pallava Mudaram!" and disappeared into his temple.

'When Jayadeva returned from bathing in the river and learnt that his beloved deity had come in his guise and completed his unfinished lines, he wept. He said, "O Padmavati, you are so fortunate to have seen Lord Jagannath! I am the unfortunate one, who could never get a glimpse of Him! *Gita Govinda* has now become sacred with His touch.' And till today the lovely sentence 'Dehi Pada Pallava Mudaram' is ingrained in every Odia's heart and is the gem of Odia literature,' concluded Prachi.

Charles repeatedly kept chanting, 'Dehi Pada Pallava Mudaram,' staring at Prachi's tender feet and wondered if Sri Radha's feet were more tender and beautiful than these, why was it so unnatural for Sri Jagannath to touch Radha's feet and beg for her love? Seeing Charles so engrossed in his thoughts, Prachi interrupted, 'Will you go there Charles? Will you visit that sacred village of Kenduli Sashana and the small shrine of Madhava? I am not insisting just because it is my birthplace, but because it is also the birthplace of the gifted devotional poet, Jayadeva!'

'I will go there, but not because it is the birth place of Jayadeva. I will go because it is where Prachiprava was born. At least I may get to see your village once in my life!'

A smile played on Prachi's face. 'Charles, you can make

fun of any situation. If a man can accept life that way he can always be happy.'

Charles was not joking at all! On the contrary it was Prachi, who had been evasive, knowing full well the serious feelings he wanted to bring up. In this country, Lord Jagannath holds the feet of Sri Radha. But he was an ordinary mortal and an untouchable! Prachiprava was like a sacred river. How dangerous was it to put his nomad feet in that water!

In India, not even a flower girl like Chitrotpala would befriend a man as Lillian did. Chitrotpala was not distracted by men around her. If anyone even touched her flower basket while buying flowers, she would step back and scream. If anyone even touched her hands, she would at once turn serious. She was betrothed already, dedicated to someone. She would not allow even a shadow to touch her. Why were Prachi's feet so out of reach? He chanted again, 'Dehi Pada Pallava Mudaram, Dehi Pada Pallava Mudaram.'

Prachiprava laughed. 'It is not enough to just read it aloud, the song of the *Gita Govinda* is to be sung with one's soul, only then will Lord Jagannath run after you, abandoning his diamond throne. When he is behind us, the road ahead is illumined by his divine light.'

Charles felt as if Lord Jagannath was showing her the way but standing in his path! That was the reason why the distance between Prachi and him remained the same as at their first meeting. In Indian traditions, even a wife would not throw herself at her husband. If that had been the case, then Queen Sita Devi would have ignored King Narasimha Deva's vows of celibacy and claimed her conjugal rights. For an Indian woman, her self-respect is far greater than her passion for physical love. That is why she is so revered by man. There is nothing wrong with Lord Jagannath worshipping the feet of Sri Radha!

Lillian had no qualms in offering herself easily to her male friends which was why her charms waned so quickly! Such women are desired by men only for blind passionate moments of sex, nothing more. When the moment is over, those women become useless and unattractive, like the shell sans its pearl!

Lillian had written that Brush had a new girlfriend and had no interest in Lillian any longer. The beaches of Goa, which had seemed like heaven, now looked like a lonely burial ground to her. She had also written, 'Charles come here soon. With your arrival, the beaches will come to life. Don't waste your youth on your boring research work. You'll regret it later!'

But Charles was did not repent. He thought little of Lillian's misfortune. Prachi had walked ahead going round the temple precincts. Charles again chanted the couplet from the *Gita Govinda*, watching her walking around on her lotus petal-like feet…

That evening Charles, Prachi and Vishnu Maharana met again to explore the palm-leaf manuscripts. New mysteries continued to unfold even as the sands of time ran out. Vishnu Maharana cleared his throat and began.

'The dance of the devadasis was over. In the old Arka temple courtyard at Konark, the sequence of the meeting of Radha Krishna would be enacted.

'Kalinga had achieved excellence in dance, music and literature during Narasimha Deva's reign. Its learned men had composed excellent dictionaries as well as works in verse, grammar, philosophy, science, astrology, treatises on figures of speech, Ayurveda, and war craft under the patronage of the king and he had rewarded them suitably.

'The country had achieved proficiency in industry, agriculture and trade. There was also prosperous diamond trading in the area. From the diamond mines of Sambalpur, stones weighing over thirty-five grams were extracted. And the products from these mines were acclaimed even abroad for their quality. There were also many iron factories in the land.

'The sea-faring merchants of Kalinga (Odisha) travelled to far-off countries like Sri Lanka, Burma, Malaysia and China to trade in silk, salt, coconut, cotton, spices and brassware. Sometimes they would also transport live elephants! The art and architecture of Kalinga also crossed boundaries and received recognition in far-off countries. The artists and sculptors of Odisha were exposed to other cultures and civilizations and recorded their experiences from the world over. They silently incorporated all they had seen and learnt on the stone walls of Konark.

'The king and his countrymen welcomed and entertained traders from abroad showering them with hospitality. The residents of Jagannath Dham[11] (were always generous towards visitors. The guest was God. That was the reason why Konark's artists thoughtfully recorded functions when foreign guests brought gifts for the king and queen. They honoured the kind thoughts behind the gifts and left the emotion alive in stone for centuries to come. The artists had recorded the greatness of the concept of "universal brotherhood" for forthcoming generations. The guests were obviously excited by these rock engravings. They spread word about the people of Kalinga and their greatness wherever they travelled. But they were surprised to see that

---

[11]The residence of Lord Jagannath; another way of referring to their land as the residence of Lord Jagannath.

nowhere were there pictures of the king himself bestowing gifts to foreigners. Neither was his hospitality ever recorded on the carved walls of Konark.

'But just as he received gifts from them with love, King Narasimha Deva also reciprocated with precious gifts and equal respect. The land of Kalinga was famed for its elephants and King Narasimha Deva felicitated dignitaries by gifting them rare and priceless white elephants which were sent from Kalinga to far-off lands by sea. Few such images were recorded in Konark.

'The Prime Minister, Siba Samantray, had put the same question to master builder Kamala Maharana. Kamala Maharana replied, "Man should remember and record what he receives from others. But to advertise what he gives does not enhance his greatness. If only the recipient remembers the donor, then the benefactor's greatness is remembered. If the benefactor forgets about his own generosity, that too speaks of his greatness. That is why the artists of Konark did not engrave the scene where the great king of Kalinga is seen gifting elephants to his guests. It was done so as not to boast themselves about the hospitality of their own king, Narasimha Deva, and thus cause the king and his guests offence." The king had felicitated Kamala Maharana that day. Another day, the king was so enchanted by Kamala Maharana's exquisite work that he said, "Artist! I am sorry; I have not honoured you properly so far!"

'"His Highness's kind gestures are the best gift and appreciation for an artist." Kamala Maharana replied humbly.

'The king said, "This only justifies your graciousness. If an artist's heart is not as liberal as the sky, he will not be able to depict the truth of life. His greatness as such is recorded on each stone piece of the temple of Konark. Time will make the artist even greater, glorify and immortalize him. Even though the images of the king and his queen have been depicted at several places in the carvings at Konark, the artist has never engraved his own name and address anywhere. Time will immortalize the magnificent artistic heritage of the Konark, but not the artist? King Narasimha Deva's name will be recorded in the history of Konark temple, but is there to be no trace of its artisans' identity? Without his name and address engraved anywhere, how can history take note of the artist's contribution? Time will one day wipe away the names, addresses and the identities of the twelve hundred masons who built the temple of Konark. That is why, oh artist; you may mention your name, your appearance and your lifestyle in the stone architecture of Konark. This is not the king's order but the genuine wish and request of the people of the country."

'Kamala Maharana was confused for a moment. But, the very next moment he said with folded hands, "It is the kindness of Lord Jagannath that the king did not order me to carve my name on the stones here. It would have defamed the great artistic tradition and culture of this country."

'The Ganga king was astonished. He asked, "Why would it disgrace the Jagannath cult and culture? It is the tradition of our country to honour our genius."

'Kamala Maharana said politely, "Lord Jagannath had granted a wish to King Indradyumna, the builder of the Jagannath temple. King Indradyumna asked of him humbly—O God! Grant me this wish that my race may come to an end with me. Let there be no offspring in my family who would take pride in the construction of your temple that was made by their forefathers. That will defile the sanctity of the sacred shrine. Similarly, the artist of Kalinga does not want his name to be engraved on the temple, which will bring a bad name to the temple or disgrace the tradition of the superb art and architecture of our land. Anyone who sees this splendid craftsmanship would say—This belongs to my country. The artists of my land, who could make lotuses bloom on stone, are the pride of my race."

' "This is not the pride of my family, Your Majesty," said Kamala Maharana seriously, "it is the honour of my country. A great country's reputation will be immortalized here."

'The king was visibly overwhelmed. He replied emotionally, "Till now I was looking at Konark with the eyes of a narrow-minded man. That is why I was searching for the names of the twelve hundred artists. But now when I look at it as a monument of a great nation, I can see that not only these artists, but the names of all the artists of my country are engraved here, on the stones of Konark! Time can never erase their indelible names. The temple builders will remain in the pages of history, but the artists of this country will be enthroned in the hearts of the people. That is why, probably, the artist has written his name nowhere on the temple walls. You are great, Kamala Maharana. And fortunate is your motherland to have you in her womb!" '

Was there no end to the spirit of sacrifice in this country, wondered Charles as Vishnu Maharana put away the palm leaves he had just read from.

Ten

—

The next morning Vishnu Maharana continued where they had left off the previous day, as soon as the small group had gathered and settled down.

'The dance presentation of the devadasis came to an end. A dance drama on the story of Radha and Krishna was about to begin in the open-air arena. Such entertainments were organized, from time to time, on the orders of the king, for the artists working to build the Sun Temple at Konark. The stone-artist was not stone, but a human being. Without hearing the song of life in the depths of his heart, why would his hands move? If not for that song, his hands would mechanically move and churn out grinding stones, wheels, pots. Without music there cannot be outstanding craftsmanship.

'The king, his queen and princess Chandrika Devi were seated on one side of the arena, on the other sat the visitors from abroad. Near them were the artists and facing them, but across the amphitheatre, was Silpa, the daughter of the Nrityacharya, Minister Sibei Samantray's daughter, along with Kalavati and a few other young girls and women. Close to them sat Nrityacharya Somya Sridatta and his band of musicians.

'Romantic interludes from the life of Radha and Krishna were now being enacted. Narasimha Deva, Sita Devi, and Chandrika Devi were absolutely engrossed, in the spirit of Radha-Krishna devotion. The guests, who were greatly impressed by the dance drama, praised it and applauded in appreciation.

'The Sun Temple artists, who were watching the drama as if in a trance, were oblivious of their physical fatigue. Kamala Maharana's eyes were transfixed. He was not looking at the subject of the dance drama. He was recalling a tranquil pond. In its blue waters swayed a beautiful tender lotus in bloom. The early morning sun had imbued it with a tint of blushing crimson. Who was she? Chandrabhaga, his bride? Her face, like an unfinished portrait, looked obscure to him. He could view her in entirety only in his imagination but this face was familiar. She was given shape by Kamala Maharana's deft hands. The same tender poetically sculpted torso, the faultlessly round and bashful face, the same melancholy, dreamy eyes! Her sculpted gaze of stone so subdued as she looked at Kamala Maharana, through the side glance he had carved and which appeared to peep like the moon through the boughs of a bakul tree. He was enticed, she was his muse, the woman of his dreams who appeared in his dreams every night. She posed for him just as he wanted her to. He carved the images one after another. But how could she actually appear before him? No woman had ever posed for the amorous images he had sculpted to appease restless souls such as Nila Maharana's and to protect the worshippers and the rituals from negative spirits, ghosts, demons and goblins.

'So how was it possible for his mystical muse to pose before him in flesh and blood? Had that been possible, Kamala Maharana pondered, then the maidens so exquisitely chiselled and engraved on the walls of the monument could come to life as well and the city of Konark could become a playground for the beautiful dancing maidens, reverberating with their graceful dances!

'He hummed to himself, "Whoever you are, stay in my imagination forever. If you appear before me in human form, it won't be possible for me to continue my task." But how could this girl's image appear in his imagination so vividly replacing the hazy image he had in mind of his beloved wife, Chandrabhaga? He thought of the days when he had been busy discussing the various postures of the dancing damsel's toe depicted on the temple wall. One morning when he went to his master's home, he found the doors wide open and stepped into the courtyard discreetly and then stood quietly for a while.

'The courtyard was washed with perfumed water. It was not raining and not a cloud sailed in the sky. An exquisitely beautiful maiden was standing in a corner. She had just finished her bath, and was wringing her wet hair. The drops of water that fell from her body had soaked the courtyard and she appeared like a painting before him. Her pet swan craned its neck to sip the drops of water that fell from her hair, like a thirsty chataka bird. On her alata-lined feet were sandals of gold. Her feet were beautiful and golden. Kamala Maharana immediately retraced his steps. But her fleeting eyes were fixed on his well-sculpted face. Kamala Maharana looked embarrassed.

'That day, the artist Kamala Maharana had given the finishing touches to the first stone damsel of the Natamandir. The image was that of the freshly-bathed Silpa. Later, though he did meet Silpa and she posed for him for a while until he began on the amorous couples, and though he was not conscious of it, the image of Silpa was everywhere in his art. He sculpted a series of damsels in different postures and with different expressions displaying his ingenuity brilliantly. Long after she stopped posing for him, Silpa appeared before him in many ways, many postures and in many beautiful forms. She posed for him in his dreams. And Kamala Maharana continued to cast her resplendent beauty in stone. He would adorn her with the most delicate garments and splendid pieces of jewellery. Along with the rhythmic strokes of his chisel he would hold continuous dialogues with his imaginary beloved. In his imagination, she too would respond to his queries.

'Now he stared at Silpa and said to himself softly, "I am indebted to you. It is only due to you that all the statues of dancing damsels at the Natamandir were successfully completed in time. They are magnificent and lifelike only because of you. The work at the Natamandir is finished. Nrityacharya's cherished visions have been successfully depicted. That is why Kamala Maharana will remain forever indebted to you. You are freed from the imaginary web of the artist and now let the artist go free as well! Like the open sky, the artist too has an open heart otherwise he would not have been able to dream and depict the dancers so clearly. That is why I bid you farewell! Kamala has recorded you indelibly. Now you too are without any bondage."

'By the time Kamala Maharana was ready to part from the muse of his art, her soul; heart and mind were already caught in the web of love for the handsome youth and his absorbing eyes. She stared at him, sighing heavily, thinking how a piece of stone was given life by the touch of God. If someone would touch her body that day and turn her into stone, it would be the ultimate ecstasy. That piece of stone would be privileged to be touched by the young artist, who would engrave on her, the poetry of his dream woven in fine threadlike designs. He would use the chisel on her body to give shape to his imagination but such a pain would be so desirable. It would be an exceptional pleasure indeed for her... Silpa closed her eyes "My Lord, turn me into stone, even if that has no life. That would be my liberation!"

'Nrityacharya was watching Silpa. He was studying the constantly flitting expressions of her face. He was apprehensive.

Was it really Silpa who had posed for Kamala Maharana? Had any relationship actually developed between them? Konark was the sacred platform on which such earthly desires had been denounced by all who worked on the temple. The artists of Konark had guarded their virtue against worldly distractions to remain physically powerful and spin their energy into outstanding pieces of art. That was why King Narasimha Deva had himself abandoned all earthly pleasures and steeled his heart into betraying no emotion for twelve long years. And yet his only daughter Silpa had set off a ripple in the unruffled and firm heart of Kamala Maharana, the king's favourite artist! She could very well destroy his perseverance as well as the sanctity of the Konark temple.

'What if the news reached the king? What would be the consequences? What would the king think of him? Besides, Silpa was already betrothed to someone. Even if she thought of any other man in her dreams, that would cast aspersions on her virginity! Her womanly virtues would be sullied. He asked to himself, "Is my daughter more important than Konark? Is art desirable or my daughter?"

'Silpa listened to her father's accusation with a shock. The more her father battered her, the more thrilled she grew. Was it a fact that the artist Kamala Maharana had painted her beauty in letters of gold in his heart? Was it true that he had depicted her torso and her face in all the dancing poses of the Natamandira? Then she was truly blessed. She felt like worshipping the feet of the great artist, but his feet too were so unattainable to touch.

'The dance master spoke gravely. "You have brought disgrace to me by modelling for Kamala Maharana night after night in his tent. You have polluted yourself and spoilt his concentration. Do you know that the king will punish me for this? Your marriage stands annulled, do you realize?"

'Silpa was both surprised and elated. She asked "Who told you that I used to stand before him posing as a model?"

'The dance master said, "Everybody has heard that Kamala Maharana talks to his model. I too have heard his conversation many times, hiding in the dark. Each sculpture of his reflects your face, eyes and expressions so vividly. How is this possible?"

'Silpa said humbly: "If my being a model for him has brought out the excellence in the temple architecture, then I am blessed. I want to worship his feet."

'"Remember, you are betrothed to someone else. It is only a matter of a few days."

'"In my heart there is only one God whom I worship. There is no place for others. I want to pay homage to the artist. Is that a sin?"

'Sridatta was stunned! "This girl will bring stigma to art. Konark will be maligned because of Silpa. It is better that Silpa pays with her life so that the sanctity of art lives eternally," he thought. He declared firmly, "The artist is married. It is considered a sin to have even a meeting of minds between a married man and a betrothed girl. It is punishable. For this crime, there may be a court order for Kamala Maharana's head. The king is very fond of Kamala Maharana. But it would not be acceptable for him to allow the disgrace to sacred Konark and annihilate his concentration. He will never forgive him."'

'Silpa cried out in despair, "If he were to give in to impulses, Kamala Maharana would not have achieved such excellence in his craftsmanship. No one can create anything with a disturbed mind and a restless heart. If there is any disgrace to the temple of Konark, then it is I who should be punished. Despite being engaged to someone else, I was blindly in love with his exceptional talent as an artist. It is my fault, not his."

'Sridatta looked at his daughter and remained quiet. He softened a little and said, "For your honesty, your punishment will be lenient by my impartiality. Otherwise I would have ordered your death for showing the slightest betrayal of your would-be husband."

'Silpa replied unperturbed. "I am not afraid of death any more. Kamala Maharana has immortalized me through the stone sculptures of the Natamandir. I do not feel distressed about my death. If by my death there will be flowers strewn on the path of Kamala Maharana and your honour will remain intact then I am willing to die happily."

'Sridatta, the father and the dance master became pensive and yet was firm. "Even a punishment like death will taint the sacredness of revered Konark. If you are banished from the land of Kalinga it will be auspicious for all. At midnight, a ship will leave for Sri Lanka from the port of Konark. Sri Lanka is 3,350 miles away by sea. You will have to spend the rest of your life there. Konark will remain untarnished. The people of Kalinga who are staying at Sri Lanka, Bali, Java, Borneo and Malaysia are called 'Kalings'. They have established their dynasty there and ruled the country for three years. A Sacred Tooth Relic of Lord Buddha is worshipped in Sri Lanka. The casket encasing the Tooth Relic has a precious pearl attached to it. It emits a bright halo and illumines the sky. From the Port of Charitra, this bluish glimmer can be seen across the sea on a dark night. Whenever I see that light on dark nights, I will feel your presence. The Kalingans have left behind a rich legacy of art, culture, architecture and the cult of Jagannath in that land. You will protect them. That is how you can pay your obeisance to the talent of Kamala Maharana. This is my verdict for you."

'Silpa listened without uttering a word. She had no reply. But how could she live alone as a sanyasini in Sri Lanka away from her beloved motherland? Seeing her pensive face, Sridatta said, "There is a group of artists from Kalinga sailing to Sri Lanka. Your uncle is also going with a troupe of dancers. He will perform Odissi dance there and will stay on for a while to teach dance. There is a great appreciation for our art and dance in that land. Some masons are also sailing with their families. They have been invited to construct Hindu temples there. You will not face any problem. Your would-be husband's home will be informed that you have met with an untimely death from snake bite. That is how my honour will be protected. Nobody will come to know that the beloved daughter of Nrityacharya Sridatta was unfaithful to her would-be husband by worshipping Kamala Maharana and bringing disgrace to the her family."

' "You will lie for me?" Silpa had tears in her eyes.

' "It is better to commit the crime of lying than to blotch the family name with dishonour. Those who cannot protect the honour, the fame and contribution of their forefathers are sinners."

'Silpa said in a subdued voice, "You have to suffer for me. I had cherished art because I was inspired by you. I had forgotten that I was an unmarried woman, and also betrothed to someone. It never occurred to me that even though she loves and worships God, a woman becomes disgraced. Please forgive me father."

'The Nrityacharya turned his eyes away. For an adoring daughter who had lost her mother in her infancy, the deportation would be more traumatic than the banishment of the virtuous Sita. But for the sake of Konark he had to swallow that pain. Otherwise the flames within Kamala would one day devastate Konark. Rather, Silpa should die, allowing the artist and his tradition to survive! He ordered gravely, "Prepare for the sea voyage. And let this remain a secret." Silpa bowed her head. She pleaded before her father for the last time, "Before leaving I want to meet my mother once." Who could forbid the unfortunate girl who had been deprived of her mother's love since birth, one last meeting with her mother?

'Goddess Gangeshwari was a living goddess. She was worshipped in an open shrine in Sain Sain Berhampur known as Bayalishibati. Before the construction of the Konark temple began, she was worshipped at a nearby mud hut. Before that she had not been properly installed anywhere. At the end of the village was a grazing field and a mucky pond. She roamed in the forests without anyone worshipping her. She suckled cows for their milk, and when milch-cows returned in the evening there would not be any milk left in their udders. One day a young cowherd kept vigil and saw an extremely beautiful woman suckling the udders of a cow, like a young calf! Mad with anger, he hit her hard on the head.

'The goddess in disguise was wounded. The same night, the boy died mysteriously. The others were alerted. They searched for the goddess in the grazing fields, bushes, forests and ponds. Drops of blood had fallen from her head. They tracked the blood marks and reached a "bel" tree. There they found a clot of blood. And uprooting the tree, they found the deity, took her and installed her in a hut. Since that day, the goddess came to be worshipped properly. She became famous as a living goddess. This happened long before the temple of Konark was built.

'The artists of Konark stayed in tents at Sain Sain Berhampur. They used to seek her blessings before setting out for work. They carried the blocks of stones that had been transported on river channels and started work, on the orders of Minister Sibei

Samantray. The stones were to be lodged one above another and the shrine for the goddess was to be completed in a single night, after which the temple of Konark was to begin. The night ended. But her temple could not be completed. Its crowning pitcher could not be lodged. Since then her temple has remained unfinished.

'Goddess Jangeshwari was the sister of Goddess Gangeshwari. She appeared in the dreams of the king one night and said, "Goddess Gangeshwari is your Ista Devi. If you do not worship her, how can you remain the king?" Thereafter, the king arranged for daily worship of the goddess and donated six acres of land to provide for the daily requirements of the temple. He acknowledged her as his presiding deity, and sought her blessings before every auspicious job. He would also pray to the goddess before leaving for war or any other assignment.

'The masons too would pray to the goddess before they started work on the stone sculptures. The blood mark remained etched on the forehead of the goddess on which three lines of sandalwood paste was smeared. Only her head was worshipped in the temple in the form of an uneven block of stone. The rest of her body, they say, had vanished into the forests.

'To the east of the Gangeshwari temple, her sister, goddess Jangeshwari was worshipped in the form of a four-armed Mahisha Mardini[12] in a thatched hut. Her trident pierced the chest of Mahishashura, the demon. In her other hand, she held a sword and a bell. The two and half feet high image of the goddess in black chlorite was believed to wake up the craftsman in the morning to start their work!

'Silpa believed in those two goddesses. Whenever she

---

[12]Goddess Durga portrayed killing the buffalo-headed demon.

thought of her mother, she would think of these deities. She could hear their voices. Her father had said that it was due to the blessings of these deities that Silpa's mother had conceived her, and she would see the goddesses many times in her dreams. When the priest came for the puja to divine the baby's destiny, he had said, "This girl is born with the virtues of a goddess. She will live a short life and go back to heaven soon." That very day, Nrityacharya had taken a vow to marry Silpa off before she turned sixteen. In a few months she would have gone to her in-law's house.

'That day she was pleading for a last glance of the goddess! At least her last wish had to be honoured. Silpa bowed before the four-armed Ganesh idol in chlorite, installed on the western wall of the temple. There was a navagraha slab at the entrance door. She bowed there. It was still dark and humid inside the sanctum sanctorum. Silpa was scared of the dark. But in that darkness, Mother Gangeshwari was waiting to embrace the girl with her stretched arms! Whenever she stepped into the temple, Silpa felt that she too, like others, had a mother. The day she had looked for her mother for the first time, her father had brought her to the temple, and pointing at the goddess had said, "Look! She is your mother! She will not respond when you call to her, but when you do not want anything; she offers everything on her own will. It is her wish. We are helpless."

'He had placed his infant girl on the floor before the goddess and pleaded, "If you are the mother of all, tell me for what fault of hers should this child suffer being motherless? Please appear before her in your form. And convince her that she too has a mother and that she is not alone." And wiping his tears, Sridatta had come out of the temple. His wife Padmavati had worshipped the goddess and this daughter was born to her as a boon. But she died before she could hear her daughter calling for her. It was the will of the goddess all along!"

'"But there was trace of milk on baby Silpa's lips when she was brought out from the temple corridor. She would later say, "There is nobody more beautiful than my mother. She is as beautiful as a goddess, how can she stay at our home? She has to be in a temple." Since then, whenever she wanted to be with her mother, Silpa would come to the temple of Gangeshwari. The goddess would appear before her and bless her affectionately and warmly.

'And yet, she was ill-fated to leave her mother Goddess Gangeshwari, her motherland Kalinga, her father, her friends, the shores of River Chandrabhaga and the greenery of Konark, to step into an unfamiliar land, sailing across the sea to live in banishment. Stepping inside the temple, Silpa asked her mother why this had to happen.

'Someone sat like a flame of fire in the dark, meditating before the mother goddess with closed eyes chanting hymns in a deep, soft voice. The sound of the chants invigorated her soul. It seemed to provide all the answers to Silpa's disturbed heart! She stood like a statue with folded hands behind the meditating figure. She saw a tall man, with strong and long arms, and long curly hair on his head—like a sculpture made by the artists of Konark.

'Silpa knelt on the ground in reverence. She could not be sure whether it was for the meditating figure or for the goddess. When she looked up, she found him standing before her. He was gesturing her to give space for him to leave. Silpa had forgotten that she was blocking his path. The meditating image that was now flesh and blood before her, by the grace of the goddess, belonged to Kamala Maharana, the artist. He was the one whose accomplishments she revered, and for whom she was going to be banished from Kalinga. She felt the urge to touch the feet of the great artist and pay him her parting regards. Her mother could certainly read her mind. How else could she know that Silpa wanted to have a last glimpse of Kamala Maharana before she would be gone permanently?

'Silpa's face hidden by her veil appeared to be pallid and desolate like a pale moon of dusk, but it appealed immensely to the artist in Kamala Maharana. One glance at her, and he became anxious. He shifted his glance at once and stared at the sky visible in patches from the temple. He said quietly, "Lady, please let me go, I have to go for work." Silpa who was readying to make way for him, stood immobile as though she was talking to herself... "Wait for a while, Oh artist! This is our last meeting." Tears flowed from her lotus-shaped eyes.

'Kamala Maharana with his eyes to the sky said calmly, "For the artists of Konark, every moment is precious. The artist has to be always time bound. Before the call of the nation, even the king does not have respite for himself. I am an ordinary artist."

'Silpa made way for Kamala Maharana. And as he stepped outside, he turned to look at the disguised face of the young girl for a brief moment. Silpa's humble, sweet demeanour touched a chord. "May God bless you!" Kamala Maharana whispered and walked away hurriedly to work. Did he ever apprehend that it was the hour of their final separation…'

'Tearfully, Silpa touched the soil where he had stood, smeared it on her forehead. She murmured in a stifled tone, "O artist! May you find glory—let my motherland exult in your success!"

'At the scheduled time, the ship departed from the Port of Charitra. Some masons with their families were on the ship along with Sudatta, the younger brother of Sridatta, and some other dancers as well. Dance master Sridatta, Kamala Maharana and many artists were present to bid them farewell. Before the ship lifted its anchor and prepared to leave, the veiled girl quickly gathered a handful of sand from where Kamala Maharana was standing just a few minutes earlier. She wrapped it carefully in her veil and softly spoke to the dance master, "Father! This is all I am taking with me as a souvenir of my motherland. If needed, I will give my life to protect her honour."

'Sridatta sighed and thought, "Really, even a palm full of sand has become like precious diamonds for my daughter today!" He said in a hushed tone "You are the daughter of Kalinga. You will nurture and preserve the art, culture and heritage of your country. Never forget this reality in your lifetime."

'"I will never forget, I promise," she murmured.

'The ship left the port. No one ever came to know about the tragic deportation of an innocent girl to protect her country's honour and her willingness to withstand her father's separation grief. It was not recorded in the pages of history. Even Kamala Maharana never came to know that his muse, the beloved of his imagination, had left the country, never to return.

'Staring at the ship fading into oblivion along with its flag at the mast, the dance master was overcome with grief and muttered to himself in distress, "My daughter's exile is far more cruel than the punishment mated to Goddess Sita. O Sea! You are my witness. I have surrendered my daughter Silpa, the source of my motivation, into your hands."

'Ironically, the same night, the episode of Sita's banishment was being enacted as entertainment opera for the artists. Kamala Maharana was also seated. To the left of the dance-master sat some young girls. Kamala Maharana's eyes kept searching for her. But where was she, his inspiration, the beautiful daughter of his dance-master? Everybody was overwhelmed with the tragic performance of Sita's exile. The women shed tears beneath their veils. The dance master was sobbing his covert anguish. In faraway Sri Lanka, his only child, the daughter of Kalinga would be looking for her mother, for her motherland. Would mother Gangeshwari traverse the sea and reach Silpa to comfort her? Would she appear before her there, too?

'The building of Konark temple was now almost near completion. He would have a glimpse of his bride Chandrabhaga now and would then give final touches to his work... Kamala Maharana's heart was at once freed from the bondage of delusion regarding Silpa. Sridatta watching Kamala Maharana's joy for his impending return to his home wondered, how could he ever feel his pain anyway? The pain of being separated from his beloved daughter till his last... he was there witnessing the temple nearing its completion where the tales of his daughter's secret sacrifice lay buried... it was a monument involving so many sacrifices from all. How could he keep Kamala Maharana's soul bonded to his daughter's memory...

'Meanwhile in the blue waters of the Bay of Bengal, the daughter of Kalinga sailed away towards the south. In front of her was a veil of mist. It tinted the clouds with hues of crimson and the sky looked even more unclear. It was going to be raining through the night, but how would Silpa know? Ever since her journey began, there were tears in her eyes and a storm in her heart.

'On the ship everybody prayed fervently to their Ista Devas. Imminent danger loomed large. A cyclonic storm was brewing and could be seen rapidly advancing towards them. A gigantic whale rushed towards their boat breasting the high waves. It looked even more frightening than the storm. There was a chance that the storm would change its direction or subside. But the whale was determined. It caused a tumult in the silent bed of the sea. In a few seconds it would twirl and devour the ship's occupants. The few artist families of Kalinga on board would die in the shipwreck, without a trace. The heritage of Kalingan art and culture, the sculptors, artists, dancers, singers, musicians and merchants they were carrying would all perish. All were tense and scared at the prospect of such impending casualty, except one. She was without sensation; she had triumphed over the pain that was more heart-rending than bereavement. Death seemed to be such a trifle before such pain!'

'Everyone was absorbed in grim thoughts. How could they protect the ship from the whale? Somebody screamed: "There is a way. But who will do it?"

'"What is the solution?" Everybody shouted at once, in unison. In a while, everything would be over. Why not attempt at a last try at survival? The answer was brutal and not easy. If a virgin was sacrificed to the animal, it would quieten and the hurricane would subside.

'There was no scope to prove the authenticity of this. Everybody thought that it was better to sacrifice one person for the lives of others. But who would that be? The mothers of the young girls on board tightly clutched their daughters close to their breasts, determined not to sacrifice them. "I am prepared to die, but I won't give away my daughter. Never! Let everybody die with my daughter. But I can't accept my daughter's death for the sake of others," they would wail.

'Silpa sat forlorn, quiet and defenceless without any parents to protect her, to hold her in their lap, ready to die with her. Everybody's eyes were on her—anxious, desperate, helpless and pleading. If there was anyone who could help them avoid such a death, it was Silpa. Her inertia vanished in a moment. She made up her mind and looked intently at the ferocious whale advancing rapidly towards the ship. She had no fear of dying now and stood undaunted and determined. Only one moment, then everything would be over. Silpa stood facing the whale bravely. Her uncle Sudatta's outstretched arms were offering her shelter. She closed her eyes and prayed to Mother Goddess. And in a moment, invisible to everybody, two arms embraced her eagerly and snatched away her life from earth.

'The dance-master did not have to suffer long. The merchants who returned brought the news that young Silpa had jumped before a giant whale to save the contingent of Kalingan people. She was lost in the sea, to become a diamond in the treasure trove of Ratnakara. Just as her father had wished, she gave her life for Kalinga.

'Now the dance master was asking Kamala Maharana, "Can you do it, O artist? Can you engrave on the walls of the temple, an image of an innocent girl who gave up her life for the sake of the completion of Konark temple and its sanctity?"

'Kamala Maharana's chisel stopped, Konark was a temple of great surrenders he thought. There were many tales of sacrifice at the feet of the God of Justice. And yet the temple still waited for another sacrifice! The picture of that submission was etched in his heart, but he did not have the strength to carve it on stone. Without imagination, art is incomplete and lifeless. Like a statue of stone, Kamala Maharana stood before the dance master, his head bowed.'

Prachiprava, Charles, Vishnnu Maharana—all looked grave as he silently put the palm-leaf manuscript away. Bowing to him, Prachi and Charles silently made their way out as he put out the lamp.

Eleven

What was once called Sain Sain Berhampur is today referred to as Bayalishi Mouja (a unit of 20 acres of land)— it was ruled seven hundred years ago by a king who was an ally of Narasimha Deva. From the bazaar of Gopa, Charles and Prachi walked three kilometres on a dusty road through Bayalishibati village. They were returning after visiting the temple of Gangeshwari. Once the revered temple of the Ganga kings, it was now in ruins and lay abandoned, a den for snakes, monitor lizards and rats.

Baladeva Padhi, the eighty-year-old priest, sat inside the temple, legs folded like a turtle and head thrust out. He had a nose like the beak of a heron, and was presently displaying his resentment. He was not in the least interested in revealing legends linked to the temple to Prachi and Charles. What would be the gain? He had narrated many legends about the deeds of Ma Gangeshwari to visitors but did any one bother to look after the conservation of her temple? After bowing to the priest, Prachi thought, how right he was!

On the way back Charles said, 'History has not recorded Silpa's sacrifice. But when I look at you, I can understand such sacrifice. People who can give their life for the sake of values and ideals, could only have been born in this land. The concept of idealism remains very much active in this country. If that was not the case, the eighty-year-old priest would have asked for his own reward, instead of begging everybody to do something about the maintenance of the temple. And he knows his days are numbered. How does it matter to him if the temple of Gangeshwari survives or collapses completely?'

They finally reached the small shed in the village temple complex where the holy Bhagabata Gita was being read out every day before an idol of Lord Jagannath. Prachi entered the complex by opening a barricade made with bamboo strips, bowed to the deity inside, and then came out of the shrine. It was a hot day and the wind lacerated their faces. The area beyond the boundary of the village was desolate. The grass in the empty rice fields had shrivelled in the harsh sun. There were only a few young cowherds playing. The 'Bhagabata Tungi', a thatched house, was the prayer hall for the villagers; it was where the villagers assembled in the evening. The thatched house was plastered with mud and a massive banyan tree spread its canopy above like a shelter.

Prachi stopped to rest for a while. She was exhausted after the day's walk. Charles sympathized, 'You took such a lot of pain to come to this temple. I am really sorry.' Prachi smiled. 'I have come to this temple many times. But this time it was a different experience.'

'How?' Charles wanted to know. Prachi sounded sad, 'Earlier I was unaware of what had happened to Silpa. I was in search of her suffering soul.'

'Did you find her?'

'Yes.'

'Where?' Charles asked her, amazed.

'Within me,' came the spontaneous reply, followed by an immediate retraction, 'I am so influenced by Silpa's story that I find myself as one soul with her.'

'Or,' said Charles, 'it is the other way round. Traces of Silpa are to be found in you!'

'It is the same thing,' Prachi retorted and began walking, but Charles stood ruminating. Prachi, who had moved on a few steps ahead, turned and asked, 'What are you thinking?' Charles stared at the cremation ground nearby and replied gravely, 'I was thinking about how by the time one reaches the outskirts of a village in India, one can have a profound understanding of the two vital truths of life.'

'What are those?'

'God and death. Each village has a cremation ground, and a Bhagabata Tungi or an image of the village goddess at its outskirts. It explains such things so easily to a mystified traveller. Trees in India must be trees of enlightenment, like this banyan here!'

'Great,' said Prachi. 'you're learning to love India, and thats's enough to sweep away my exhaustion. But we still have to catch the last bus before sunset,' and she began to walk even faster along the ridges of the paddy fields. Charles followed her, talking to himself. 'Yes, I have begun to love India. It is because India has you, your culture, your idealism and values.' Prachi had a bouncing gait like that of a hill stream, and Charles flowed with it as if to a dream destination of absolute contentment.

'I have been roaming throughout the night looking for Chandrabhaga, I'm sure her soul is wandering around Konark. I have come across a ghost at times,' said Charles, and asked, 'Could Chandrabhaga and the ghost be connected in some way?'

Vishnu Maharana looked up and gazing at the sky and sighed, 'Perhaps it is the grieving soul of Chandrabhaga wandering without salvation even today.'

'How did Chandrabhaga die?' asked Prachi looking visibly

disturbed as though Chandrabhaga restless soul might suddenly show up in front of them, seven hundred years later still looking for Kamala Maharana, or demanding answers from the sculpted walls of Konark!

Vishnu Maharana smiled enigmatically, 'Who knows, Chandrabhaga may even be alive today. Ever since she disappeared so mysteriously into the jungle that day, nobody, not even King Narasimha Deva, ever found a trace of her.'

'Possibly King Narasimha Deva never ordered a proper investigation,' rued Charles.

'Where did he get that much time? Night after night since she went missing, he rode through villages in disguise, combed the forests and hills looking for her; he even explored the caves. He employed special messengers and policemen to gather information about her. But before all these efforts could bring fruit, the warfront called,' said Vishnu Maharana gravely.

Continuing from where they had left the palm-leaf manuscript yesterday, he read aloud: 'Senapati Rama Govinda, Minister Sibei Samantray, Suru Mahasenapati, all advised him, "Take rest, Maharaj! In the north, the enemy is terrified of us. There is peace and prosperity in the land. The Sun Temple is almost complete. Why a war now?"

'But Narasimha Deva was having none of it. Enraged, he roared, "The Paika soldier of Kalinga is not hungry for war! But he is not scared either, nor does he want to only defend his country. He wants to establish his power and his might; display his valour and outstanding warcraft beyond Kalinga boundaries and teach Nawab Yujbeg's forces in Bengal the measure of the real strength of Kalinga."

'And so in the twelfth year of his reign Narasimha Deva went again to war. Queen Sita Devi offered prayers to their presiding deity and marked the king's noble forehead with a bright daub of vermillion wishing him victory and a victorious return. En route to the battlefield, he told his commander Akhtaya, "If I am killed, you will ensure the completion of the chariot-shaped monument to the Sun God, with a pitcher at the crown and a splendid Natamandir dancing hall in front." Whenever he set out for war, such instructions always brought despair to his subordinates.

'Soon war ensued in Bengal, its fury unabated. Narasimha Deva charged into battle on back of Nishanaka, his white war-elephant, with such ferocity that the last shred of thought for self left his soldiers and they screamed into battle, lances, swords, and daggers ready to be bloodied.

'Undaunted that its northern borders had turned into a battlefield, Kalinga preparations for the consecration and installation of the pitcher at the pinnacle of the Sun Temple carried on in full swing. Minister Sibei Samantray, and master-builder Kamala Maharana worked even harder to complete the temple on time. The tempo on both fronts—war and temple—was aggressive, determined and relentless.

'Until the day they received news that King Narasimha Deva had fallen on the battlefield. The king of Kalinga! The invincible one! They heard that Nawab Yujbeg had sought assistance from the Sultan of Delhi and with this help, regrouped. The king, struck by an enemy arrow, had fallen from his war-elephant and lay motionless in a pool of blood. The soldiers, finding their brave king lifeless, fled the battlefield. Only Nishanka, the king's favourite, stood like a rock next to the lifeless body of his beloved master, tears streaming from his eyes drenching the blood-soaked earth. He was a war-elephant, he belonged to a king, and so he did not move. He was that special, and still unafraid.

'As the devastating news reached the palace, Queen Sita Devi fainted. Chandrika Devi wept, she had also lost her husband in a war, and had now lost her beloved brother and king. The entire nation was engulfed in darkness and the sea turned grim with sorrow. In the temple complex at Konark, the masons could not lift their chisels. Prince Bhanu Deva was only an adolescent—how could he face the enemy?

'Minister Sibei Samantray was furiously mulling over the pros and cons—if Kalinga's victorious sun set like this who would install the image of the Sun God within the massive temple? Kamala Maharana was also wondering the same thing—would the idol of Lord Surya never be worshipped at Konark? If Nawab Yujbeg succeeded in defeating Kalinga let alone the completion of the Sun Temple at Konark, he would have every small piece of carved stone crushed to dust. Kamala Maharana's chisel rose and began to hammer the stones, pausing to perfect the sculpture, and then polishing a lotus in stone.

'These lotuses were his offering to the soul to the great king who had died fighting. And he too was fighting for his nation. The image of the Sun God had to be installed in the temple before the Sun God arose in the eastern sky and his first ray struck the sacred diamond throne inside the sanctum sanctorum. Only then would the soul of the King Narasimha Deva rest in peace. If the God of Justice and Strength was established in Konark only then would the army of Kalinga be strong enough to once again fight and defeat the enemy Muslim soldiers. That was why the artist of Konark did not drown himself in sorrow, he stayed unswerving on his path.

'Prayers were offered and rites held for the departed soul of the mighty king and offerings made to gods and goddesses invoking their blessings to keep the freedom of the country intact. Queen Sita Devi was praying at the temple of Ma Gangeshwari seeking her blessings. Chandra Devi had abandoned food and water and was worshipping Lord Jagannath. The moment the body of the fallen king arrived at the capital, Crown Prince Bhanu Deva would be installed as the new king and his mother Sita Devi would leave her ante-chamber the Rani Hamsapura. She would be rechristened 'Rajamata' or Queen Mother. The last rites of the deceased king would then be conducted as per royal tradition. The Prime Minister was supervising everything with a heart heavy with grief at the king's death, and fear that it was just a matter of days before Kalinga freedom was snatched away by the Muslim invaders.

'Meanwhile the battlefield lay bathed in the crimson rays of the setting sun. The last rays of the sun fell on the pool of scarlet flowing from the king and reflected it back into the darkening western sky, painting it the colour of grief. The great king lay as though lost in the tender embrace of Mother Earth. The battlefield lay covered in the bloodied bodies of the injured and dead, the darkness of the night being pierced with their anguished cries for help. Death had levelled both Hindu and Muslim. As night descended the blood began to clot. Like the stars in the sky, the soldiers-souls lit up. The sky too wept with the inconsolable earth, as the soldiers' cries for help began to fade and were extinguished.

'But Narasimha Deva regained consciousness. Someone's soft caring hand was putting life into his dying body. He opened his eyes and was surprised to see a dark-skinned boy nursing him tenderly; he appeared like a luminous faint blue flame to the king. By his side was another fair-skinned boy. Overwhelmed, the king tried to open his mouth, but he was weak with the overwhelming emotion. His eyes were filled with tears. He trembled with excitement. The boys lifted him off the ground and placed him carefully on Nishanka's back. The king closed his eyes once more. Nishanka began to walk, with the boys leading the way. The king did not know for how long he slept or how far they had travelled.

'When he woke up he found himself lying on the sandy beach at Mahodadhi Puri. He could clearly see the Nilachakra—the blue wheel—in the dark sky. At a little distance, a lamp burned in a hut, a sign of life nearby. He had reached Purushottam Kshetra. Who had led him there? Everything appeared like a dream. The king folded his hands and prayed to Lord Jagannath. Nishanka sprinkled some water from the sea on his body. Suddenly the king felt thirsty. Sea water does not quench thirst. He signalled Nishanka to take him to the hut nearby. Nishanka was hungry too, and was visibly tired. He lifted up the king slowly and laid him down gently at the entrance of the hut. He himself sprawled on the sand, exhausted.

'The king knew that without food and water he would die. Nishanka too felt the same. But would the family living in that tattered hut be able to quench his thirst, let alone feed him? Inside, a lamp burnt feebly. It was about to flicker out. After sometime it would be dark. Before that, the presence of a hungry visitor had to be announced to the inmates. The king coughed a little. A woman, her face hidden in a veil, came out; her lips trembling slightly. "Who are you? What do you want?" she asked.

'"I am an injured soldier," replied the king. "I have been brought here from the battlefield. I am extremely weary from lack of food and water. My elephant too is hungry and thirsty, he is lying nearby. If you could arrange something for us…"

Before the king could finish his sentence, the woman stepped back startled. She said in a choked voice, "The king is dead in the battlefield. Yet, you being a Paika soldier of Kalinga could escape? I do not know whether the magnanimous king would have forgiven you for this, but I certainly cannot. Alas! What misfortune has fallen on our country with the untimely death of the king?"

'The king wondered if it would have been better for him to have died on the battlefield than beg for sympathy from this woman! But he continued, "Lady! I was hurt when I was fighting the enemy, and then I lost consciousness. I have not come here on my own. It is Lord Jagannath who has brought me to your door. Nishanka, the king's war-elephant, has carried me to Srikshetradham on His orders. I do not know what the purpose behind this is. But I promise you, if you save my life tonight, I will go back to the battlefield to fight again. The Muslim army, celebrating the death of the king, must be feasting and making merry with music and dance. I have renewed strength in me now to defeat them. If you can arrange for my meal for the night, Lord Jagannath's purpose will be fulfilled."

'"Forgive me, sir. I said such cruel words. Whoever you are, you are my guest tonight. It is my great joy that a soldier of the Maharaja has reached my door. If you will start for war tomorrow morning, I will light an earthen lamp for you at the Srimandir. Please come in, step into my poor hut."

'The king entered her hut with difficulty. The woman in the veil was startled. It was her saviour, the Mahadandapasha! If he recognized her, he would ask for explanations of the day that she had fled. He might even punish her! But she had not left on her own. It was Lord Jagannath who had led her. Since that day, she suffered no sorrow. She lived all alone in that lonely hut, but she never felt helpless. Somebody was always with her and resided inside her, in her soul. He arranged for her food. She never had to remain on an empty stomach. She made earthen lamps and sold them at the temple. It was enough for her livelihood. The rest of the time she would sit at the temple and pray for her husband Kamala Maharana. She would pray for the victory of King Narasimha Deva. She lit a lamp every day at the temple in Puri for the successful completion of the Sun Temple at Konark.

'She would never meet Kamala Maharana in her lifetime. But that did not deter her from wishing her husband a long and fulfilling life, or for the completion of the Konark temple, or even for the good fortune of the king of Kalinga. An earthen lamp's thin wick burns itself, but provides light to the world. That was the fruit of her life. Chandrabhaga was not inferior to a thin thread; she was a human being, a woman. She was an unfortunate daughter of Kalinga It would not be fitting for her to be alive and live only for herself. She had to dedicate her life to the well-being of others, and that was her principle of life. She pulled her veil further down in case her guest should recognize her!

'Her heart wept at the sight such of injuries on his body. Blood had clotted in the wounds. But she could realize how painful it must be for him. He was hungry as well! He had to be given food. Outside, the white royal elephant, Nishanka was hungry too. Yet she had cooked only a handful of rice that night and boiled a bunch of green leaves. It was sufficient for her consumption. She did not have even a grain of rice in her hut. Why should she anyway? She had nobody to feed. No children, no husband. Her daily provisions were collected on a daily basis. If she could sell some lamps the next morning, only then could she purchase some food for herself.

'Chandrabhaga was disturbed. She could go without food that night and serve the guest whatever she had. But would it be sufficient for him! Could he eat it? What would she do about Nishanka? She was at a loss. And yet she could not turn away her guest. It would speak ill of her and of Srikshetra too. No one goes back from Srikshetra on an empty stomach. She prayed to Lord Jagannath: "Lord! What ordeal is this! Chandrabhaga has to face all sorts of adversity. Without your will, nothing happens in this world. Srikshetra has the palace of the king, the palaces of many rich merchants, and there are monasteries, hermitages, inns and the temple of Lord Jagannath. But why did you lead a brave soldier and the royal elephant from the battlefield straight to my cottage? I, who survive on a handful of soil from Srikshetra... Lord I have no fear of humiliation, but you have to rescue me from this, my Lord! The one who has reached your temple hungry and thirsty, is your guest. Who am I? What can I do without you?" And so praying, Chandrabhaga decided to serve the guest the rice porridge she had cooked for herself. She did not feel ashamed.

'But when she entered her kitchen she fell to her knees and was moved to tears. For before her were pots of Mahaprasada, sweetened rice, dal, besara, khata and kheer. As she set a thal from these earthen pots, tears of happiness rolled from her eyes and fell on the food. She wondered why Lord Jagannath had so many blessings for a poor woman like her. He listened to everybody's problems at the temple, but she had never thought that he also listened to her pleading, her problems! She would never feel low, useless, or unwanted again. Her life was not without purpose. Henceforth, she would spend the rest of her life in the secure love of Lord Jagannath. She served her guest with a merry heart, humming a couplet from the *Gita Govinda*. The sweet aroma of the divine food filled her hut. The king asked her in surprise, "Who has brought Mahaprasada at this odd hour? And it is so deliciously warm too!"

'Chandrabhaga replied softly, "The one who has led you to my doors! Except Him, I have nobody in this world to call my own. Everything is his wish, his mercy." Chandrabhaga was choked with overwhelming emotion and as he took a mouthful of rice, tears of joy fell from his eyes too. He thought, "The Lord has blessings for me! He stands with my country, or else why has he fed me to keep alive?" While he ate the Mahaprasada, his wounds began to heal as if by a miracle! In the flickering light of that earthen lamp, his body regained its divine glow.

'Chandrabhaga, staring at him, thought the young man was definitely a blessed son of Lord Jagannath. His blessings would definitely help him succeed. Although the entire nation was demoralized for a while by the sad news of the king's untimely death, victory was now assured for the kingdom of Kalinga. This young man was definitely the able saviour sent by the Lord of Kalinga. There was no doubt of that. Chandrabhaga felt she was blessed to have him as her guest.

'After he finished his meal, Chandrabhaga took the leftovers to feed the elephant. She said affectionately, "I do not have anything more than this. I am sure it will satiate your hunger because even a little of divine Mahaprasada rice from Puri temple can fill the soul."

'Nishanka ate Mahaprasada to his heart's content as though he understood everything she said. He then thanked Chandrabhaga, caressing her softly with his trunk. Chandrabhaga was thrilled with the affectionate touch of the royal elephant. Her eyes were filled with joy. She was overwhelmed. "Nishanka, if only the king could be brought to life once again within my life-span, how fortunate and happy I could be! Though I have never seen him in person, I have felt his kindness. Who says he is no more! As the builder of the Sun Temple of Konark, he has become immortal. Today, this unfortunate woman is lucky to be able to serve his elephant, in however small a manner."

'The elephant nodded in agreement. The king, overhearing the conversation between his elephant and the innocent woman was elated.

'Although Chandrabhaga had forgotten to keep aside a little of the food for herself, she was not hungry anymore. Her heart, mind and soul were filled with a strange, unspeakable satisfaction. All her sorrows vanished in a moment and were replaced with a new song of life. The king was grateful to Chandrabhaga. "Lady!" he said humbly, "now you can rest. I will start for the battlefield as soon as it is past midnight. I am now perfectly cured. May Lord Jagannath bless you."

'Chandrabhaga was so overcome with the happenings, she stood still as if rooted to the ground and uttered feebly, "Everybody is expecting the dead body of the king to reach Cuttack by tomorrow morning. The sorrow and anxiety regarding his death has taken away my sleep. You need some rest now. Please go inside the hut and lie down for a while. I will sit outside and pray for the soul of our king the whole night."

'The king was touched with the reverence of the young woman for the king and said, "I am sure that your devotion will lead the king to regain life and he will also become strong enough to face the enemy. But you do not have to abandon your life for his sake. Rather, a new life will begin for you. As a representative of the king, I will send for you tomorrow morning. Your devotion to the king, love for the country, and this hospitality should be adequately rewarded. Only then can it benefit the country. Lady! May I know your identity? Why are you living alone by the sea shore at this young age? If you tell me everything, I may be able to help you."

'Chandrabhaga kept quiet.

'The fear that had caused her to flee that night faced her like a question mark and she had no answers. This kind man would take her to the capital. If her identity was revealed to the king, her husband Kamala Maharana would be devastated with grief and humiliation, but it would not lessen her sorrow. Society would never accept her as his bride any more. One who had stepped outside the boundary of her home could not regain societal respect, no matter how virtuous she was. It was better if her husband Kamala Maharana returned, re-married and started a family. Let him also believe that his first wife Chandrabhaga was dead.

'Chandrabhaga's silent stoic bearing affected the king. He said sadly, "I know you do not believe me. You have made it a tendency to bear all pain without ever putting up a protest. But by Lord Jagannath's will, your sorrows will come to an end for sure. Please have confidence in me."

'Chandrabhaga was thinking that as one who had surrendered to Lord Jagannath so completely she did not have to look for help elsewhere. She was above any mundane despair.'

'The king came out of the hut and said, "It is against a man's nature to rest inside the house leaving the woman outside. Lady, you go in. I will relax on this bed of sand, under the open sky without any fear. With the sacred blue wheel on one side and the blue sea on the other, what do I have to fear?"

'The king lay down on the sands. Nishanka caressed him lovingly and lulled him to sleep. Meanwhile, Chandrabhaga was inside singing hymns for Lord Jagannath, while searching for a way out of the situation.

'The sonorous noise of the sea and drops of rain that fell on his face woke the king from his deep slumber. There was a huge globe-like crimson orb rising from the embrace of the seabed and illumining the dawn gloriously. The king murmured to himself, "How generous is nature! She has woken me up just at the right moment. Had it been a little late, the priests and other attendants of the Puri temple who come to the sea to have a pre-dawn bath would have certainly recognized me. The news of the king being alive would spread like wild fire. Everybody would have celebrated with joy and ecstasy forgetting that enemy soldiers were at their doorsteps! This is not the time for celebration. I have to go back to the battlefield instantly. The Muslims, anticipating a certain victory, will be revelling in wine, women, and song; and will be careless now. They have to be attacked and conquered." But before that something had to be done about the kind woman.

'The king stood at her doorway and called out softly, "Lady, kindly burn an earthen lamp for me on my mission for victory! Bid me farewell. I will come back very soon. Then my foremost duty will be to put an end to your woes." But there was no one inside that leaf-hut. Its door was open. Inside a little earthen lamp burnt dimly to symbolize victory for Kalinga. There was no trace of the woman. A few unburnt lamps lay in a corner. The king, now worried, peeped into the room. There were two saris hung on a rack. One of them caught his eye and a flash of the memory rushed in. A Khandua sari with exquisite motifs that Chandrabhaga had worn when she had collapsed in the arms of the king in that jungle by the well, alone in the dead of the night!

'It was this sari that had first drawn his eyes. The king had been impressed by the intricate dexterity of the weavers of Kalinga who could produce such matchless beauty on cloth. He had realized that the craftsmanship of Kalinga artisans was indeed the best in every field. Meanwhile, he had forgotten Chandrabhaga's face, which he had seen only hazily, he had forgotten her voice too, but his perceptive heart remembered the sari with a temple border and a beautifully designed pallu with motifs of fish, lotus and elephant. Was this Chandrabhaga herself then?

'The moment the king remembered all this, his heart was filled with both happiness and sorrow. The fact that he had found her so close and lost her again just as mysteriously, made him grieve with a pain that he could not overcome. Maybe the sari belonged to someone else! It was possible, he tried to comfort himself. He did not remember the design that perfectly. But if a woman living in a tattered hut of leaves could afford to wear such an artistic sari, it had to be Chandrabhaga, nobody else.

'The king came out and looked for Chandrabhaga. There was no other sign of any habitation in sight. Poor woman! She had been leading her life quite peacefully making earthen diyas and selling them at the Puri temple. Once again, his entry into her life had disturbed her solitude.

'The king rode on his elephant and saw small footprints in a serpentine line on the damp beach. Chandrabhaga had walked away to some unknown destination by the seashore. She could not have gone very far. She had to be told at least that her life would not be caught in a whirlpool any more. She would be left in peace at Srikshetra to spend her life as a devout Vaishnaivite, immersed in the love of Lord Jagannath, in peace and happiness. Who else but Jagannath could provide shelter to Srikshetra's Chandrabhaga?

'After a while, the king lost hope. The waves had wiped away the footmarks. Could it be that the waves too were searching for her, crashing at the shore! The sea was not satiated with the dust of her feet, and it wanted to devour her. Had the sea then taken Chandrabhaga to the bottom of its unfathomable womb? The king pleaded with the blue waters of the sea, "O Ratnakara, please do me this favour; return me Chandrabhaga, the woman who has saved my life. If you cannot do so then treasure her carefully, tenderly in your womb. Let her pious soul not be further affected by any injustice of the world." He turned to leave. It was not right for him to roam the sea beach searching for Chandrabhaga. He had to reach the battleground before daybreak. Chandrabhaga might be very precious to him, but she had no relevance before the freedom of the country. Each moment was crucially important in the new dawn. The early rays of the morning sun touched the 'blue-wheel', the filial crown of the Puri temple. The gallant king bowed and proceeded to the battlefield on his war elephant, Nishanka. Lord Sri Jagannath was his invisible guide all along the route.

'Was it a dream! Narasimha Deva, the invincible king of Kalinga returning home? A hero and a conqueror? Everybody had expected his dead body to arrive instead. The nation was in deep mourning, its people drowning in a sea of despair at the news of his death. But he was alive! The conqueror was back in flesh and blood.

'The king and his fearless soldiers, with Lord Jagannath's blessings, had trounced Nawab Yujbeg as well as a contingent of the Sultan of Delhi. The glorious victory could only be possible due to the blessings of Lord Jagannath who helped the king all along. The sky of Kalinga resounded with cries of thanksgiving and praise for the beloved Lord Jagannath. Otherwise how could the king, who died on the battlefield, regain life to once again fight the enemy valiantly and send them packing!

'Not just Kalinga and the eastern parts of Kalinga but parts of Andhra Pradesh, eastern Madhya Pradesh, southern Bihar, entire Bengal province, Kamrup and Manipur reverberated with praises of Lord Jagannath. Hundreds of temples were built in commemoration of His glory. In Muslim-ruled Bengal too the famous Dwadasha Yatra of Lord Jagannath was celebrated with pomp and splendour.

'Lord Gokarneshwara of Mahendragiri was the royal deity of the Ganga dynasty. But the devout Vaishnaivite, King Narasimha Deva, had adhered to Lord Jagannath as his presiding deity. Lord Jagannath was the virtual king of Kalinga. To celebrate His role as the protector of Kalinga, arrangements were made for many rites and rituals. The fame of Purushottam Dham of Puri was to spread all over the world.

'Queen Sita Devi who had given up food and water and was praying to mother Gangeshwari, was unconscious. She had a dream that the Goddess was applying the traditional streak of vermilion to the parting of her hair. When she regained consciousness, she learnt about the king's arrival. Her eyes filled with tears. Her desolate life was once again beginning to fill with colour.

'Once the news of the King's being alive and his imminent homecoming spread, elaborate arrangements were made at the Sun Temple for his welcome. A huge slab of chlorite weighing 742 maunds, with the Navagraha[13] depicted on it, was placed

---

[13]The nine planets as per Vedic astrology, so placed at the temple to bless the visitors at the entrance.

on iron railings and installed at the entrance of the porch of the Sun Temple for the king's prosperity. Each of the nine planets was placed in separate blocks. The idols of Rabi, Chandra, Mangal, Buddha, Bruhaspati, Shukra, Shani, Rahu and Ketu were depicted in Padmasana posture from left to right, and were heavily adorned with ornaments, as if assuring Kalinga of its unconquerable future!

'The king proceeded to Konark with his queen on his return and knelt before the Navagraha slab. Sculptor Kamala Maharana was giving the finishing touches to a stone image of the king in his moment of victory. The king said, "This victory belongs to Lord Jagannath and the best soldier is my favourite elephant, Nishanka. It is because of him that I am blessed with a new life today. First you should depict his image on the walls of Konark, and then carve the images of the elephants and horses who gave their lives fighting for the country. Only then can Konark become a victory memorial for Kalinga"

'Great was the king who recognized the immense contribution of men and even animals in battle. Kamala Maharana asked the artists to carve the image of the war elephant Nishanka. As a result, two giant replicas of Nishanka were installed on both sides of the north entrance door of the porch of the temple. The elephant was armed with weapons but was chained tightly and looked so real that to spectators it appeared that he was tied with actual iron chains! He was also depicted crushing enemy soldiers with his trunk and trampling soldiers lying beneath his feet.

'The king was very impressed with the sculptures of Nishanka. He thanked the artists. "Nishanka demonstrates his strength exactly like this on the battlefield. But kindly release him from the iron chains. He is never unfaithful or arrogant, he is truly a loyal friend on the battlefield. It pains me to see him in chains."

'The artist, kneeling before the king, replied humbly, "My Lord, please forgive me. The elephant and the chains are carved together. The chains cannot be removed now. If it is done, it will be disfigured and the statue will crack."

'The king was astonished, "You are great! Your craftsmanship is superb. If you remove this iron chain, the elephant may not be injured but I will be upset. It is a faultless carving in the artistic tradition of Kalinga; let it remain intact."

'Two war-horses were depicted at the end of the steps of the southern gate. The king honoured the artists with royal saris. But how could he honour Kamala Maharana? Time and again, Chandrabhaga had escaped him. Who would know of his continuous failures and his agony?'

'There were four strong forts in Puri town—Bhagavati, Naga, Maricha, and Indradyumna. The Srimandir temple was guarded on all sides by those forts. If any suspicious-looking person entered the city, he could not escape. Without a permission letter or satisfactory answers, nobody could leave the city too. It was thus impossible for Chandrabhaga to leave the city secretly. The night guards who were employed to keep the records of people entering or leaving the city did not have any entry in her name. Where could she have disappeared to?

'The king, kneeling before the Diamond Throne, prayed quietly, "My Lord! Where have you concealed Chandrabhaga? I will search for her on the earth, in the water, in the sky and across the entire universe. What will happen to Kamala Maharana's life when he returns home after sixteen years of dedicated labour only to find that his beloved is not there!

'Lord Jagannath sat on his Diamond Throne, unmoved like a piece of rock, without arms and legs, but with a glimmer of a smile on his red lips, as if telling the king, "I do not have legs, so how can I move from my diamond throne? I do not have ears, so how did I hear your prayer for help on the battlefield? Oh brave one! Work is God. Self-confidence will be your guide, confidence is divine. Keep doing your duty, there can be no defeat for a valiant hero."

'The smile remained etched on the red lips of Lord Jagannath. "A river charts its own course. It does not mingle with the sea. If you pursue the course of a river, you may land up in a dense forest and lose your way! Oh King, your destination is the battlefield and you are not destined to get lost in a forest!"

'The king was trying to check his tears and prayed, "All knowing Lord! If Chandrabhaga is at all alive, please make her meet Kamala Maharana. If she is dead, keep her buried in your mercy. This unfeeling society has tormented her for no fault of hers! Let her soul rest in peace after her death at least!"

'He observed the women who sold earthen lamps at the temple complex. All looked elderly, well past their youth. Could Chandrabhaga ever sit with them and sell her lamps? If that was possible, then whoever bought lamps from her hands and offered them at the temple must have washed away all their sins. If only he could buy a lamp from the hands of that virtuous woman, he too could be in heaven!

'The king came and stood at the site on the seashore, where Chandrabhaga's small leaf hut had once stood. There was no trace of the hut any longer. The sea had washed away even traces of the leaves and the twigs. Her footprints had long since disappeared.

'The sea shore was lonely, desolate.'

At a little distance from the southern entrance door of the

temple, stood two huge images of Nishanka and Nirbhaya placed on separate pedestals. Those sculptures had withered with time. The two war-elephants too had crumbled. Prachiprava caressed the dislodged tails and ears of the elephants. Charles took a photograph of Prachi with them. He smiled, 'Your facial expression is exquisite. While nursing the king, Chandrabhaga must have had this same expression on her face—melancholic and so enchantingly beautiful!'

Prachiprava said softly, 'It reflects the love of patriotism, nothing else. Without Nishanka's devotion for his master and his bravery, the Sun of Kalinga's freedom would have set that day, never to rise again. That is why I adore this elephant. Chandrabhaga would have loved the injured soldier for his valour, power and patriotism.'

'Poor Chandrabhaga! Other than her patriotism and devotion for God, what else did she have for comfort?' Charles sighed.

Chitrotpala was walking away with her basket of flowers atop the boundary wall. She had attained puberty recently and she did not jump around like a child anymore. Her movements were slow, steady and rhythmic. But her expression remained same as before. She would talk to Charles with downcast eyes. She told him, 'Saheb! Why don't you postpone your departure a little longer? My marriage will take place in the coming summer, in Baisakh.'

Charles laughed and said, 'I will stay back even if my work is over. This year I am not going without witnessing the Rath Yatra. I will eat a sumptuous feast at your wedding, too.'

'We are a poor family, how much can we afford? My father will be relieved to get rid of me. I am a burden to him. Last winter, during the Samba Dashami Mela, I sold flowers to help my family. If I can earn enough in the coming Magha Saptami

Mela, my wedding can take place without any financial hurdles. After this I will not sell flowers any more. I will not have to come so far from home. Only a few days remain until my wedding anyway.' She would blush shyly, turn pink and draw her veil to cover her head. Those days she mostly kept her head covered with her pallu.

Charles asked her playfully, 'When is your Prachi Didi getting married?' Chitrotpala would curl her tongue, and with widened eyes, whisper, 'Do not even mention it. She will be angry. I do not know why she gets upset whenever the topic of her wedding comes up.'

Charles replied, 'Your Didi is a devout Vaishnaivite. I too am planning to become a Vaishnaivite. I will become her disciple. Will she agree?'

'Shall I ask her?'

Charles smiled, 'Let it be. I'll ask her when the time is right.'

But he could never ask her, although he was used to talking with girls, Prachiprava was entirely different. The kind of relationship Charles wanted to establish with her was also different from others. He wanted to have her in his life as his life-partner. He was deeply influenced by the man-woman relationship and family life of Indian culture. Whoever she married, she would never divorce her husband over trivial issues like Charles's mother had done.

Prachiprava had in the meantime descended from the pedestal where the war-horses stood. Noticing Charles's abstraction, she asked, 'What is wrong? What are you worried about?' Charles gathered his wits together and smiled. He pointed to Dharmananda, who was standing at a little distance, 'I was thinking about Dharmananda. He has improved a lot, is earning handsomely, eats well, wears better clothes. He is happy.

The ruins of Konark even today feed so many mouths. I was wondering about that.'

Prachi looked at Dharmananda, and became unhappy. 'These days, Dharmananda eats good food at good hotels. He wears good clothes. His appearance, behaviour, everything is changing rapidly. Meanwhile, he has earned enough to marry off one of his sisters and send his brothers to better schools. The fifteen-year-old Dharmananda, is handling his family burden so well—by selling pictures of the erotic sculptures at the Sun Temple. He is actually sacrificing the art and culture of his country to feed the lust and desires of sick minds. If necessary, he could trade even the nude pictures of his own mother or sister to meet food and clothing requirements!'

Prachiprava sometimes chastened him, 'Look Dharma, give up all this. Find some other work. You can sell pictures of other sculptures of Konark. You are deliberately choosing these obscene pictures and polluting the artistic treasures of Konark. You are tarnishing your own country's image before outsiders.'

Dharmananda would smile and reply. 'Didi, I do not understand any of this. Country, nation, art, culture, whatever. I only know poverty, disease, hunger and want. I have no other means to defend myself against all these.'

Prachiprava had no answer for him. She understood that what Dharmananda told her was true and irrefutable. Sometimes the truth could be so cruel and unbearable! She went ahead to light a lamp at the Navagraha temple. It was a Saturday and hence there was quite a rush at the temple. Charles bought a flower garland from Chitrotpala and handed it over to Prachi, 'If you please, do offer these flowers to the deities to appease them, so that my planetary problems are over.' Prachi looked at Charles, surprised. Charles smiled, 'Here, one cannot talk from the heart to another person, and that is why so much trust is reposed on an idol of stone... Here one can trust this medium only to convey one's thoughts. As long as I am in this country, I must obey the rules of this Lord!'

Prachi turned pale. 'What are you referring to as stone, Charles? You do not know about the powers of these nine planetary gods. Would you believe it if I told you this is not fiction, it is a historical fact?'

Charles looked at her, a little amused, as she explained to him like an expert guide. 'The British Government had tried to transport this chlorite slab of nine planets to the museum at Kolkata. But despite all their equipment they could move it only two hundred yards! When they failed in their effort, they cut it into three parts. And only the portion containing the nine planet idols was to be taken away. But they could move even that just one mile. All efforts failed. The Navagraha idols were put up in Konark and once again worshipped. Charles, these stones are living stones and possess a divine spirit. With simple faith you, too, can see this.'

Charles laughed heartily, and replied, 'Prachiprava, I am waiting to see you in your attire as a Vaishnaivite. When are you going to establish your own monastery? Come to my country, you will have many disciples. You won't have any problem with funds too.'

Somewhat hurt, Prachi replied sarcastically, 'It is not dollars we need to establish monasteries. We need twigs, stones, flowers, leaves, clay, faith and devotion. We do not lack all these here. Why should I go to your land?'

Charles laughed, 'You don't understand. I want to take you to my country. I thought it would prove lucrative for you.'

Prachi smiled back, 'I too wish to go on a world tour. But

all our wishes do not get fulfilled.' Saying this, she went inside the Navagraha temple, offered obeisance, placed the garland Charles had given her, and lit a lamp. She prayed, 'Oh God! Bless Charles with happiness, peace and stability.'

After coming out of the temple, Prachi realized that she had prayed only for Charles, completely forgetting her own self. Did she love Charles more than she loved herself, she wondered. She held out the offerings to Charles. Taking a small piece of it, Charles said, 'You will find everything in my country, except this. This is my favourite picture of India.'

'What?'

'The clothes of a woman when she goes to worship at a temple, the spiritual aura of kindness she wears. I have never seen my mother like this. When I see you like this, I feel a strange longing. I feel, if only you were my mother!'

Prachi laughed, 'It is not impossible, Charles! Now you can think of me as your mother too. In Indian culture, a man has to view a married woman as his mother and an unmarried girl as his sister.'

'But you are not married. And you are also not my mother's age!' Charles exclaimed.

Prachi, slightly anxious, said, 'I am like a mother to Dharmananda! He is not of a son's age for me. There is no age requirement to see somebody as a mother! There is no need to be married to experience the sacred feeling of motherhood. Satyabati and Kunti of the Mahabharata had become mothers without getting married.'

Charles was slightly irritated. 'No way can I address you as mother. Impossible!'

'Even if you do not call me mother, you can think of me as one! It is not necessary that you need to express everything.

All relationships do not require verbal communication.'

Charles sighed. 'Leave it. Even without any expression, you still occupy an important position in my heart.'

'Thank you! I am proud to have an immensely meritorious son like you,' said Prachi, a little amused.

Charles did not respond. He strode ahead and came face to face with Dharmananda. Charles put his hands on his shoulder and addressed him like a friend, 'Mr. Dharmananda, I am happy that you are doing well. My research is almost complete. Before leaving, I have a request for you. You will take photographs of Chitrotpala's wedding. I want the pictures of her wedding ceremony, complete with all its rituals. I want her photo when she is decked up as a bride. To me, an Indian woman looks her best as a bride. I would have been happy if I could get such a photograph of your Didi, but I do not think she is going to get married before I return. You click plenty of photographs of Chitrotpala. I will pay for them. Agreed?'

'I have no problems. But will Chitrotpala agree? She appears to be very annoyed with me these days. Perhaps she is jealous because I am earning more than her. But Saheb, she does not understand that there are lesser devotees than tourists who visit Konark these days. Nobody comes to Konark anymore to worship the Navagraha deities. They come to see the lovely carvings of Konark temple, the amorous couples. Naturally, my photos would sell more than her flowers.'

Charles did not reply. Chitrotpala was returning with her empty flower basket, counting her steps on the boundary wall of the Konark temple. The golden sunshine framed her like a lovely image. Dharmananda stared at her adoringly. Charles thought that the girl who was betrothed to marry someone in the near future was far above any jealousy or hatred. She did not crave to be rich. Her greatest dream in life was to get married. And she was trying to raise enough money for her dowry. Why should she be envious of Dharmananda, who was earning only to become rich?

Charles waved at Chitrotpala. She looked at him, smiled sweetly, and nodded in response. Charles said softly, 'Oh Chitrotpala, if marriage happens to be the best dream in your life, then I will definitely partake in that happy celebration. Before returning to America, I will stay on to witness the wedding ceremony of Chitrotpala, and the world-famous car festival of Lord Jagannath. These two incidents will be noted down as the most memorable events in my nomadic life.'

Twelve

On the second day of the bright fortnight of the month of Asadh (July), was the chariot festival of Lord Sri Jagannath. The three deities at Puri Temple descend the twenty-two steps in a swinging motion called Pahandi Bije. On the main road in front of the temple, called Mahakhala or Ratha Danda, three huge wonderfully-decorated chariots are put in front of the Lion's Gate facing the Balagandi square at a distance. The three chariots have sixteen, fourteen and twelve wheels, respectively. To the north of the sacred River Malini lies Maushima's home called Gundicha Ghar or Adapa Mandapa. The three chariots are built at Indradyumnapatana. Initially, there were two sets of these three chariots for the three travelling deities, so that the deities could leave their vehicles at the river bank and climb into the waiting chariots across the river to reach their aunt's abode. The chariots across the river were smaller, called Patana Ratha and had four wheels each only.

Numerous devotees waited anxiously at the Bada Danda, meaning main road, for a glimpse of Lord Jagannath and his siblings. Their eyes were suffused with happy tears; their hearts throbbed for the Niladribihari Golakanath.

Vishnu Maharana opened the palm-leaf manuscripts, looked to see if Prachi and Charles were ready and began reading.

'During the reign of King Narasimha Deva, this chariot festival of Lord Jagannath was famous as the Ghosha Yatra—the victory procession of Lord Jagannath. It celebrated the victory of the brave soldiers. The eastern parts of Odisha were surrounded by Muslim rulers, and enemies continually threatened to capture the land. In fact, Kalinga the land of Lord Jagannath, was the last independent country in the whole of India to succumb to the British in the 18th century A.D. Its sovereignty was protected by Lord Jagannath himself!

'The joy of victory, the news that the king was indeed alive, the proponent of the Konark Temple's completion date and the ensuing festival in Puri for the annual sojourn of Lord Jagannath reverberated in the air. The resonance of the musical instruments, shinga, karatal, pataha, dambaru, khemata, bells, veena and the jingling of the ghungoors mingled with the chanting of hymns. Fervent prayers filled the air, rose from earth to the sky and reverberated back to earth. Nothing was impossible before God's will, and that too the will of wide-eyed Jagannath! In the turbulent mortal world inundated in earthly desires, devotees longed to find ultimate bliss in spirituality, in God, ever kind and considerate. The hearts of the devotees were now far removed from mundane happiness, sorrow, meeting, parting, success, youth, old age, the feelings of gain or loss, hope or despair. They all waited for the self-manifested wooden images of Lord Purushottam with hope and devotion, eager and anxious to surrender themselves at the feet of that great God. There were waves of devotees who thronged to have a glimpse of the mysterious Lord Purushottam, who had rescued Kalinga kingdom many times, and maintained the pride and glory of the Odias.

'King Chodaganga Deva had built the massive temple to install Lord Purushottam in the temple at Puri. His son King Anangabhima Deva added many more structures to the complex at a later stage. King Narasimha Deva, from this great lineage, opted to build a shrine for Lord Surya at the Padma Kshetra instead. The temple was to be unique and in the shape of a chariot. But he had the temple at Puri renovated, maintained the broad road facing the temple, made provisions for the massive timber logs required to construct the wooden chariots transported from the Tribhubana Sundar forests.

'Nayak Damodara Mahapatra was assigned the task of transporting the logs through river routes as per the king's instructions. That is why the king had felicitated him with a royal sari. Earlier, King Anangabhima Deva had made provision for Chhatisa Nijog or 36 servitors clans to look after the daily rituals of Puri Temple, and now Narasimha Deva provided landed property to these servitors. King Narasimha Deva established exclusive colonies for them—the wood carvers were settled in Haribamshapur Mauja, Chitrakara lane was for the painters, and Mali Sahi for gardeners who supplied flowers to the temple.

'Three sacred chariots, kept in a row on the main road, were the Nandighosha, (for Lord Jaganntha), Taladhwaja (for Lord Balabhadra), and Debadalana (for Goddess Subhadra). King Narasimha Deva had sent a messenger to Kashmir for delicate pashmina shawls to drape these three chariots. At the pinnacle of these temple-shaped wooden chariots were the glistening pitchers of gold. And atop the thrones of the deities were canopies studded with diamonds. The flag swayed as the strong south-western winds blew in. As the deities were seated on their throne, musicians in ecstasy played their instruments vigorously. And devotees thronged to offer bhog—sweets, coconuts, saris and ornaments to their beloved deities.

'When the rituals by the priests were over the first servitor of Lord Jagannath, the king himself would arrive in his silver palanquin to offer his service to sweep the floors of the chariots and then pull the massive ropes. Only then would the devotees break loose and grab the ropes to haul the chariot to their heart's content. After that, six white elephants would be employed to pull the chariots a distance of forty-eight feet to reach Balagandi Square, from where they would be pushed on to boats to be ferried across Malini River. The charioteers held the ropes firmly in their hands, while King Narasimha Deva ceremonially laid his hands on the ropes.

'The Ratha Danda was reverberating with the noise of people making ululating a shrill hulahuli sound and playing musical instruments loudly. The ground throbbed, the earth shook with the vibration, the hearts and minds of everyone were aflutter with joyous emotion. The deities on the chariots were also moved by the emotions of their devotees. Lord Jagannath smiled enigmatically.

'The valiant king, who had crushed enemies many a time, now pulled the ropes with humility, like an ordinary devotee. Before the Almighty, all are equal, be it the king, his subjects, the sick and ailing, rich or poor, big or small. One crore people chanted in unison, "Oh God rescue us from our mundane, sorrowful life and help us to surmount our difficulties!" The chariots moved from the Niladri Sikhara to Sharadhabali gathering a cloud of dust. Without this, there would not be any respite for the world. "You are immobile, unmovable like a mountain. Even Lord Brahma has no clue about your invisible feet. If you do not move on your own, nobody can move you even an inch farther." '

'The Dahuka or the announcer, who was holding a cane and sitting at the front of the chariots called out loudly:

"Jau Ratha jau
Balaganthi thi thau
Vaha chaula khanda nadia
tau tau kari khau"

(Let the chariot move and rest at Balagandi, where they
will quickly eat semi-cooked rice and coconut.)

'The chariot of Jagannath called Nandighosha, moved ahead
on the road, accompanied by the victory cries of the crowd,
who kept heaving their hands towards the sky. The whole world
joined in the ecstasy. The pilgrims who had come from far-off
lands were at a loss. What could they ask the Lord as a boon?
They had all come to Srikshetra to ask for many things, but
one look at the Lord and everything was forgotten. All sorrow
and pain vanished; death seemed to be sweet as nectar. Saint
Shankar Deva, too, had forgotten everything after beholding
the wooden deities and had prayed:

"Na baijache rajyan na cha kanaka manikya bibhabam,
na jachyehan ramyan sakalajanakamyan baradhutam
sadakale kale pramathapatina gita charito
Jaganntha Swamy nayana pathagami bhabatu me."

(I am not asking to conquer any country. I do not need
gold or precious jewellery or riches. I also do not desire
the most beautiful woman for a bride. The one whom
Lord Maheshwara prays and sings to his glory, I wish
He becomes the guide for my eyes.)

'The mighty king said with quiet fervour, "Let Him guide
me as my archangel."

'The king wondered about this Ruler of All who would so gladly leave his diamond-studded throne, the elaborate rituals conducted in his honour, the lavish feast-like meals served up with sixty-four delicacies every day, simply to appear before his believers on a rainy day on the main road outside his massive temple, to greet them with his wide open embrace; people of all religions, castes and creeds.

'His large benevolent eyes blessed them all, his wide red lips drawn in a gracious smile that spontaneously brought cheer to his devotees' faces. He greatness was so vast that his throne was insignificant compared to the boundless warmth and affection of his devotees.

' "A royal throne can be gained by inheritance or by force," thought the king, "but to rule the hearts of one's countrymen indeed requires enormous sacrifices, dedication and humanity. If Lord Jagannath can forgo his Diamond Throne to reign in the hearts of his beloved devotees, then why cannot I, Narasimha Deva, the mere servitor of Purushottam (another name of Jagannath), follow his example?" And Narasimha Deva tearfully looked at the Lord seated on the chariot and prayed, "Show me the way, O' Lord! Show me the path so that I can remove all the pain and suffering of my countrymen. He chanted with eyes shut, "Jagannath Swamy nayana pathagami bhabatu me."

'Meanwhile, honey poured as rain from the sky in the month of Asadh (July). The Gods were showering their blessings from heaven when suddenly, amidst the ocean of devotees, the king caught a glimpse of a devout Vaishnaivite woman. She was gazing at the deity single-mindedly, lost in devotion as streams of tears poured down her face. "Who was she? Who was that beautiful Vaishnavi? Chandrabhaga?" wondered the king.

'For a fraction of a second her eyes met the king's and

instantly she hid herself, vanishing into the surging crowds. Soon the crowd, vast as the sea, parted in the middle to allow the chariots to move to Balagandi. But there was no trace of the woman. "Was it simply an illusion? Had God made him realize that while the king was praying to Lord Jagannath, he was actually searching for Chandrabhaga in the core of his heart?"

'Lost in the crowd, Chandrabhaga was trembling, body, heart, soul. She had come across the mighty king himself, so close to her, so many times! Like a fool she had abused and condemned him when she was going through the pangs of separation from her beloved husband for so many years! And yet the all-forgiving king had rescued her! He had assured her that he would look after her proper maintenance in the capital city. Alas! if only she could have recognized him then! She would have gathered the soil from beneath his feet and her life would have been redeemed. Due to her alone the king observed a twelve-year sentence of celibacy! He had moved out in disguise to look after her night after night, forsaking the comforts of his palace! One, who serves Lord Jagannath, is also a great and sacred soul. So why did she feel disgraced by his touch?

'When she saw the king up close, pulling the ropes of the chariots, she recognized him. But her joy was offset by her sorrow. That noble soul had been her guest in her leaf-hut that fateful night. Had she known that, she would have smeared the dust of his feet on her head and sung his glory. She was now fully assured that her husband was fine and happy at Konark.

'On that night too she had managed to escape. She had been afraid that the man she then knew as the Mahadandapasha would take her back to the capital. She had walked along the seashore, wondering where she could go thereafter. If she sold her earthen lamps at the holy temple, the king's messengers would recognize her. If taken to the capital, her agony would increase and so would her husband's suffering. For him she was dead, that was acceptable to her. After completion of the Sun Temple at Konark, he would return to his village and would remarry. He would start a new life. He had never lived a conjugal life with Chandrabhaga, why should he then suffer unnecessarily?

'Chandrabhaga's mother-in-law had always cursed her, "Go back to your father's house. Do whatever you want. Remarry if you want. I will send a message to my son that my daughter-in-law has died of cholera. When he comes back, I will find a good and virtuous girl for him and marry him off." Maybe her husband took her for dead. That was good. If she went back to the capital, she would never get her lawful place as his wife, so why should she trouble him by making him feel remorseful?

'While she was thus walking along the shore with no destination or direction, that she came across Mekhala, the devadasi. Dawn was yet to break, but Mekhala had finished bathing in the sea and was about to return. She was chanting a couplet from Sri *Gita Govinda*. Her melodious voice soothed the agitated soul of Chandrabhaga, who stood listening like a hypnotized doe. Taken aback, Mekhala asked her, "Who are you? Why are you alone at this untimely hour?"

'Chandrabhaga replied in a tear-soaked broken voice, "I am helpless. I do not have a place of my own in this world. I do not know where I am heading. I feel blessed listening to your divine song. If I can listen to this song every day, all my pain may disappear."

'Mekhala asked her excitedly, "Will you stay with me? My attendant has quit after marriage. I am searching for a suitable attendant for myself. Will you stay in my house?"

'Chandrabhaga folded her hands in reverence to the

Almighty and said, "Who can defy Lord Jagannath's wishes? My God has understood my plight and has landed me at the perfect place for a safe shelter. What more is there to worry?" So saying, Chandrabhaga followed Mekhala. The Morning Star was just about to melt into the blue expanse of the sky.

'But even at Mekhala's, Chandrabhaga continued to live in hiding, in solitude and spent her time worshipping Lord Jagannath. Lord Jagannath is also called Patitapabana meaning the one who cleanses all sins—devotees who could not get a glimpse of the deity during the annual chariot festival—could not be redeemed of their sins. That is why Chandrabhaga went to witness the chariot procession and it was here that she came across King Narasimha Deva. Her heart could not bear the burden of such happiness and sorrow, thrill and pain, hope and fear. The only man whose actual presence had kindled affection, sweetness and tender emotions within her, and who had defended her honour and her life, was the noble king Narasimha Deva himself, the first servitor of Lord Jagannath!

'Chandrabhaga counted herself fortunate to have gained his sympathy and the opportunity to serve him as well. Despite all this good fortune and his efforts, she was castigated by society; she was so ill-fated that she was deprived of her husband's love and driven out! Strange indeed are the ways of God.'

'Now fleeing the king's eyes, Chandrabhaga escaped to her secluded abode and once again bowed to Lord Jagannath accusing him with tearful eyes "My Lord! For how long will you punish me like this in this mortal world? When will you give me a place at your feet? I am weeping at my good fortune—how ironic that seems!"'

In the lovely play of light and shadow, each and every stone of Konark sprang to life. Each dust particle throbbed with life. Its open-air theatre was showcasing the dance drama of Dharmapada, enacted by local youth. Dharmananda in the role of Dharmapada was extremely sensitive and spectacular. Charles asked Vishnu Maharana, 'Do you know anything about Dharmapada?'

Vishnu Maharana replied sentimentally, 'Dharmapada's existence could be a fact, legend or even folklore, but there is no doubt that each and every artist of Konark is the reincarnation of Dharmapada. It is their sacrifice, dedication and love for the country that is reflected in each of the carved stones of Konark. Alas! Where have those great artists gone! Konark is today being ruined under the cruel hands of time. Who will save it? Who will build another Konark?'

Prachi said passionately, 'Grandfather, Dharmapada is not dead. He is alive in the throbbing of Odisha's heartbeat. I see his shadow every night these days. I hear the sounds of his chisel and mallet. Every night, the soul of the Konark artist comes to the temple complex to resurrect the ruined temple. Even seven hundred years later, Dharmapada comes to the temple to carve some more.'

Charles laughed. 'Prachiprava, can you kindly arrange a meeting for me with the soul of Dharmapada? I want to learn about the matchless artistic heritage of Konark from him.'

Prachi was offended, 'You do not believe me? If you try to listen carefully in the dead of night, you will be able to hear the noise of chisel and mallet from the temple courtyard. When I keep my windows open I can hear it. Vishnu grandfather is an eyewitness.'

Vishnu Maharana nodded in agreement. He whispered, 'I see him every day. A hazy shadow of a boy of Dharmapada's age. He roams the temple courtyard throughout the night. Sometimes he carves the stones. How could he scale those high iron gates every night, get past the guards and enter the temple courtyard, were he not a ghost? But can a ghost build a new Konark temple?'

Charles asked excitedly, 'Can you introduce me to him? I have some urgent business with him. There could even be a new angle for my research!'

Vishnu Maharana smiled enigmatically and replied, 'No one can meet a ghost face to face. You have to watch him from a distance. He may disappear in your presence.'

'All right, I'll watch.'

'Then wait at the masonry walls of the temple tomorrow, at midnight. I will wait for you on the verandah of Dharmapada Hindu Hotel,' said Vishnu Maharana.

Prachiprava said in a trembling voice, 'Grandfather, I too want to see Dharmapada. I will come after taking permission from uncle.'

'If you have no fear in your mind, then you can also come. Others do not believe me.' Vishnu Maharana said with despair in his voice.

Charles tried to comfort him, 'I also never believed in ghosts. But after coming across that ghost of a woman many times, I believe you.'

'Thank you, Saheb. It does not matter whether you believe in ghosts or not. It will bring stability and peace to your mind for you have begun to trust people. That is enough.' Vishnu Maharana sighed deeply, 'There was not so much mistrust, discontent and betrayal those days!'

Then the curtain rose as the crowd cheered and clapped. A silhouette of the Konark temple in its dazzled against the white background. A plaintive tune was played in the memory of Dharmapada's sacrifice and Prachiprava wondered, 'Why does such a painful memory lurk behind such a beautiful creation of man, it's like the bright moon concealing the darkness. Who knows how many ill-fated men and women like Kamala Maharana and Chandrabhaga sacrificed their blossoming youth for these fine works of art to come into being—who has kept a record of their sacrifices?'

Dharmananda stood before Prachiprava dressed as Dharmapada. Prachi stared at him for a moment, bewildered. Charles congratulated Dharmananda for his outstanding performance and Prachi said affectionately, 'Dharama, I did not know that you possessed such artistic talent. You depicted the sad tale of the making of Konark so sensitively. I had underestimated you till now.'

Dharmapada said shyly, 'Didi, my acting was superficial only. Of course, I love Konark just as Dharmapada did. But for Dharmapada, Konark was his life. While for lowly Dharmananda, Konark serves as a source of livelihood. A great difference,' and he quickly left the place and disappeared into the darkness ignoring the cheering crowd. Prachi knew Dharmananda was unhappy about his life, parents, family, profession and the world at large. Her heart softened for his wretchedness as they walked back.

She and Charles headed again for the Konark Temple a little past midnight, with Dinabandhu Babu's consent. Ganesh, who served at his house, tagged along carrying a stout stick, and a lantern in hand. The surroundings of the temple were already crowded with devotees visiting to take a holy bath in the River Chandrabhaga and attend the sacred Magha Saptami festival on the beach.

Shops, bazaars, lodgings and hotels stayed open late at night. There was nothing to fear. Besides, Dinabandhu and Charukala had immense faith in Charles. They liked the colour of his skin, his mind was fair, bright and open, they would say. He was transparent in his thoughts and expressions, and was clear about what he wanted. He never hesitated to express his feelings for Prachiprava before them. Sometimes he would tease, 'Had Prachiprava been a little more of an extrovert, I would have proposed to her long back.' But it was impossible for a nomad like Charles to marry such an introverted girl, a girl like Lillian would be a better option and so saying, Charles would burst out laughing. Charukala and Dinabandhu would smile too but would keep quiet. Then Dinabandhu would say, 'Prachiprava won't put up with such a jest, Charles! That girl is exceptionally soft-hearted and sensitive. Remember, she does not tolerate any jokes about marriage.'

Charles promised he would talk to Prachi in a measured manner. He kept his word too. Prachiprava and Charles walked side-by-side, engrossed in their deep thoughts about the souls of the dead. Both were inquisitive. Could it be possible that that the spirits of the artists still remained unrequited seven hundred years later, and they still wandered waiting for salvation?

By now the little food vendors and other shops were closed. There were no big hotels, lodgings or market complexes near the temple, lest they interrupt its peace and tranquillity.

Vishnu Maharana was waiting for them on the verandah of the Dharmapada Hindu Hotel. Prachi and Charles came up to him and Vishnu Maharana silently motioned them to dim the flame and hide the lantern behind the stout pole.

Konark temple shimmered in the moonlight and Charles was hypnotized by its heavenly aura. He was least afraid of the speckled shadows, and was not scared of any ghosts. Somehow he felt assured that life would continue and look up. But Prachi was standing transfixed as though in a trance. She was searching for answers to her past, present and future in the stones of Konark. As if her life was bound to the temple by some invisible thread; as if Konark's story was the epic of her own life as well. She bowed to the souls of the artists in reverence. Charles realized how incomplete his life would have remained had he returned without having witnessed such a sight!

Unexpectedly, the moon hid behind a hanging cloud and a thin veil of darkness quickly shadowed the temple of Konark. At that very moment, a silhouette moved along the boundary walls on the western side of the main temple. Vishnu Maharana whispered, 'This is the time of his arrival.' Prachi was perspiring heavily, all her bravado gone; it felt as though the trees, leaves and branches, were all spreading their long dark limbs and advancing towards her. Prachiprava moved closer to Charles and held her breath watching the silhouette. It seemed to have been alerted by something too, and was moving cautiously. The silhouette halted for a moment and scrutinized the stone carvings of the temple. Slight sounds of a chisel and mallet could now be heard. The silhouette was busy at his job.

Charles asked in a low voice, 'I have a powerful camera; I can take a photograph of the shadow, what is the harm.'

Vishnu Maharana replied in a muffled voice, 'No, no. Do not. Do not disturb the peace of that mortified soul. Perhaps he is getting some solace standing atop the ruins of a creation that he built with his blood and sweat. No one can capture the picture of a ghost anyway. Let him wander. What is the harm?'

'I wish I could meet him in person,' said Charles. 'I have a lot of questions.'

As if it could read his mind, the silhouette stepped forward and moved towards the temple of Chhaya Devi. Prachi was numb with fear. In a few moments, it would appear close to them! She retraced her steps, but Charles stood like a rock wall behind her. She did not have the courage to walk. She could not even utter a word to warn Charles. The ghost was coming towards them!

Prachi's ice-cold hands caught hold of Charles's warm hands and she whispered, 'Ch..Charles!' in terror. She could not speak another word. Charles had already taken her in his protective arms, and was whispering assuringly, 'Don't be scared, Prachi, I am here. I always carry weapons for self-defence. I can shoot that ghost if you want, even if it is the spirit of Dharmapada!'

The moon broke free from the grasp of the clouds and a splash of it fell on the shadow. It stood still for a second. Prachi whispered, 'Charles!' once more before fainting against his broad chest. She was pale and cold like ice. The warm body of Charles could not warm her. He gently placed her on the wooden bench of the hotel.

The shadow had disappeared by the time Prachi slowly opened her eyes. Vishnu Maharana had left quite some time back. Charles assured Prachi, 'Look, there is nobody now. He's gone. There's nothing to be scared about, I've come across that ghost many times before. It has never harmed me. What's to fear? I am with you!' Prachi was sitting quietly, stunned at the turn of events, not responding. She looked white as a sheet, her eyes still wide in fear.

A frightened Ganesh commented, 'Didi is under the spell of the ghost now. I had already warned you at the outset.'

At a distance, they saw the glow of an approaching lantern. Someone was coming towards them. Charles held Prachi's hands tightly and tried to comfort her, and also give her some warmth. He thanked the ghost because of whose presence, he had got to hold Prachi's hands, take her in his arms; normally Prachi always kept him at an arm's length, as though he were an untouchable.

Now he said tenderly, 'Prachi calm down, I'm here. Have faith in me. With me around, you don't need to fear anybody. Why are you feeling so helpless?' Her tender hands still shook. She was still not responding, as though some unbearable sight had stifled her voice. Charles had never suspected his composed Prachiprava would ever come apart like this. His male heart throbbed with a strong protective rhythm and he felt he was burning up to just hold her again. But it was not lust he was burning with, it was the passion of love.

Very softly, almost inaudibly, he whispered in her ears, 'Prachiprava! At this moment I realize I am in love with you. I need you desperately. If you think that is audacious of me please pardon me.'

Tears streamed from Prachi's eyes and fell on Charles's hands.

Charles startled, said sadly, 'I am sorry if I've hurt your feelings, I am extremely sorry.' She continued to sob uncontrollably, trying hard to control her tears, but failing. 'Let's go back. You need rest. I take back all that I've said to you.'

Dinabandhu Babu had arrived by then, lantern in hand, and he said to Charles, 'After you left, I felt very uneasy. Prachi is a timid girl. If she gets frightened, there will be problems. As a child she used to fall sick whenever she got scared.'

Charles was remorseful. 'I'm sorry, Prachi is still suffering and scared. I don't know whether she understands my words now, she is not responding to me.' Dinabandhu was very upset and put his hands on her forehead and said, 'Let us go home, there is nothing to fear. Have faith in Lord Jagannath. Everything will be all right.' Prachiprava started weeping uncontrollably once again. Dinabandhu Babu murmured, 'My dear, forget the past.

Learn to live life afresh. Everything will be all right. I knew the view of Konark on a moonlit night would make you cry,' patting her as she wept on his shoulder. A perplexed Charles wondered what could have been in Prachi's past, that caused her so much suffering, and which she did not want to share with anyone.

A few more chapters of the palm-leaf manuscript remained to be read. Charles' had gathered sufficient material for his study. Chitrotpala's marriage and the Chariot Festival were now close. After these events, Charles would return. What remained unfinished, would now never have a beginning either. Because, after this, wherever he travelled, Prachiprava would no longer accompany him.

Since that day, Prachi had been bedridden, sick with fever. The doctor said, 'She went into a state of shock; some serious incident affected her badly.' But what could be the cause?

Charles was sitting by her bedside, Prachi was asleep. She looked ashen and lifeless, like a dry, shrivelled flower.

She opened her eyes and looked up blankly speaking almost in a whisper, 'I saw the shadow. But that ghost did not belong to Dharmapada.' Prachi stopped. She looked at Charles despairingly, 'Charles is it possible?'

Charles got worried and asked, 'Who are you talking about?'

Prachi said faintly, 'It was not Dharmapada, it was Dharmananda that I saw. In the moonlit they appeared identical. Can Dharmapada be Dharmananda?'

Charles laughed and said, 'Is that what's been worrying you—seeing Dharmananda, instead of Dharmapada's ghost? Prachi, you watched Dharmananda play the role of Dharmapada the night before. I think that affected you, and you were still under that influence when you thought you saw Dharmananda the other night. You are attached to both of them so it's not at all strange that both appeared similar to you.'

Prachi hummed to herself, 'If Dharmananda wanted, he could become Dharmapada today. Yet he sells the art of Konark for a livelihood instead,' and she closed her eyes.

Charles said calmly, 'My job here is almost finished, but I'll return home only after you are fully recovered. It was possible to gather so much information about Konark only because of your help. I am so grateful to you.'

Prachiprava did not respond. Charles was like a nomad. She knew he would go away one day. Still, farewells were very traumatic for her. Tears sparkled in secret between her closed eyelids, as she tried to control her emotions. As if those silent tears answered many unanswered questions.

Charles asked her very tenderly, 'May I ask you something?'

Prachiprava opened her eyes and looked at Charles questioningly.

'What lies behind your sorrow?'

'It is so easy to ask about my pain, but it is not so simple to answer in a few words. Let it go, Charles! You are like a bird of the sky, happy and without a care. Do not burden your mind with somebody else's sorrow.'

Charles smiled with tender sadness and said, 'Do you know, Prachi, what my only sorrow is?'

'What?'

'That I do not have any bonds to hold me,' he sighed.

Prachiprava looked at Charles, surprised. She had thought that someone who always appeared to be jovial and lively would have no sorrows to speak of. Was there no life then, without sorrow?

Charles looked at Prachi's tear-filled eyes and said, 'I am alone in this world. There is no one to share the joy of my achievement. If I am killed in an aircrash on my return journey, there is no one to shed a tear for me. Will you understand me Prachi? Will you be able to understand the pain of my footloose, carefree life? You just had a fever and your uncle and aunt stopped eating food, kept awake nights, and kept a vigil over you for so long. You are blessed with so much happiness.'

Prachiprava was filled with sympathy for her foreigner friend, who was longing to be loved. Her heart softened with emotion, she said, 'If I die of this illness, won't you feel sad for me, Charles?'

'May God bless you. You will get well soon. Let's not talk about your misfortune again. I have no words to describe how it will hurt me.'

Prachi said tearfully, 'It will hurt me, as well as uncle and aunt the same way if we hear about your pain or any misfortune. You have become part of our family. Relationships are not restricted to blood, caste, creed, religion, or country.'

'Who am I to you?'

'Every relationship cannot be explained.'

'An aimless life and inexplicable relationships are so tiring.'

'Why don't you take a decision about where your life should be going, and define your relationships? Lillian is still waiting for you in Mumbai,' said Prachi calmly, looking at Charles. Charles remained silent for a while. Then he raised his head skyward and said, 'Forget about Lillian. Let her spirit rest in peace.'

Prachi was startled to hear this, 'What do you mean?'

Charles said sadly, 'You have been sick for over two weeks. The doctor says it is due to shock. That is why I didn't tell you. Lillian is no more. Brush had written to me and informed me before he left India.'

Prachi almost screamed, 'Lillian was like a spark of fire. How could she die such an untimely death? What happened to her?'

Charles replied with bitterness, 'Lillian wanted to enjoy life to the hilt, she overdosed and died asleep on the beaches of Goa. Many of her lovers, including Brush, used her dead naked body and then laughing, dumped her corpse into the sea. Later they got together on the beach and called her a bitch, said she thought of herself as an angel, but showed her true colours fast enough. It was disgusting. Let her soul rest in peace and let her not return to earth and disturb its peace.' Charles hung his head and sat quietly, while Prachi lay stunned, gripped with sorrow.

Charles sighed. His mind was now free of Lillian's thoughts and from all the tragic memories of disgust. He said lightly, 'Lillian is now gone. It is not very difficult for me to imagine a life without her.'

'Then plan a new way of living. At least Lillian is not there anymore to distract you now.'

'I am pretty impressed by family life in India, I'm sure I've reached my destination.'

'Then raise a family soon, Charles! We will also partake in your happiness.'

Charles looked at Prachi straight in the eye, 'Once I used to hate the concept of marriage because my own parents' marriage was a disaster. But Lillian's lonely death and the true loving bonds of your family have convinced me otherwise.'

'Then get married, Charles! We will all be very happy.' Prachi sounded enthusiastic.

Charles found himself unable to express what was on his mind. He had never yet felt at a loss of words. He had never felt any discomfort relating to girls or even married women in his country. He could not understand why he felt so tongue-tied with Prachi. He could not decide what to tell her, and said. 'I'll also be very happy when you get married just as, you are about mine. When are you getting married? If you marry sometime in the near future I'll be fortunate enough to attend it!'

She became pale. Charles had expected just the opposite! He had seen that the topic of marriage always brought a glow to a girl's face in India. There were a couple of framed photograps on the table next to Prachi's bed. One of them was of a smiling girl and looked very old. The girl in the picture looked even paler than Prachiprava.

Pointing to the photograph, Prachi asked, 'Do you know who this girl is, Charles?'

'Who?'

'You tell me.'

'Your friend?'

She just smiled. Then changing the subject she asked, 'Who is the one person you can wait your whole life for?'

'Never heard of waiting for anyone my whole life—be they man or woman, friend or not.'

'But that is the Indian tradition and a distinct characteristic of our culture. Chandrabhaga had also waited for her husband till the end. She was not prepared to accept the kindness of the king himself! That is why she lived as a recluse, as an attendant of a devadasi. And I hide myself in my studies, my research, Dharmananda, Chitrotpala and you. Let me be. In any case, fifteen years of waiting have passed.'

'What!! Fifteen years!' said Charles. 'Who waits fifteen years for someone, and when you're young!' Charles couldn't believe his ears, what a colossal waste!

'The wives of the twelve hundred artists of this land

spent sixteen years of their youth waiting for their husbands. Chandrabhaga's entire life was dedicated to waiting for her husband. There are many such cases of sacrifice and an endless wait in the history of my country,' said Prachi, sadly, but resolute and resigned.

'Times have changed Prachi,' Charles said, desperate to shake her out of this. 'History is just ideologies. Man's history was written in keeping with his notions of happiness, comfort and self-interest. You are pushing yourself to the past! If you face the future but walk backwards, you're going to fall, and often. Life is for living, and living it happily, it's meant to be enjoyed. It's not healthy to search for sorrow and actually treasure it. For whom have you been waiting for all these years? Who is he?'

'My husband.'

Charles was stunned. Prachi went on, 'My hand was given in marriage to him before Lord Jagannath. By the time my eyes met his, he had already become my husband. The large round eyes of Lord Jagannath were witness to our wedding. Can anyone cheat his eyes? Charles! I am confident, he will come back. He does not have the strength to evade Lord Jagannath.' Prachi looked at the sepia-tinted photograph on her table with firm confidence.

Charles followed Prachi's eyes and his gaze remained fixed on the photograph. He had come to her room many times when she was sick and bed-ridden. He had stayed for some time and returned with the doctor after enquiring of her health and medication. But he had never looked at anything in her room, but her.

That day was the first time he was alone with her in her room, that too after seeking Dinabandhu Babu's permission. Now, looking at the photograph of a young man next to Prachi's photograph on the side table, he thought, 'How unreasonable and stubborn of Prachi to wait for such an unimpressive man all her life. There's nothing extraordinary about him.' Charles noted that he was dressed ordinarily, and his eyes and face had a look of distaste and indifference. Articulate and extraordinary Prachiprava seemed no match for him.

Charles asked her, 'Where is your husband now?'

'I have no idea.'

'When will he come back?'

'Only Lord Jagannath knows.'

'Is he lost?'

'Perhaps.'

But what if he does not return... Charles wanted to ask this question but did not. It would hurt her; but what if he did not return? What would she gain out of such waiting! Why did he vanish after marrying a woman like Prachiprava?

Prachi could read Charles's mind. She said, 'Charles! Don't go back to your country with any misconceptions. If you ask Uncle, he will explain everything to you. He trusts you and has enormous affection for you. I am sure you will understand me as well,' and she closed her eyes, exhausted. After many years of silence she had removed a heavy curtain of her life before a foreigner. At least Charles should know that Prachi never hated him. But love was forbidden to her. She was a married woman. She was a stone sculpture of Konark, frozen in an eternal wait! The call of youth had to return after knocking at the door of her heart, and finding it shut.

The fragrance of perfume wafted in from the door. Chitrotpala stood there like a willowy cloud, with a bunch of freshly-plucked tuberoses in her hand, looking beautiful and refreshing. May be she would stop selling flowers the very next day. After that she would bloom herself like a flower in someone's courtyard. As he was stepping out of that room, Charles paused before Chitrotpala. He looked at her appreciatively. 'Chitra, you are looking very beautiful today. Are you very happy?'

Chitrotpala smiled shyly and looked even lovelier, but the very next moment her eyes filled with tears. 'Yes Saheb, I stop selling flowers from tomorrow. The day after, is the day of the holy bath in the Chandrabhaga River. I will not come here anymore. The courtyard of Konark temple, the vast beach of Chandrabhaga river, the casuarina jungle—I will now visit them only in my dreams. I may not be here, but my heart, soul and mind will be around the temple. I have known Konark, played around here from my birth. Konark is my teacher, my protector. It has supported me financially. How can I forget it? I will also never forget you and my Didi. She is sick. That is why I came here to meet her for the last time.'

She wiped away her tears with her pallu.

Charles took the bunch of flowers from her hand and told her, 'I will also never forget you, Chitra! Like India, you too are unforgettable.' He took out a hundred rupee note and handed it over to her. Chitrotpala pulled her hand away, 'No, no. I am not selling flowers today. I have sold enough flowers. This is my gift to you.'

Charles looked at the small knot in the pallu in which Chitrotpala had tied a few notes and some loose change, and said, 'I have accepted your gift, but this money is also my gift for you. Your flowers do not cost that much. Please accept my gift.'

Chitrotpala's eyes filled with tears. She said, 'You have always given me a lot, much more than my flowers were worth; I earned more this year than ever before, only because of you. I can never repay your debt in this lifetime. You are like an elder brother to me. Wherever I may be, I will always have regard for you.'

Charles was overwhelmed. He had never known the love and affection of siblings or a family. His heart was touched by the love and affection of the innocent village girl. He said affectionately, 'Chitra as an elder brother it's my duty to help you. So if I've done something for you, how are you indebted? Besides, I only paid you for the flowers. Whatever gift I give, I will give it when I see you dressed as a bride. And that gift will be a surprise. You look really beautiful dressed as a bride!'

Chitrotpala, bashful, brightened with happiness. She said softly, 'That will be my good fortune, Saheb! You will attend my wedding that's enough for me. I do not want any other gift.'

Charles nodded. 'I'll be there, I'll definitely come to your wedding and I'll take photographs. The film stars in my country will be so jealous, your photographs will put them to shame. I'll hold an exhibition of your wedding photographs!'

Chitrotpala could not follow everything Charles said and shyly laughed. Charles looked at her adoringly but wondered, 'Why is she so sad, now that she's getting married—marriage was her one dream and it's coming true,' nevertheless he wished her, 'Chitrotpala be happy. You have always seemed a source of boundless joy to me. May grief never touch your soul.'

'Move Charles!' said Prachi, 'I also want a glimpse of Chitra before she is married off. I will not get an opportunity to see her as a girl again.' Charles stepped aside and Chitrotpala came and stood by Prachi's bed, with Charles behind her. Prachi sat up, her eyes full of joy and filled with blessings for Chitrotpala, thinking, 'How different the real world is from a bride's rosy dreams! Let Chitra be happy, absolutely joyful; let there be no sorrow in Chitra's life, even for a day. May Jagannath keep this gentle girl always cheerful and bless her with fulfilment and peace!' Chitra stooped to touch Prachi's feet, almost sobbing for she was going to part from Prachi. 'I am going, Didi! This is our last meeting. I do not know whether it is happiness or sorrow. But you will not forget me, will you?'

Prachi hugged her and planted a kiss on her cheek, overwhelmed with emotion. 'You are unforgettable Chitra! How can I ever forget you? Lead your life with faith in Lord Jagannath. Never think of yourself as a nobody, never demean yourself. You will find He will make you happy. This much I can wish for you because of your attachment to me.'

Chitra burst into tears, 'Didi! I wish I could sell flowers at the temple forever, keep getting your affection; I would have been happy just thinking about getting married. The days would have passed. God knows why I am beginning to feel very scared about my future. I've heard in-laws torture brides a lot and make their life hell. Even though we are poor and very often I don't get two meals a day in my father's house, I am better off. How can I be guaranteed a happy life there when my in-laws are forcing my father to cough up so much dowry?'

'Don't talk like that, Chitra! I am sure nobody will ever torture you. Not even in hell.'

Chitra wiped away her tears and bent to touch Charles's feet as well and said, 'I am leaving for a nightmare, Saheb! This is our last meeting. If I survive, I will always remember you.'

Charles became serious, he had understood every word that Chitra had spoken. Even now for girls like Chitra, the in-law's house was hell. He had read about the torture and murder of daughters-in-law so frequently in the newspapers. Chitrotpala's fears were justified. She could have continued selling flowers, would have fallen in love and would have survived. Why did she decide to get married at all, wondered Charles.

Chitrotpala left. Before evening she would sell the rest of her flowers and go back to her village. It was difficult to move through the crowd at Konark because of the Magha Saptami festival of holy dip at River Chandrabhaga. In a few moments her flower-basket would be empty and she would take leave of Konark. She would touch the sculptures for the last time.

Charles's thoughtful stare followed Chitrotpala as she went through the door. He continued staring at the door long after she left, thinking how the kind of simple affection that Chitrotpala expressed had become so rare among human beings. Had he been give such warmth at any time in his life, he would never have ended up so footloose.

Man craves freedom and many will cheerfully place their burdens and dissatisfactions upon others if they feel that will make them happy. But not Dinabandhu Babu. He had always blamed himself for Prachi's marriage and for her tragic life. Charukala would say, 'Who can go against the wishes of Lord Jagannath? Everything hinges on fate.'

Years ago Dinabandhu Babu had come across a former student Jagannath who was a poor orphan but a meritorious one, well behaved and always respectful. Moving on from Konark High School, Jagannath had enrolled in a local college but continued to face tremendous financial hardship. He worked at whatever odd jobs he could, but with his widowed mother and younger sister also dependent on him, he usually never had enough money for his college fees. So he dropped out, decided to earn enough and then safely give wing to his academic dreams.

By the time Jagannath was a matriculate he had turned twenty. He often worried that his dream of studying further would remain unfulfilled, but ploughed on valiantly turning to the temple of Konark for work as a part-time guide. His sister was nearing the age of marriage and he still hoped, at times, that he would be able to save once he had married her off, and acquire a graduation degree. Only then, he felt, would he be able to explain the exceptional craftsmanship of Konark to the tourists in a professional manner.

Sometimes he would reveal his thoughts to his friends. But they would make fun of him, 'What are you going to get with a degree at thirty? You'll be past your prime!' Jagannath would retort, 'Not for a job, I'll study for knowledge. I'll learn foreign languages and describe Konark to foreigner visitors in a much better way. I'll explain how Konark is a place of sacrifice, sanctity and dedication, not for erotic visual pleasure. Konark is not a ruined temple. It symbolizes the soul of a great nation, a country and a culture. Only then will they be able to enjoy and understand the heavenly beauty of the Sun Temple.'

Jagannath was passionate about the beauty of the Sun Temple's carvings but he never, unlike the other guides, sought to make a fast buck by describing the erotic couples at the temple and making cheap comments. He would narrate the tantric and religious elements behind those erotic images, his expression animated, his love and regard for the temple's long-gone artists manifestly evident. His deep philosophical insights impressed some tourists. But the ordinary tourist did not come to Konark to acquire deeper knowledge of its history, twelfth-century social life, religion, martial skills and administration.

And so, Jagannath was never a crowd puller. Only research scholars, or tourists eager for knowledge, sought his company. He would lose himself in the tales and history attached to the Sun Temple and would stop only when his guests were satisfied. He never charged them a hefty fee and that is why perhaps his condition never improved. He found it tough to meet his little family's daily needs, let alone saving enough to marry off his sister and continue his studies later.

Jagannath was a favourite with Dinabandhu Babu, who had observed him since he was a child. He had never come across another boy like Jagannath in the locality. He was impressed by the way he presented Konark to the tourists. Dinabandhu had written a poem on Konark which Jagannath had memorized and often recited it before his audience, explaining its meaning. Sometimes, Jagannath would visit Dinabandhu Babu and teach the alphabet and numbers to Dinabandhu Babu's son Dinesh who was then just beginning to learn. He would take him around the temple courtyard in his arms. He had immense regard for Dinabandhu Babu and would lay bare many of his dreams before him. Dinabandhu Babu's encouragement somewhat helped to relieve his burden.

One day Dinabandhu Babu asked him suddenly 'Jagannath, will you study in a college?' Jagannath was astonished. His father-figure, the teacher, was aware of his dream! He also knew that such a dream would remain just that. Jagannath did not reply. Dinabandhu said, 'This year you enrol in college. I will take care of your expenses. You can work as a guide during the holidays. In four years' time you will be able to graduate. If you do well, it won't take a miracle to win a scholarship for post-graduation. And I feel my niece Prachi will be a suitable bride for you. She is pretty and scholastic and will make a good wife for you. That I can vouch for. What do you say?'

Jagannath looked at his benefactor in dismay. What was the meaning of such generosity? Was he being exploited in return for all the kindnesses shown to him? His sister had recently committed suicide because Haramohan Babu had promised to improve their lot and had duped the family. Haramohan Babu was quite influential and well known to his family. He worked as a social worker and had lots of contacts in the city. When he visited the family, he promised Jagannath's mother he would find a suitable groom for her daughter. Harmohan was close, almost like a son and often brought several proposals from prospective grooms. He also said he would shoulder all the wedding expenses. There were no reasons why anyone would doubt his intentions.

One day Haramohan Babu had come with a proposal, 'The groom is a busy officer. It is not possible for him to come to Junei village all the way from Bhubaneswar just to have a glimpse at the prospective bride. The girl has to go to Bhubaneswar. The groom wants a beautiful girl. He will definitely like Gouri.'

Haramohan had brought a taxi. So Gouri and Jagannath accompanied him to Bhubaneswar. The taxi stopped in front of a palatial two-storied building. The matriculate Jagannath of Junei village shouted in surprise, 'But this is a hotel!'

Haramohan Babu smiled, 'These days everything takes place in a hotel—choosing a bride, job interview, literary meet, discourses on religion, weddings, thread ceremony, feasts, anything. It will look indecent to take the girl directly to the boy's house. That is why I have hired a room on rent. It might be expensive, but the image of our daughter should be protected. Let everything be finalized. In this manner, they cannot humiliate her later.'

Jagannath was overwhelmed with gratitude. Haramohan Babu was a true friend! So concerned about the honour of someone else's daughter! He made up his mind to campaign for Haramohan Babu in the forthcoming elections.

Gouri stepped out of the car nervously. She looked beautiful even with minimal make-up. Now fate would be kind to her. She would have a life of her own. Haramohan Babu sent Jagannath to his residence in Bhubaneswar, 'Go and take rest. Who knows when they will arrive? What will you do here? They may reject your sister when they see you. They think Gouri is my sister. That is why they have agreed to this proposal.'

Jagannath felt bad. He compared his dirty and crumpled clothes with the snow-white dhoti and kurta of Haramohan. He decided that Haramohan Babu was right. What was the harm if he stepped aside for his sister's future? He ate rice and dal at Haramohan Babu's place and then rested on a wooden cot in the outer room. Hopefully he would soon be freed from the burden and responsibility of his sister's marriage! If it was destined, he could even study further. There would be nothing to worry about anymore!

As he dozed off, the bugs started biting as if warning him, 'Wake up, get up, life cannot be this easy,' and Jagannath tossed and turned impatiently the entire afternoon. Gouri and Haramohan did not return that day or the next. Three days later, they all returned to the village. Haramohan said, 'Not one, I brought five prospective grooms to have a look at Gouri. It is expensive to bring the girl so frequently to Bhubaneswar! One party may agree, provided she gives her consent. That is essential these days.'

Jagannath looked at his sister expectantly, why shouldn't she agree? Gouri looked lifeless like the pale moon. She hid her face in her veil and was absolutely quiet. Her eyes met Jagannath's and two large tears rolled down her eyes. She looked away and tried to check her tears. Gouri was crying because her marriage had almost been fixed, thought Jagannath. It was natural for girls to do so. He was very happy for her. His sister would get married.

Haramohan continued, 'Gouri is completely rustic. But they have chosen her for her beauty. In every other respect she is unfit for today's lifestyle. Let us see what happens!' When they reached home, Gouri wept continuously holding on to her mother. Everybody knew that her marriage was fixed. All praised Haramohan Babu. He continued to smile and kept saying, 'This is my duty. Gouri's father was a freedom fighter who went to jail many times for the sake of his motherland. If we do not look after his daughter, who will? Poor Gouri, let her be happy and lead her life in peace!'

The next morning, Gouri's dead body was found floating in the village pond. She had committed suicide and left a note behind saying, 'Nobody is responsible for my death. I have lost my moral strength to live. That is why I am leaving.'

Haramohan Babu stunned everybody by saying, 'Gouri was involved in an illegitimate affair. She was not agreeing to the marriage. That is why she chose this path!'

The simpleton Jagannath could not understand why a sentimental girl like Gouri should lose her mental strength to live. It was much later that he realized that it was Haramohan who was responsible for his sister's death. But he did not have any proof. Since then Jagannath had always mistrusted anyone who came forward to help him of their own accord.

Dinabandhu continued, 'I know you are wondering why I am trying to help you. I have always had a weakness for meritorious students and have tried to help brilliant and poor students in whatever way I can. Also, I treat you as my son. Your father's noble character, his sacrifice and love for the country have influenced me tremendously. If I can be of any help in fulfilling your life's dream, his immortal soul will bless my son from heaven.'

Gratitude rendered Jagannath speechless and tears flowed copiously down his cheeks. He enrolled himself in college in an Honours course in English, and Dinabandhu financed his studies for four years. Jagannath earned money in his spare time to sustain himself, and ended up topping the University in his final year. Dinabandhu decided to send him to Delhi for his post-graduation. He could learn a few foreign languages there and earn as much as he wanted. Dinabandhu's dream for Jagannath's future was beginning to come to fruition.

Jagannath belonged to the warrior clan of the Paikas, his forefathers had fought against the Muslims during the Ganga Era. They had also fought the British soldiers. Jagannath's father, Niranjana, had gone to jail for participating in Gandhiji's famous Salt Satyagraha during the independence movement. By the time he was released and came home, his wife had become old and he himself was fifty-four and ailing. Jagannath and Gouri were born at this juncture. His father died when Jagannath went to primary school, and Satyabhama his widowed mother, had to fend for the whole family. They were a poor but reputed family. Dinabandhu knew Jagannath would never be a disgrace to him. That is why he became very close to Jagannath and showered his affection on him.

For Jagannath, an M.A. degree was a distant dream. He was now a graduate, could speak fluently in English and that should be enough, he consoled himself. His friends and relatives, too, agreed. His sister was dead. When he was still completing graduation his mother had died. He could earn some money working as a guide at the temple premises. But Dinabandu Babu stood in the way. He told him firmly, 'You will complete your post-graduation and that too at Delhi University. If you wish, you can also learn a few foreign languages there. Your dreams are not yet over. Get ready. The rest is up to me. Two years may alter your whole life.'

Jagannath said reluctantly and humbly, 'It pains me to be an unnecessary burden on you. You have your family to look after too. The burden will only increase, it will never lessen!' Dinabandhu Babu sighed, 'I have only one son, Dinesh. He is in school now. Is this a family? Dinesh is my son. If he studies well, he will prosper. But the person who could have been a burden is no more a responsibility.'

His daughter Anupama had been married to a doctor, a handsome man from a well-off family. But after the wedding they came to know that Anupama's husband was involved with a staff nurse called Sushama. By then Anupama was pregnant. Dr Nilakantha told her, 'Go back to your father's home. I will marry Sushama. I can't live without her.'

'Then why did you marry me?' wept Anupama.

Nilakantha retorted, 'I was forced by my father. He would not have agreed to this proposal if your father had not given such a hefty dowry. After a few years my father would have bowed to my wishes. Your father is responsible for my condition today. That is why he has to shoulder your responsibility. Along with you he has to take care of your unborn child too.'

Dinabandhu had then received a letter from his son-in-law that his daughter Anupama was returning to his house for good. A few days later Anupama died from severe burns and it could never be established for sure whether it was an accident, a murder, or whether she had committed suicide. Seeing Dinabandhu Babu's tear-filled eyes, Jagabandhu said, 'I agree with you. But I won't be able to repay your debt even in seven lives!'

The date for his departure for Delhi was fixed. Dinabandhu told him suddenly, 'You must get married before you leave for Delhi. By the time you come back after finishing your studies, it will be too late.'

'Marriage?' Jagannath almost screamed. He had never thought of his own marriage. After his sister's death he had become scared of marriage and openly scorned the possibility—who would marry an orphan like him?

Dinabandhu continued, 'I know you well. I have treated you as my own. It is thus my duty to get you married. I want to forget the tragedy and guilt of my daughter Anupama's death by marrying off my niece Prachiprava to you. I am responsible for my only daughter's death because I had judged Nilakantha on his family reputation, his educational qualifications and his good looks. After my daughter's death, I have considered Prachiprava as my daughter. If I can get her to a good husband, I can redeem my sins.'

Dinanabdhu Babu had mentioned Prachi and her marriage to Jagannath much earlier, but since nothing had happened since then, Jagannath had thought no more of it. Now he felt cheated. Dinabandhu Babu had not educated him selflessly, there had always been a secret motive behind Dinabandhu and Charukala's affection, help and graciousness. They had been nurturing him carefully as the prospective husband for their niece, Prachiprava. He was disgusted. Could there never be a relationship without an ulterior motive? His education paid for by Dinabandhu Babu, was the dowry given to him in advance. Nevertheless, he agreed for he was indeed grateful.

It was a simple ceremony before Lord Jagannath as witness. Prachi leaned onto Charukala. Her small soft hands were put into his already hard and coarse hands. Jagannath's resentment melted at once with that touch. What was the harm in accepting destiny in the auspicious presence of the Almighty Lord Jagannath?

A few soft words from Charles had rekindled all those old memories in Prachiprava's mind. She ignored the memories of her marriage, husband, and wedding night, and had concentrated only on the two large round eyes of Lord Jagannath, expanding to contain the whole Universe. She had been just thirteen and still in school. She had gone to Puri with her uncle, aunt, brother and sister-in-law. She wore a new sari and put on new ornaments. Only when she reached Puri, did she learn about the wedding. The groom's name was Jagannath. He was studious, well-behaved, of good character. He would leave for Delhi for higher education after his marriage. His future was bright and promising. Prachiprava was like a puppet and took whatever God and the elders gave, as being for her good.

On their wedding night a frightened Prachiprava looked at her husband, Jagannath. He was dark, well-built with a firm expression on his face. He looked unmoved, like Lord Jagannath. She felt like worshipping him. But she was also terrified of the unknown. Jagannath, too, had become rude and rough with the various struggles he had to overcome. Yet somewhere, there was a soft, human side to him. Jagannath embraced his bride lovingly, and found himself embracing a thin, emaciated body and pulled away at once.

'How old are you?' he asked.

'Thirteen,' she replied.

He was filled with remorse and pain. The erotic images at Konark mocked at him. Filled with sorrow and shame he said disgusted, 'Stupid! Had I known how young you were, I would never have touched you. Your uncle told me you were eighteen. I am twenty-eight. Forgive me Prachi. I feel ashamed to force myself and hurt you. Go to sleep. You are tired. I will sleep outside. It is extremely hot inside the room. I feel suffocated.'

Prachiprava could not understand her husband that day. She was actually very tired. She immediately went off to sleep. Outside, Jagannath sighed heavily.

The next morning there was no trace of Jagannath. He was gone.

There was a letter lying by Prachi's bedside. It said, 'This world is beautiful and is being renewed always with the meeting of a man and woman. But that meeting should not be a lustful union. Prachiprava, an ideal groom's age does not matter to your uncle. But if I live close to you, I may turn into an animal with a man's lusty desires. I don't want that. Konark has taught me about restraint and self-negation. That is why I am leaving you behind. You are not yet of marriageable age. I have made a mistake by marrying you. You can deny this marriage. Even if you accept me one day, I will be too old by then. Marriage will become a compromise. Prachiprava, become highly qualified yourself, braving the social discriminations against women. Only then can my sister's soul be redeemed. I am leaving to search for ways of selfless service to mankind. If I find my destination, I will come back. Please forgive me for my faults, committed unknowingly. Goodbye.' It was signed, 'Your well-wisher, Jagannath.'

Prachi read that letter over and over, but could not understand anything at first. But when she did, her heart softened for Jagannath, filled with regard and reverence. Her soul was content. Jagannath was not a beast, he was a noble man. She had taken a vow to prove her own worth to him one day. She did not blame her uncle. His genuine concern for Prachi's future had made him act that way, she conceded.

Some said Jagannath had become a family man. Others said

he had become a celibate, a sanyasi and that he roamed all over the world spreading the message of universal brotherhood, unity, peaceful coexistence, harmony and fraternity. He campaigned for the soul of India through the message of Lord Jagannath.

Prachiprava remained unaffected by the news regarding her husband. It was difficult to fathom whether she was waiting for him or she had already forsaken his memory. Every bit of news regarding him had been proven false in the past fifteen years. Only Dinesh had informed them in a letter that Swami Jagannath was a celibate and was admired by all as a 'Mahatma'. He was an Indian, but it was difficult to know if he was from Odisha. He was fluent in many languages. When asked about his origin, he would reply, 'The entire world is my motherland. I am a human being by caste. God is my parent. The animals, insects, all are my friends, relatives.' He had no permanent home but roamed like a nomad, wrote Dinesh, adding that he was hailed for his wisdom and his discourses on every religion. Whenever asked for his address, he would say, 'Wherever I am, that is my address.'

If he was Prachiprava's husband and if he would ever come back to Odisha, how would she receive him? What would he give her? Dinabandhu and Charukala blamed themselves for Prachi's fate. But she was nonchalant.

Thirteen

—

The seventh day of the bright fortnight of the month of Magha was the day of the birth of Lord Surya. A holy dip in the river Chandrabhaga on this day cleanses one's sins. Numerous pilgrims, devotees and tourists had thronged to the river Chandrabhaga to take part in the auspicious event. Lord Iswareshwara, Tribenishwara and Dakshineshwara had graced the site of the colourful fair. There were strings of shops, make-shift bazaars. The commotion contaminated the ambiance of Konark. But its tranquillity remained intact.

Children and old people waited on the beach in the biting cold of February for the sun to rise. The night of waiting was slowly coming to an end. Charles was an engrossed witness. It was a moment that would forever remain in his memory.

Daybreak was marked by loud bhajans and kirtans and the bustling of gathered devotees. The deities were given a holy bath in the sacred water, after which the pilgrims went in for their dip. Dinabandhu Babu was also taking a holy dip in the river, chanting mantras. Charles repeated these mantras after him. He had become one among the frenzied crowd, his own identity merged in the surroundings. He was simply a human being now. He was a worshipper of the Sun God, who made no distinction among people, in the land of the Sun.

Seven hundred years ago, Narasimha Deva, the invincible king of Kalinga, a devotee of the Sun God, had laid the foundation stone for his tutelary deity and it was to become the portal of mankind. Konark seemed more beautiful to Charles that day. Perhaps, he had understood the real meaning of Konark by then!

The eastern horizon turned crimson. Eager eyes were glued to the edge of the red sky anxiously. From the endless spread of the blue sky, a burning red ball of flame began to appear slowly. The crowd became ecstatic. The riverbed throbbed with cheering crowds, chanting the names of the gods and ululating. The orange ball leapt and rose above the horizon and the sky now embraced the dawn. Charles was spellbound at the spectacular sunrise over the river.

After the early morning worship, the pilgrims returned to Konark. Charles, Prachi, Dinabandhu Babu and Charukala went along. Prachi, who had just bathed in the river, looked fresh and enchanting. Charles could not take his eyes off her. He broke the silence, 'Have you now recovered? Only a few chapters of the manuscripts remain to be read. I am eager to learn about Chandrabhaga's fate now. Only twenty days are left for Chitratpola's wedding. After these two events, I will visit Puri for the Chariot Festival. I can have a glimpse of the Patitapabana riding the chariot in the open road. During the Rath Yatra, many holy men come to Puri. If your husband turns up as well, I will consider myself fortunate to meet him.'

Prachi was disinterested and said, 'My aunt and uncle have been visiting Puri for the past fifteen years to spot him. They consult seers and monks for my husband's whereabouts without any results. They believe he will come back one day. How long can he evade Lord Jagannath, they ask.'

'You also believe that?'

'That is what keeps me sane and alive. Or else I too would have gone astray like Lillian. What can you say of a human heart?' and she smiled. Charles wondered how Prachi could talk about the hard facts of life so effortlessly! She continued, 'As per my knowledge when sorrows come to an end, the soul gains salvation and attains nirvana when all desire is satiated. If any desire is unfulfilled, one has to go though rebirth many times on this sinful earth. I am sure Lillian has attained her "nirvana". She is freed of all bondage.' She glanced sideways at Charles. His face looked disturbed with unfulfilled desire.

'Charles! Gratification of your desires does not assure complete fulfilment and does not guarantee enjoyment. In surrender lies the real joy. Can you show me a man completely at peace with himself? Lillian's soul must be wandering too in emptiness. You are more sensitive, you will realize how discontented she was,' said Prachi, and walked ahead leaving Charles behind.

The casuarina jungle became denser. A crowd had gathered in the forest beside the roadside to the right. The tourists who were returning had joined the crowd. Charles presumed there was another holy site in there. After taking a dip in the holy river one had to gather some virtue! One had to visit that holy site! The crowd was surprisingly silent. Some elderly pilgrims were uttering 'Héy Ram' and moving away, closing their eyes. Prachi asked one of them, 'What's happened?'

'Kalyug! It is all kalyug,' murmured one of them, and turned his face away. A police van drove up and halted and some officers got down from the vehicle. The crowd split. Prachi and Charles followed the policemen out of curiosity and were horrified by what they saw. There lay Chitrotpala dead, naked and her body bruised. Her sari lay at a distance. The bundle of her hard-earned money which she had tied to her pallu, was missing. The payals on her feet, the silver bangles she wore on her hands, the gold nose pin, everything was gone. The tender tip of her nose was injured and was swollen with clotting blood. Her whole body bore the marks of a terrible and barbaric physical assault. 'Rape, and murder followed by theft,' said the police. Chitrotpala, who was on her way back had fallen prey to those devils. She had fought to save herself. Some boot marks were clearly visible nearby. Charles took Prachi's cold, lifeless hand in his hands as she screamed, 'Oh my God....' He pulled her away to the road and walked away speedily. She was in shock and murmured, 'The climax of sexual desires releases one's soul in salvation. Did Chitrotpala too achieve her nirvana?'

Charles's face looked pale with pain and sorrow. Dharmananda stood leaning against a tree. Seeing Charles, he said, 'I would have taken the wedding photographs of Chitrotpala. You had asked me to. It was not to be. I had taken her photographs before the police reached the spot. I will give them to you. You were advising me that people prosper in life if they are honest and obey rules, regulations, rites and rituals. What happened in the end? Unfortunate girl, if she gave away her savings and offered herself to those brutes, she could be alive today!' and Dharmananda burst into heart-rending wails, like a child.

Charles walked away. Without Chitrotpala, Konark was deserted for him despite the crowd. In the morning air, a distant, obscure cry pulled at Prachiprava's soul. She sat down at the entrance of the Konark temple, exhausted, at the spot where Chitrotpala used to sell her flowers. Tears, so far gathered in the corners of her eyes, flowed freely. She murmured inaudibly, 'For sexual gratification, man can become a brute. Can the path to salvation be so ghastly and so frightening?'

Charles accepted defeat and hung his head in sadness. One comes across all sorts of distress in life. Charles too had suffered distress many times since childhood. But Chitrotpala's cruel inhuman murder had upset him completely. Ever since he'd been in Konark he had known Chitrotpala. The relationship was sacred, pure and without any expectations. He would remember her forever. And yet she slipped away. He knew that such murders happened quite frequently, but he had never been so devastated. As if Chitrotpala was a part of his family! Unknowingly, she had occupied a corner in Charles's heart. Could anyone feel so distressed for others? Charles discovered this fact for the first time in his life. He had discovered that feeling in himself on the soil of India.

Before he could recover from Chitrotpala's tragic death, another tragedy occurred. But Prachi was the most devastated—Dharmananda was taken into police custody. He was arrested on charges of theft of ancient sculptures from the Konark temple. The case against him was irrefutable. He had been entering the temple complex secretly every night and removing the small statues exquisitely carved with copulating images. These were the decorative, carved statues he used to sell. That night some people caught him red-handed with the sculptures and handed him over to the police. When Dharmananda was asked he had replied straightforwardly, 'I am not a thief. I simply carry out orders. I get a small commission but my masters get a large profit.'

'Who are they?'

Dharmananda kept quiet. He refused to answer.

When the news arrived, Prachi went to the police station. Who else would provide bail for him! Dharmananda's father refused to leave home out of shame. His mother was wailing uncontrollably. Prachi had thought of Dharmananda as her own son and now she came to rescue him. The moment she looked at him she broke down in tears. 'I know you are involved in the smuggling. I have seen you in the temple courtyard at midnight. I thought I had seen Dharmapada in you that night. And you were roaming around night after night to construct a temple at Konark. Today you are the iconoclastic Kalapahad in my eyes. You have become well-off selling the artefacts of your own country. Had you dreamt you would become rich in this manner? You are a traitor. Dharmananda, I am very ashamed of you.'

Dharmananda had no sense of sorrow, shame or fear. He retorted, 'Kalapahad was not a criminal. The society that transformed him into Kalapahad is responsible. I need a career to live like a human being and have two proper meals a day. I have done just that much. They've become rich. In what way have I gained beyond securing two proper meals a day?'

'Who are they, Dharmananda?'

'I was warned not to reveal their names.'

'If you do not disclose them, you will be punished. But they will continue to flourish in society as respectable citizens.'

'If I tell their names, my family and I will be finished.'

'If you do not tell, society will be destroyed.'

'I am not bothered if society is destroyed. I have no place in this society.'

'You will live Dharamu, I promise you. If you speak the truth, you will be released with honour. The real culprit will be punished. I will fight the case for you.'

'Will you spend that much money for me?'

'Not I but Charles will bear the expense. He will write to his father. He has opened a social welfare organization there with the help of Indians. That organization spends a lot for the development of Indian society.'

Dharmananda laughed sarcastically, 'The people who are selling these antiques and the ones buying them abroad will never be caught. Corruption is deep-rooted here. Nothing can happen. Only my family will be destroyed.' Prachi was visibly irritated, 'Dharamu, you are unjust. It is a criminal offence to protect those who are trading with India's heritage.'

Dharmananda laughed again, 'Chitrotpala never committed any injustice and was never wrong. She never took a single paisa more than what her flowers cost. She was pure. Why did she die? And such a ghastly and barbaric death? Can you answer why?' and tears rolled down his face. He was least concerned or sad about his own impending fate. Yet sorrow over the manner of Chitrotpala's death still brought tears to his eyes. Neither Prachi nor Chitrotpala knew that Dharmananda had a soft corner for Chitrotpala.

As time passed almost everybody forgot about Chitrotpala and the manner of her death. Her murderers were still at large. Dharmananda was unable to forget her. Prachi would cajole him affectionately, 'Dharamu, everything exists in our world, be it sin or virtue, truth or lies. If you argue about sin and lies, society will not change. One particle of truth may expose and uproot many untruths. If you reveal at least one name, many things will come out into the open about the smugglers.' Dharmananda remained silent for a while, and then said almost inaudibly, 'I am afraid.'

'Of whom?'

'There may be a threat to the lives of my parents and my siblings, and my own life too. Can you assure me protection?'

'I promise you. That responsibility is mine. I am sure truth will triumph. You will be released on bail tomorrow. The rest is up to me. Charles has promised me. There won't be any shortage of money to fight the case.' Dharmananda replied firmly, 'I will tell you Didi, I will tell you everything I know. If they can escape by lying why should not I ensure my life by telling the truth? I do not know whether God will be pleased by my action, but will you be satisfied?'

Prachi's eyes filled with tears. Her heart went out to the poor, talented boy who had grown up through poverty and pain into a hardened soul but yet softened due to her softly convincing him. Prachi understood that in this world there was at least one person who valued her words; she had not been totally rejected because her husband had left her!

She came out of the police station glowing with confidence. When she had entered, her heart had been filled with contempt for Dharmananda. Now that was gone. Dharmananda's words echoed in her ears. 'A society which gives birth to such Kalapahadas, is the real culprit.' Kalapahada was a victim of his situation! But the next morning there was no need to release Dharmananda on bail. His freedom-seeking soul had already been released from the bondage of his body under mysterious circumstances. The previous night, his father had been informed that his son had escaped from jail. Two policemen came to his house to search for him. The next morning Dharmananda's corpse was found on the Marine Drive road hanging from an electric pole with his face downwards. Those who had seen Dharmananda's dead body said, 'There were injury marks due to beatings on his whole body. His neck showed clear marks of the fingers that suffocated him to death.'

There was no scope for a post mortem. Dharmananda's father had immediately cremated his body. Some leaders and important persons had come forward to help financially with the cremation, donating Rs 1000 to the father. The sorrow of losing a son faded before their magnanimity. The old man consoled himself, 'At least he got my daughters married off. Now the boys can manage somehow. Dharmananda is dead, but Konark is still there. What is there to worry?'

By the time Prachi got the news it was too late. When she reached the cremation ground Dharmananda's short life of pain and misery was at an end, his long-suffering body having survived many struggles, had been reduced to a handful of ashes. Dharmananda's soul, which was committed to reveal the truth, had left behind its mortal body for the path of truth. It was free. Prachi blamed herself. Although it was true that Dharmananda had been murdered because he agreed to reveal the truth, she had no proof.

It was a memorable sunrise on the shores of the sacred Chandrabhaga. The morning sun was coming out of the sea to accept felicitation and greetings on his birthday. His first rays would touch the idol on the diamond throne at Konark and would bring with it a glorious seven-coloured rainbow. Numerous devotees waited for the holy event.

Charles could never forget that sunrise on Magha Saptami at Chandrabhaga because the memories of Chandrabhaga were involved. His stay at Konark was coming to an end. Vishnu Maharana's readings had completed the construction process of the Konark temple. All hope, curiosity and enthusiasm had died within Charles following the tragic deaths of Chitrotpala and Dharmananda. Whatever little remained only sought to know what happened to Chandrabhaga and Kamala Maharana in the end. Only that would bind him to Konark. After that he would continue his life as a nomad once again.

Fourteen

⌒

Vishnu Mahrana cleared his throat and began the closing chapters of the palm-leaf manuscript. Charles and Prachi's eyes looked empty and sombre. Now only Chandrabhaga's fate hung in the balance.

Maybe seven-hundred year old voices would reveal what had happened to her, maybe they would not. Charles, Prachi and Vishnu Maharana could only wait and see.

'Konark was the testimony of King Narasimha Deva's passion for art and culture. The combined effort of the twelve hundred masons for twelve years was taking its final shape. King Narasimha Deva's vow of celibacy was also coming to an end. It was a time for peace and prosperity. Ikhtiyaruddin Yujbeg, who had been defeated repeatedly by King Narasimha Deva, was at last killed in war. The constant wars and bloodshed which began with the Muslim invasion in 1246 AD had finally ended. Every household in Kalinga was celebrating the victory because it was the only state in India that had fought off subjugation by the Muslims. It was a great moment of homecoming for the brave Paika soldiers. The masons of Konark too were to return home and were being felicitated by the king. Holy pitchers had been placed at the entrance of their homes which had been decorated and the walls painted. Delicacies were prepared in every home.

'It was now 13 January 1258 AD, the Sunday of Magha's seventh day in the bright fortnight—the day for installing the deity in the Konark temple. It was sheer coincidence that the holy day fell on a Sunday.

'Sunday is the birthday of the Sun God. The royal priest Bhaba Sadashiva had done his planetary calculations for the auspicious day. Invitations were sent to neighbouring kings, pundits, learned men and poets. Musicians were invited from abroad to participate in the grand event. Many came by the sea route. Numerous people came down from Purushottam, Kruttivasha, Varanashi, Remuna, Narayanapur, and Debakuta, as well as many other places. Many villagers and artist families came from small and big villages like Dhanyapur, Sindurapada, Itipur, Jaipur, Nabagrama, Malidarada, Botanda, Mangaleswar and Janarapara, among others. Rich and poor, irrespective of their social status, were treated as guests. Everybody was equal at the abode of the Sun God.

'All the artists were honoured by the king at a special celebration. The king himself bestowed on Kamala Maharana, a diamond medal called the "Silpi Siromoni". Kamala Maharana's old mother had come too. The old woman travelled the long distance to cleanse her sins in the holy water of the Chandrabhaga River. Kamala Maharana was delighted to see them. But the very next moment he looked around, where was she? How could his mother leave her behind? After years of separation their meeting would have been all the sweeter. Chandrabhaga would have learnt that her husband was the master-craftsman. She would have felt blessed.

'As though she could read her son's mind, the old woman said, "The world moves as per God's wish. What can a man do? She was stubborn about wanting to live in her father's house. There she died of some mysterious disease and caused my house to become empty." Dhabala Maharana looked away impassionedly at the temple, where the flag of justice was fluttering aloft. Kamala Maharana stood stunned in silence.

'The image of the maiden he had etched in his heart and carved on stone, that lotus-smelling girl carved in an eternal waiting, was dead long ago! She was beyond any meeting and separation, happiness or sadness! That news had never reached him. It would have tormented his heart for his beloved wife. It would have destroyed his concentration. His family never let him know of the painful news and helped him to fulfil the king's wishes! Actually how many of the families of the twelve hundred artisans must have gone through the same tragedy! If the news had reached them it wouldn't have been possible to complete the temple on time.

'But why did Chandrabhaga disappear so untimely? Before he could catch a proper glimpse of her, she was gone! Maybe Chandrabhaga was an angel, and the artist Kamala Maharana was not fit for her! Staring at the pinnacle of the Konark temple Kamala Maharana whispered, "Chandrabhaga at least tell me once, whether I was worthy of you or not!"

'His mother could understand her son's sadness and pain and said, "The process of creation and destruction goes on in this world. You don't have to lose your family forever, I've found a suitable bride for you. She is much more beautiful than Chandrabhaga, and is barely ten years old. I've chosen a bride for Dhabala too. After you come home I will bring both daughters-in-law with pomp and splendour to my house. My family will be complete and happy. Why mourn for someone who is no more?"

'Kamala Maharana did not respond for he had risen above happiness and sorrow through the twelve years of abstinence while building the temple. He had become an ascetic in body, mind and soul. He had been in rapture at the thought of meeting his beloved wife, but he was never desperate or excited. He was moved and inspired by divine love and had carved lotus flowers on stone and images of Shiva, Jagannath and of Goddess Durga. He had carved the Navagraha slab, pouring all his devotion and love into the idols. Today he was not devastated at parting from his beloved. He thought it was a hint from Lord Jagannath for him—he could never leave Konark. He would have neglected Konark for his family, children and mortal gratification. Today he was free, without any bondage.

'The king had granted the masons and artists permission to settle around Konark with their families. He had rehabilitated some artist families in Sain Sain Berhampur, Ganeshwarapur, Bhairipur and Achyutpur villages. He had also sanctioned plots at Puri for their permanent settlement. The idea was that they would care for and protect the temples of Konark and Jagannath. Who else could better protect those timeless creations than the artists themselves, who had poured their blood and sweat into their work?

'On the southern banks of Kushabhadra River was a garden of ketaki flowers. Inside that garden, was an old ruined temple of Dakshineshwara Mahadeva, where both Vishnu and Shiva were worshipped. The temple stood on the outskirts of Begunia village. Kamala Maharana had visited that temple many times. He could not be too sure whether it was the enchantment of the ketaki garden or whether it was the ethereal presence of Lord Dakshineshwara. He had gone to the area many times for supervising work—there were many villages like Bhairipur, Bedapur, and Achyutpur near Dakshineshwara, through which stone blocks were ferried across the river for the Konark temple—and while supervising the work there, Kamala Maharana would always go to pray at the temple. He was enchanted by the ketaki flowers and the gurgling waters of the Kushabhadra.

'He had wished many times to construct a small hut in that garden of ketaki flowers and live there with his beloved wife, Chandrabhaga. Now he knew he could spend the rest of his life worshipping Lord Dakshineshwara. He would stand on the banks of the river and look at the Sun Temple of Konark, against the background of the pale sky. He would offer holy water to the Sun God after taking his bath early in the morning and then pay obeisance to the temple of Konark.

'The king extremely pleased with him said, "O artist! Tell me what is it that you most desire, I will fulfil it immediately." And Kamala Maharana replied instantly, "Maharaja! If you can grant me a piece of land near the ketaki flower garden of Dakshineshwara Mahadeva, I will be obliged. Every morning after taking my bath in the Kushabhadra, I will worship Lord Biranchi Narayana Dakshineshwara with fresh ketaki flowers. I will have a glimpse of the Konark temple on the horizon. I don't want anything else in life."

'The king had wanted to honour him as a great artist. He wanted to construct a grand palace for Kamala Maharana. He could visit Lord Jagannath's temple every day. His beloved Chandrabhaga had disappeared at Purushottam Kshetra, perhaps Lord Jagannath would someday unite their souls, thought the king. But Kamala Maharana had opted for a lonely abode on the banks of the Kushabhadra in a garden of ketaki flowers!

'Devadasis were to perform a dance at the temple on its inaugural, as per the king's orders. They were to travel from Srikshetra to Padma Kshetra. Among them was Mekhala who was now getting ready for the journey. Chandrabhaga was accompanying her. Why should she refuse the last wish of Lord Jagannath? At least she would look at the glorious creations of her husband! She would bathe in the holy waters of the Chandrabhaga on the sacred day of the Sun God's birthday and attain salvation! She would be redeemed. If she could glimpse her husband from afar, and have an opportunity to recognize him, then she would not have any want unfulfilled in life. She had never thought that one day she would go to the sacred site of Chandrabhaga. Everything was God's will. What could she do?

'The ritual of the holy dip at Chandrabhaga River was over. Mitraditya Surya had completed his diurnal course in the south and was rising from the north-east corner. The pilgrims had celebrated the event of the Sun's northern course with a holy bath at Chandrabhaga. The chanting of "Jaya Suryanarayana Jaya" rent the air, drowning the sonorous sound of the sea—the early rays of the new Sun had touched the diamond throne inside the temple of Konark. The consecration of the holy temple was celebrated with great splendour, amidst chanting by Brahmans.

'King Narasimha Deva had made provisions for more land for the worship of the Sun God and his daily rituals. He had gifted 3,500 pots of gold for the offerings. The Sun God's worship had begun with proper rites and rituals. The moment He awoke, his idol was given a holy bath with a nectar prepared from five ingredients. The first early morning offering made to the idol was simple and was followed by offerings at noon and later in the afternoon, after which the deity rested till evening. In the evening, there would be prayers and light offerings were made. Thereafter, there would be elaborate prayers and offerings. Before the final offering called Bada Simahara Bhog the Sun God was decked up with eight types of ornaments. The idol of Surya Narayana looked breathtakingly beautiful. He partook the lavish dinner of Monohi before he went to sleep. During prayers in the morning and evening, as a part of the deity's ritual, accomplished devadasis performed at the Natamandir. Everybody, along with the Sun God, then went to sleep to overcome the fatigue of the day.

'But Nrityacharya Somya Sridatta was awake. His younger brother Sudatta had come with his family from the Suvarnadwip of Java to take part in the inaugural function of the Konark festival. He had informed Somya Sridatta about the deep regard Silpa had for her father, her boundless love for her motherland and her incredible courage. The fame of his daughter should have added to the happiness and honour of her father, but, in fact, it added to his burden of sorrow. Somya Sridatta was heartbroken.

'He quietly bore the burden of pain and was standing in the dark at the Natamandir before the statue of a woman in the posture of an eternal wait. He reached out in the dark to touch the image of his own daughter carved by the artist. His tears fell silently in her beloved memory as he softly asked, "When will your bath in the sea be over, Silpa? When will you come up to the world? When will you play again in the courtyard of Ma Gangeshwari temple?" He thanked the artist Kamala Maharana from the depths of his heart, "O artist! You made my beloved daughter immortal. You are worthy of my admiration. I offer you my respect."

'Kamala Maharana and his mentor Sridatta stood face to face on that desolate moonlit night and had no words to share their agony. Chandrabhaga's soul had merged into Kamala Maharana. Their untold sufferings and sacrifices would be told many a time on the walls of Konark. They would be gone but their art would last and survive sickness and death.

'There was no trace of the sun on the horizon. The sky was overcast. Only yesterday joyous celebrations of dance, music and prayers had filled the place. Today everybody was exhausted. As if nature had spread sheets of soft clouds to soothe their limbs. And the morning sun too would wake up lazily from slumber that dawn. He too had a hectic day and had beamed in all his glory before the pilgrims. It was as bright a sunshine as they could crave. But pilgrims at the Chandrabhaga waited anxiously for the sunrise again and cursed the clouds that shielded the sun! They were afraid that their waiting for the auspicious sunrise would be futile.

'The artisan families had left for the nearby villages to set up their habitation. They had early morning baths before sunrise. There was no time to wait for the Sun God to emerge. They would start life afresh with their families in their new villages. They would never know sorrow, misery or want by the grace of the king. They would excel in their artistic inheritance and live happily. Their hard work and passion in the building of Konark would bring glory and a good name for generations to come.

'Kamala Maharana would depart for his new abode in the garden of the ketaki flowers, on the banks of the Kushabhadra. There would birds for company from the nearby forest. The quiet flowing waters of the river would be waiting for him; he would build a temple for Dakshineshwara there. He was facing Chandrabhaga, the river soothed his mind when he pined for his beloved wife. He would feel close to her when he came to the river. And then he wondered why Chandrabhaga, his muse, had drowned herself. Kamala Maharana's ennui was broken by someone's dulcet voice singing hymns nearby. He saw her in front, standing in the river water, smelling of lotus but completely unadorned like a hermit. Her ethereal beauty had illumined the surroundings and she was more beautiful than anyone could have imagined. Her eyes, shut in prayer, resembled two lotus buds and her folded palms were nothing less than lotus petals, too. Her sacred saffron robe enhanced her beauty and spread serenity all around. Kamala Maharana felt as if he had known her from time immemorial and took her to be his muse of lasting beauty and sacredness. After her prayers were over, she opened her eyes and wondered what she could ask of God. What can a courtesan ask for? A husband? A child?

'Tall and handsome, Kamala Maharana stood on the river bank, sculpted, motionless and beautiful as a statue. Dense curly hair crowned his head enhancing the beauty of his large forehead. He wore large earrings and a diamond necklace which were gifts from the king himself. His eyes were deep and sensitive, an artist's eyes. The woman in the water now saw him and was instantly assailed with fear, apprehension and shame; she dived into water again as she realized it was not an ordinary man looking at her. Her companion, bathing nearby whispered, "He is a great artist of Konark. The king had himself honoured the artist with the diamond medallion. Some had touched his feet with reverence saying, 'We are blessed to meet you. You are the pride of our nation. The artist of Konark is greater than Konark.'"

'The woman now quietly bowed to the artist from a distance, she considered herself blessed as she had seen many such artists in the morning hours. She thought all the artists of Konark looked as handsome as he did. Again she looked at him timidly. She could not resist staring at him. But before she could concentrate on the face of the artist, her eyes fell on the old woman standing behind him. And there was another young man too who was just a replica of the artist! She became paralysed with fear. The old woman's eyes hissed with hatred, intolerance and reproach as if she was cursing her, "You are not yet dead? Where were you till now? If my son comes to know that you are alive, he won't be able to live with dignity anymore. Go away! Don't stand on my son's glorious path."

'Chandrabhaga immediately turned back and stared at the horizon. With sorrow and fear she plunged into the water once again and prayed silently, "Lord of Death! Do bear the burden of my pain and shame. I've got a glimpse of my husband. In this life there cannot be greater joy for me. I've left society, quit home. Your lap is my only shelter. I've no fear of death: at long last, an impossible desire in my life is now fulfilled." She plunged into the river with her back to the artist. Tears flowed and mingled with the river. The Sun God had hidden his face behind the thick clouds because he could not bear to see those tragic tears. Rain and thunderstorms were closing in to soothe the pain of a virtuous woman. The sky, the earth and the sea all were being united to protest against the injustice of society. Kamala Maharana had already turned away and disappeared. He was cursing himself in repentance and shame because he thought he was standing in the way of a young bathing woman! Before purity and beauty the artist is always defeated, oblivious of his self. What was his fault? The one who created such heavenly beauty. He himself would have been intoxicated by his creations on earth. He bowed to that great Creator again and again and walked away with long strides.

'The old woman was saying, "There will be clouds, thunderstorms soon. There is already a hint of such misfortune, early in the morning. Such a temple may not be there even in heaven for the Sun God. The sky is apprehensive in case the Sun God would choose to descend to the earth and stay at this temple permanently! I can foresee signs of disaster at Konark. Let us quit this place and go to our new house at Begunia village. Many people have already left. Why delay?"'

Fifteen

⌒

Vishnu Maharana continued from where he had left off the previous day.

'The sky, angry, jealous and full of hate, unleashed devastation upon the city, as the terrible arms of the storm embraced Konark. The driving rain, lightning strikes and raging thunderstorm left many dead, and villages and habitations destroyed. But the newly consecrated Sun Temple of Konark stood unshaken and unperturbed, like a monk free of all desire. Inside, rituals to the Sun God continued unabated. The idol had been installed in the consecrated temple just a day before. Why then had nature turned its wrath on Konark?

'At the palace with his queen, Sita Devi, King Narasimha Deva realized that all his powers as a king had failed before nature's fury; he had been unable to protect the lives and property of his countrymen and pilgrims against the assault of nature. Nevertheless, the grand and successful inauguration of the temple was a crowning achievement in an already glorious career. History would not mention the architects of Konark, but would glorify him. He was the king who had the Sun Temple built with the nation's revenues over twelve years, and history would record his achievements as the golden era of the Ganga dynasty. His name would dazzle in the constellation of great rulers through history. He would be immortal.

'Since the entire credit of erecting such a magnificent monument lay at the feet of King Narasimha Deva, his heart felt light as the sky. He felt as though he were floating on a wave of eternal success; though his mind was heavy with pride.

'His minister, Sibei Samantaray was happy that Konark would stay intact for ages to come, and through it the great accomplishments of Minister Sibei Samantray would also survive. History would sing the glory of Sibei Samantray. In fact history would record in golden letters that it was more due to Sibei Samantray's contribution, than due to the king's desire, that such a glorious monument had been erected.

'The chief architect, Kamala Maharana, was looking at the completed temple and wondering whether history would recognize only one artist of Konark, and if that artist would be Kamala Maharana. He after all, had been instrumental in sprouting a lotus on each piece of stone. The names of twelve hundred masons would be recalled by his name. There was no doubt that as a representative of those twelve hundred artists, Kamala Maharana would become immortal.

'Man, though mortal, aspires to immortality. His greatest desire is that his honour and establishment be protected even after death. But the nameless labourer who had poured his sweat and life blood into cutting and lifting the stones to their rightful places on the temple site, and carried endless bagfuls of sand for temple construction, had no such thoughts. He was happy to see how magnificent the temple looked now that it was complete. He was happy because the king, queen, crown prince, ministers, clergymen, and citizens were happy with the temple. The thought of immortality never arose, he did not even realize that it was because his dedicated effort, and the dedicated efforts of thousands like him, that the twelve hundred masons had been able build the temple. Without him and others like him, there would have been no Konark Sun Temple. But his simple heart never thought of all this.

'The devastating storm on Ashtami day had scattered corpses around Konark and broken many limbs. The shrine stood amidst this devastation like a silent spectator, as though admitting silently, "Konark is not indestructible. Time will one day wear it down, too." But the effort and labour of the nameless masons and the labourers would be written forever in the hearts of future generations. They would attain immortality, not as individuals, but as the spirit of a great nation. Man dies, but a great nation sees no death.

'Today King Narasimha Deva was cremating the dead bodies of unidentified dead pilgrims and workers on a common pyre. His ego had finally been annihilated by the flames that devoured the heap of bodies, irrespective of religion, caste or creed, wealth or poverty. They'd all suffered the same fate. He was now praying with a bowed head for the salvation of those souls who had contributed their all to building the temple. Although he had fought the war as the king, Konark had been built by these masons and artists. He, the king, never had such strength.

'The storm swelled and swept by the banks of the Kushabhadra and the ketaki garden, which now also had lotuses which reminded Kamala Maharana of Chandrabhaga. The ketaki flowers brought Silpa's ethereal beauty to mind, transporting him to another world—one where Silpa's dark hair fell in long lustrous waves, adorned by ketaki flowers; the petals falling from her loose hair like lightning from dark clouds. An image he would never forget.

'When the lotus flowers bloomed he hazily recalled Chandrabhaga's shy face. His brother Dhabala Maharana would tell him about Chandrabhaga—whatever he knew, heard about, or imagined about his beloved sister-in-law. Chandrabhaga's memories were linked to the lotus; while Silpa's love like the ketaki flower, was pure and dedicated. Both Chandrabhaga and Silpa had won Kamala Maharana's heart.

'Now he lay in the ketaki garden searching for the moon and his beloved's smiling face on it. But the moon had been obliterated by the dark storm spread across the sky. The face he imagined as Chandrabhaga's was no longer visible. In its place were two sad tear-filled eyes of the woman he had spotted emerging from the waters of the Chandrabhaga yesterday, after bathing in the river. Those eyes now looked helpless, as though helplessness had come down from the skies yesterday night to ravage her like the storm.

'She was as simple, tearful and lovely as the wild ketaki flowers. Who was she? Whose daughter, whose sister and whose wife? These questions vexed him but as the night deepened he dozed off in exhaustion. She appeared in his dreams with ketaki flowers in her hair, writing letters on ketaki petals, before vanishing in front of his eyes in the ketaki garden.

'When he awoke, Kamala Maharana faced a rain-washed morning and felt compelled to search for her. His feet took him to the banks of the Kushabhadra where he spotted a few withered and pale ketaki flowers lying in a heap. Even though it is the nature of flowers to wither, it is the nature of artists to be sensitive towards fallen flowers. He sat down. The river was scented with their fragrance. He bent to scoop up a handful of water to wash his face and saw a fresh flower amidst the pale fallen flowers. It was more clear, calm, and lovely, than the blue sky cleared by the storm. It was the same woman he had spotted bathing in the Chandrabhaga. She lay dead among the ketaki flowers. Yesterday's violent storm had offered this beautiful flower at the feet of Lord Dakshinishwara as if to make amends for its sins.

'Kamala Maharana was too bewildered to react, the corpse was floating with its face to the sky. The merciless storm had scattered her clothes but the flowers had draped her like a veil. Her pale arms lay stretched and one had a Radha Krishna tattoo. Her feet were swollen and had lotus tattoos on them. He controlled himself.

'The corpse had to be identified and cremated. He informed the village guard, and the police came. Details about the dead body were put on record and the report presented before the Inspector General of Police. The dead woman was declared an orphan; she was an attendant of Mekhala, a devadasi. Mekhala knew nothing more about her.

'Details of the corpse were presented to the king, along with Kamala Maharana's inputs. Going through the report, the king saw Chandrabhaga before him—long, dark curly hair; a pale left arm with tattoos of Radha-Krishna, and lotus flowers on her feet. When he had first seen those tattoos on the tender body of that beautiful woman in the courtyard of an abandoned temple in a dense forest, he felt like abolishing the cruel practice of tattooing one's flesh just because it was the custom to do so.

'But was this woman Chandrabhaga? If she was, then there was no parallel on heaven or earth to her single-minded devotion. Even though she was an orphan, her dead body had followed and finally reached her husband, Kamala Maharana. Who else but Kamala Maharana should cremate her; but the king was tempted to look at her one last time. After the devastating storm he had planned to visit the temple of Goddess Gangeshwari and Lord Dakshineshwara Mahadeva to pray for his people. He decided that Kamala Maharana should complete the last rites of that unknown woman in his presence.

'The news of the king's arrival reached Dakshineshwara just as darkness began setting in. The pyre was ready, and a conch was blown announcing the king's arrival. The village guard kept a vigil on the corpse. A dark cloud loomed on the western horizon and its shadow fell on the deserted riverbank. A westerly wind was causing swells to rise, and the heart of the dead body also quivered, tossing in the water. The village guard stepped back. It looked as though the corpse would spring to life; he hastily climbed onto the verandah of the boatman's hut. Rain clouds had appeared and he did not plan on getting wet while guarding the corpse. And what if the dead body actually sprang to life? He would not be able to escape!

'The king had finished his prayers at the Lord Dakshineshwara temple and was standing before the pyre along with the others. There was no distinction between a king and his subjects at the temple or cremation ground. Everybody was equal before God and Death. Suddenly a policeman appeared with the news that the corpse had vanished, probably swept away by the river currents to fathomless depths. There was no trace of it.'

And Vishnu Maharana looked up, having reverently placed the last of the palm-leaf manuscripts back in its cloth wrappings.

Partings are painful for everybody, everywhere and at all times. Charles would leave Konark, Dinabandhu, Charukala, and Prachiprava behind in Odisha. Who could say whether they were not meeting for the last time? After all, Kushi Mausi, Chitrotpala and then Dharmananda—were no longer with him. Chandrabhaga would remain a haunting memory.

He had wanted to take Kamala Maharana's handwritten manuscript from Vishnu Maharana, but he wouldn't part with it. Besides, money can't buy everything. He visited the Sun Temple for the last time. And in that rain-swept afternoon, the temple seemed to him akin to a woman shrouded in mystery. The fading rays of sun made the awe-inspiring images of Bhairava more animated, as if the temple had come to life.

Mitradev, depicted on the southern wall with matted hair, heavily adorned with ornaments had a sacred thread on his shinning chest. His two wives, Chhaya and Sangya and daughters Gayatri and Savitri flanked him. At the feet of this glowing Mitradev or the Morning Sun God, were depicted King Narasimha Deva and Queen Sita Devi praying. On the wall to the west of the Sun God was Baibaswata, representing mid-day. Charles photographed this ornate idol in polished chlorite. Then he came and stood before the idol of Haridashwa (the afternoon Sun) on the northern wall. This idol rode a horse and the image exerted immense vitality. The horse and Sun were so immaculately sculpted that they looked as though they were frozen in action. Charles knew there was more to be seen and in the ruins lay many treasures. He knew he was mistaken in believing that he had learnt and seen all there was to learn and see about Konark. Konark's mysteries would never cease to overwhelm.

Charles came and stood where Chitrotpala once used to sell flowers, and a sigh escaped him, then Dharmananda's face too flashed before him, and he strode away with long strides in the light of the pale and listless July moon. As he headed away it began to drizzle. Charles was drawn to the sound of wailing from the casuarina jungle and saw a shadow flit past.

It looked just like the one he had seen many times from a distance. Was it the ghost of Chandrabhaga? He moved closer but each time the shadow slithered away. Charles advanced slowly. Now the shadow stood facing the sea. Charles thought if only he could get a closer look at her feet and see lotus tattoos there, he would be sure. His heart beat with excitement not only because he was chasing a ghost, but because he felt it was Chandrabhaga's spirit.

'Chandrabhaga,' he called out passionately, 'I want to tell you what King Narasimha Deva could not. Chandrabhaga, I love you, I love you! I love your soul, I love the artistic heritage of this country. I call that love. Please forgive me if I offend you....'

The shadow looked back once and then disappeared in a flash into the blue waters of the sea. Whether she had walked into the sea or whether the leaping waves had embraced her was difficult to ascertain. The sonorous sound of the sea and the now deserted shore made everything seem unreal; had he imagined the whole thing or had it really happened? His whole body trembled. Perhaps it wasn't Chandrabhaga and somebody had committed suicide before his very eyes. What could he do? Man is so helpless before the sea and Time! Behind him, appeared the faint glow of a lamp. Charles turned to see Dinabandhu Babu standing behind him, a lantern in hand. Ganesh was hurrying them both saying, 'Let us go home. It is not proper to roam around at such an unearthly hour of the night. Ghosts roam here at midnight.'

'What time is it?' Charles asked, retracing his steps.

'Twelve o'clock! Your aunty is getting agitated,' replied Dinabandhu Babu. 'We will leave for Purushottam at daybreak to witness Lord Patitapabbana on the Grand Road, tomorrow is the Sri Gundicha festival of Lord Jagannath, remember? And after two days we will be forced to bid you farewell, when you will leaving Odisha by Nilachal Express,' he said, his voice trembling with tearful emotion. The drizzle became a full-fledged shower. Dinabandhu Babu took Charles's arm affectionately leading him away from the rain, 'We will bid you farewell at Puri Station and always pray to Lord Jagannath for your happiness and prosperity.'

Charles couldn't take his eyes from Prachiprava. She was wearing a red Benarasi silk sari, and jewellery. Her forehead bore a vermilion dot and the parting of her hair shone brightly with vermilion powder running through its length. He was enamoured. She had come with her family to bid farewell to Charles at Puri. But why was she dressed like a bride? Dinabandhu read Charles's mind and said softly, 'Every year during the Rath Yatra, the Chariot Festival, lots of wise men, ascetics, scholars, and philosophers travel to Puri. Charukala believes one day Jagannath will return with them too.'

'And what about Prachiprava?' Charles asked.

'If she did not have faith, she would not dress up like a bride and come with us to Puri year after year.'

A crowd had gathered at the Chandrabhaga River. They got down from the car and learnt that someone had drowned last night and her corpse lay on the shore. The police had arrived. The corpse had been identified as the body of a pilgrim who had come to Konark as a bride two years ago, only to lose her husband when he drowned at sea. She had turned mad and wandered about with no fixed abode, like a ghost. In the end she had walked into the sea. Charles became grim; he was an eyewitness to the episode. He had called out to her as the ghost of Chandrabhaga.

'May her soul rest in peace,' he prayed quietly.

Sri Sri Jagannath is the lord of Odisha, the Saviour. He is the fulcrum of Odisha's religion, art, literature, civilization, culture, pride and spiritual heritage. He symbolizes love, brotherhood, and unity among mankind. Charles, standing on the main road and witnessing the festival and the deities being brought down from their abode, believed all this. Devotees hurled abuses at the Lord, and he would smile. His bright face had tanned in the sun. The rain had smudged his kohl-lined eyes. But he was unperturbed. He was smiling at his devotees, swaying backward and forward amid the cheering crowds.

Lord Gajapati was seated on a palanquin, with an attendant holding a cotton umbrella above his head. He wore a crown and was dressed all in white. He would sweep the floors of the chariots with a golden broom to keep alive the centuries-old tradition. Then the chariots would move. The charioteer was ready.

Charles, moved by the cult of Jagannath which made no distinctions among people, began to dance with the crowd, his heart filled with compassion and ecstasy. The resounding cheers of 'Shankirtan' filled the surroundings. The giant wheels rolled. Since one is redeemed of one's sins by touching those ropes, Charles pulled them too. Prachi touched them as if she was touching the deities, with utmost reverence.

Dinabandhu, Charukala, Charles and Prachiprava walked in a line through the crowd, under a clear blue sky. Charles did not feel lonely here, unlike some Americans. He had a family. He had relatives. Whatever he lost in America, he had gained in India. Charles bowed to the deities on the chariot and prayed, 'He whose feet stay earthbound for sake of the poor and the orphaned, let that Lord Jagannath be my guide through life.'

The next morning, they found Vishnu Maharana standing knee-deep in the sea, meditating. Seeing Prachi and Charles, he waved. He had consigned the sacred manuscripts along with the Silpa Chandrika treatise, to the waters.

The tragic moment of parting had arrived. Charukala never went to the station, it hurt her too much to say goodbye. Charles touched her feet with reverence and said, 'I've taken Dinesh's address. Do want me to carry any news for him?'

Charukala trying to conceal her tears said, 'You tell him not to forget his motherland. Even Lord Jagannath visits his birthplace once a year,' and caressed his head saying, 'Be careful. Write to us on reaching. I will keep worrying till I receive a letter from you,' and tears streamed down her motherly face. Charles nodded and came out. He knew parting would be difficult. But he never knew tears would come to his hardened eyes.

The train was at the station. Dinabandhu Babu was standing at a distance trying to hide his tears. Charles thought, almost prayed, 'Goodbye Prachi, stay well. Thank you for all your help, sympathy, care and affection. I wish I could stay longer, perhaps forever. Stay near you, if only as your friend. Maybe you wanted that too. But you are made of stone, a damsel of Konark. You've to stay behind, but I'm a nomad, with no place to call my own. I've to move on, but we will keep hoping that we meet again, sometime, somewhere.'

Maybe Prachi was also thinking along the same lines, but neither spoke. Thoughts touched one another bridged by the profound ripple of sadness that linked one to the other, lips still and silent. This was possibly the last time they would ever see each other; perhaps they would never meet again. Neither could bear to accept that as the truth.

Did Prachi know that the time they spent together had been the happiest in his life, wondered Charles bleakly. Something had to be said. The silence was unbearable.

'Values have deteriorated in every country, but despite the tragic way in which Chitrotpala and Dharmananda died,

India still holds Dinabandhu, Charukala, Vishnu Maharana, Prachiprava, Konark and Lord Jagannath, the symbol of universal fraternity, for me,' he said. 'The gap between Chandrabhaga and Prachiprava is not all that big—Chandrabahaga, Prachiprava, Kushabhadra, Chitrotpala, all the same, just different names of one eternal river. I'll remember everyone... will always hold everybody in high regard. I love them and that's why I love India, and everything about this country.'

'Thank you Charles,' whispered Prachi finding it difficult to speak through the tears she held back, 'thank you.' The last bell sounded, the train was ready to depart. Charles spoke through his grief once more before boarding the train, 'I know Prachi, farewells are very painful. But I will come again, I'll definitely come back.'

Prachi finally looked up, the tears still valiantly held back, 'Thank you for that Charles, may your journey be pleasant, and your life auspicious,' and the tears escaped.

They stood motionless before each other. When the heart is smashed, the language is speechless, silent. Their story was age-old, magnificent and, for the moment, in ruins like Konark. Charles held her hands. Two more tears followed and she took back her hands; Charles climbed into his train compartment.

Only after the train had started to move, did Prachi look up again at him. She waved and then quickly walked to the windowpane behind which he sat. Charles whispered to her, 'I love you, Prachi, you've overwhelmed my soul. There is no end to this love.'

Prachi was split into two in a fraction of second. Her body of flesh and blood, and her duty, hopes, desires, enthusiasm, emotions. One was mortal, the other immortal. One was the body, the other her soul. Her body remained where she stood, but her soul had flown in search. But in search of whom, she thought, distressed. She had been searching for so long—for King Narasimha Deva the key to the mysteries of Konark, for her husband Jagannath whose discovery of her had led him leave her searching for him, or was it Charles? Had they been reborn? Was he Narasimha Deva to her Chandrabhaga?

Charles was looking at her transformation amazed, from behind the windowpane. Suddenly she looked like one of the statues of Konark, a temple without a deity, just the edifice. Charles saw only a lovely sculpture waving at him. Slowly the hand became still and her eyes came back to life, distressed. Then her expression changed again. Now it seemed she was no longer bidding farewell, but waiting for someone; like that timeless sculpture of the waiting woman at Konark, thought Charles. The train began to gather speed and Prachi's image began getting blurred, soon her motionless figure looked like a bright spot, a flame burning in the darkness as if guiding Charles to his destination.

Epilogue

—

When I gazed at the temple for the first time as a young girl, I was fascinated by the outstanding workmanship of the Odia stone carver artisans who had chiseled the numerous nymphs, animals and lotuses so skillfully that they seemed to have an almost lifelike appeal. I was moved by the sacrifice and dedication of those artists who were away from their families for twelve long years. They had to make the temple unparalleled in craft and art, while living in makeshift hutments around the temple, surrendering absolutely to the task.

There are several stories glorifying the temple and fictionalizing about its ruins as well. The temple is no longer there, only the porch remains along with the edifice of the main temple which collapsed from its mid-level. The remains of the temple still stands with the enormous lotus in granite, intricately carved, though the idol of the reigning deity Sun God has been removed and placed in the Jagannath Temple at Puri.

This novel was written in 1983, titled *Silapadma* in original Odia language, based on the backdrop of the famous Sun temple of Konark. The novel received the Sahitya Akademi award in 1985 and has been subsequently translated into several Indian languages. I remember after the novel was published in Malayalam, noted writer and critic, Asha Menon, had written to me saying that he wanted to view the sculptures of the Sun temple the way I had described them in the book. The damsel in waiting, the woman drying herself after bathing in a lotus pool while a swan drinks the water falling from her long wet hair, the women busy at cooking and detailed art pieces like that. One artist in an art exhibition had depicted a dancing woman of Konark after reading the Hindi translation of the novel.

Konark receives attention worldwide for the erotic sculptures that adorn the stone walls. Women in waiting posing for her lover or her husband, is the most captivating sculpture that had overwhelmed me then. One such stone image at the southern gate of the Natamandira, the roofless dancing hall of the Sun temple, had impressed me the most—a woman leaning onto the half open door, waiting for someone. There is sadness and longing as she is all dressed up and ready to meet her man who never comes. She waits indefinitely. She could be the wife of one of the artisans who remembered and immortalized her in his artistic excellence. She inspired me to write the novel, the saga of sacrifice of the artisans who had left their home for more than a decade and could not go home or meet their family till the temple reached its completion. There were men who had to join the team, leaving their bride and family, from the wedding platform itself; many were engaged, many were newly married, many with young children. But no such personal life mattered when the nation united to build a magnum opus monument.

Konark for me was never a seat of erotic sculptures. I was moved by its religious significance; by the Suryavamshi king Narsimha Deva and his subjects who devoted their prime youth to build such a magnificent edifice. Critics opine that the temple collapsed so early because of too much eroticism. They say both the king and his subjects were immoral, and harbored a lustful lifestyle. That is why the thirteenth century temple lost its glory. For me however, the supreme sacrifice made by the warrior king and his subjects who never deviated from their path of commitment and observed celibacy, matters. The aesthetic appeal of this unique Sun temple moves me even today.

There are many characters I have encountered during my several visits to the temple when I was conceptualizing the novel. I met an adolescent boy selling erotic picture postcards who dogged me to buy his wares. I was aghast to find how a little bit of money had wiped away his innocence at such a tender age. I met foreigners too who frequented India as hippie culture was in its peak during those days. It was a time of cultural decadence. Moral values were declining, even cases of rape were frequently happening.

I have referred to a lot of texts related to the temple to gain factual accuracy. I travelled extensively in the adjoining villages to find the characters related to the Sun temple that only myth had immortalized. But I built my stories the way I imagined the situations. The love stories woven around Kamala Maharana and his wife Chandrabhaga, his muse Silpa, the chief architects' beautiful daughter, the King's encounter with Chandrabhaga are all fictitious.

One night in the month of August, it was raining incessantly. I was there at the Konark, surrounded by swaying casuarinas. I felt as if one of the nymphs carved on the walls of the Konark sprang to life. Her steps were audible to me because she had jingling ghoongroos on her feet and her gait was rhythmic. She came so close that I was almost hypnotized and then I heard her saga. How moving that was… even though it was my dream, my imagination…! One may not believe in such supernatural happenings, but I felt the shiver in my veins and I was driven to write her story the way I felt it, the way I experienced it.

Prachiprava and Chandrabhaga are the two rivers that flowed in the periphery of the temple. My two women protagonists symbolize the rivers, flowing eternally, keeping alive the heritage. Chandrabhaga has dried up, while Prachi is a thin stream today. Maitreyabana, the green forest belt fringing the Bay of Bengal at Konark, no longer exists the way it did. Many things have disappeared with time, like many sculpted stone slabs have been replaced with polished plain stones, many carved sculptures have been pilfered, defaced, damaged.

Konark remains a mystery; its celestial women carved in stone remain hauntingly mystifying as well. The stories of the Konark Temple can be abundant, unending... I have taken only a petal of the numerous lotuses carved on the base and walls of the temple, and tried to tell my tale, be it romance, or unrequited affairs of the heart. The pain of not being able to deliver the poignant feelings always torments me.

I am grateful to Dr Karunasagar Behera, the eminent historian; Mr Maloy Mitra, the journalist who lived in Begunia; the 80-year-old priest Sri Balaram Padhy of the Gangeshwari temple at Baialishibati area; the illustrious stone carvers, Sri Sridhar Mahapatra, Raghunath Mahapatra and Bhubaneswar Mahapatra of Pathuria Sahi of Puri, who helped me enormously by clarifying my doubts and providing me with lots of resources when I was writing the novel.

The novel *Citadel of Love*, *Silapadma* in Odia, has stories, historical essentials and folk elements. History only records the episode of the great king and his ministers. That is why history mentions about King Narasimha Deva, his queen Sitadevi and his chief architect Sibei Samantaray, but there is absolutely no mention about the artists who sacrificed their lives. There is no mention even of one artist amongst those 1,200 artisans engaged at the temple building. That is why there is no mention of Kamala Maharana and his wife Chandrabhaga who made supreme sacrifices. Even then it is hard to ignore their longing for each other, which got suppressed under their high moral value, celibacy, and virtues.

I have depicted my truth as I felt them. The sacrifice of those artists, and their dedication, honesty, the imaginative and artistic excellence of the Konark is a reality, a truth. The truth is depicted on the walls of Konark, recording the brilliance of Kalinga's splendid art and craft heritage, for eternity.

I have completed the novel with the hope that I could acknowledge the truth, the heritage of my land and my people and pay my homage to those artists of Kalinga and the king Narasimha Deva. This novel is my tribute to them.

Pratibha Ray

www.ingramcontent.com/pod-product-compliance
Lightning Source LLC
Chambersburg PA
CBHW060426030726
47495CB00003B/759